Earl W. Reichert

CHRISTIANITY AND THE NEW WORLD

An Approach to Christian Ethics

BY

F. R. BARRY

M.A., D.S.O.

FELLOW AND TUTOR OF BALLIOL COLLEGE, AND VICAR OF ST. MARY THE VIRGIN, OXFORD
CHAPLAIN TO H.M. THE KING
EXAMINING CHAPLAIN TO THE BISHOPS OF SALISBURY AND SOUTHWARK
FELLOW OF KING'S COLLEGE, LONDON

MCMXXXII
HARPER & BROTHERS PUBLISHERS
NEW YORK AND LONDON

PRINTED IN THE UNITED STATES OF AMERICA

"THERE IS A CITY BUILDED AND SET IN A PLAIN COUNTRY, AND FULL OF ALL GOOD THINGS; BUT THE ENTRANCE THEREOF IS NARROW, AND IT IS SET IN A DANGEROUS PLACE TO FALL, HAVING A FIRE ON THE RIGHT SIDE AND ON THE LEFT A DEEP WATER: AND THERE IS ONLY ONE PATH BETWEEN THEM BOTH, EVEN BETWEEN THE FIRE AND THE WATER, SO SMALL THAT THERE COULD BUT ONE MAN GO THERE AT ONCE."

2 Esdras vii. 7, 8.

"THE KINGDOM OF HEAVEN IS LIKE UNTO A MAN THAT IS A MERCHANT SEEKING GOODLY PEARLS: AND HAVING FOUND ONE PEARL OF GREAT PRICE, HE WENT AND SOLD ALL THAT HE HAD, AND BOUGHT IT."

S. Matt. xiii. 45–46.

"WHATSOEVER THINGS ARE TRUE, WHATSOEVER THINGS ARE HONOURABLE, WHATSOEVER THINGS ARE JUST, WHATSOEVER THINGS ARE PURE, WHATSOEVER THINGS ARE LOVELY, WHATSOEVER THINGS ARE GRACIOUS; IF THERE BE ANY VIRTUE, AND IF THERE BE ANY PRAISE, THINK ON THESE THINGS."

Phil. iv. 8.

GENERAL INTRODUCTION

THE Editors of this series are convinced that the Christian Church as a whole is confronted with a great though largely silent crisis, and also with an unparalleled opportunity. They have a common mind concerning the way in which this crisis and opportunity should be met. The time has gone by when "apologetics" could be of any great value. Something more is needed than a defence of propositions already accepted on authority, for the present spiritual crisis is essentially a questioning of authority if not a revolt against it. It may be predicted that the number of people who are content simply to rest their religion on the authority of the Bible or the Church is steadily diminishing, and with the growing effectiveness of popular education will continue to diminish. We shall not therefore meet the need, if we have rightly diagnosed it, by dissertations, however learned, on the interpretation of the Bible or the history of Christian doctrine. Nothing less is required than a candid, courageous and well-informed effort to think out anew, in the light of modern knowledge, the foundation affirmations of our common Christianity. This is the aim of every writer in this series.

A further agreement is, we hope, characteristic of the books which will be published in the series. The authors have a common mind not only with regard to the problem but also with regard to the starting-point of reconstruction. They desire to lay stress upon the value and validity of religious experience and to develop their theology on the basis of the religious consciousness. In so doing they claim to be in harmony with modern thought. The massive achievements of the nineteenth and twentieth centuries have been built up on the method of observation and experiment, on experience, not on abstract *a priori* reasoning. Our contention is that the moral and spiritual experience of mankind has the right to be considered, and demands to be understood.

Many distinguished thinkers might be quoted in support of the assertion that philosophers are now prepared in a greater measure than formerly to consider religious experience as among the most significant of their data. One of the greatest has said, "There is nothing more real than what comes in religion. To compare facts such as these with what is given to us in outward existence would be to trifle with the subject. The man who demands a reality more solid than that of the religious consciousness, seeks he does not know what."[1] Nor does this estimate of religious experience come only from idealist thinkers. A philosopher who writes from the standpoint of mathematics and natural science has expressed the same thought in even more forcible language. "The fact of religious vision, and its history of persistent expansion, is our one ground for optimism. Apart from it, human life is a flash of occasional enjoyments lighting up a

[1] F. H. Bradley, *Appearance and Reality*, p. 449.

mass of pain and misery, a bagatelle of transient experience."[1]

The conviction that religious experience is to be taken as the starting-point of theological reconstruction does not, of course, imply that we are absolved from the labour of thought. On the contrary, it should serve as the stimulus to thought. No experience can be taken at its face value; it must be criticised and interpreted. Just as natural science could not exist without experience and the thought concerning experience, so theology cannot exist without the religious consciousness and reflection upon it. Nor do we mean by "experience" anything less than the whole experience of the human race, so far as it has shared in the Christian consciousness. As Mazzini finely said, "Tradition and conscience are the two wings given to the human soul to reach the truth."

It has been the aim of the writers and the Editors of the series to produce studies of the main aspects of Christianity which will be intelligible and interesting to the general reader and at the same time may be worthy of the attention of the specialist. After all, in religion we are dealing with a subject-matter which is open to all and the plan of the works does not require that they shall delve very deeply into questions of minute scholarship. We have had the ambition to produce volumes which might find a useful place on the shelves of the clergyman and minister, and no less on those of the intelligent layman. Perhaps we may have done something to bridge the gulf which too often separates the pulpit from the pew.

[1] A. N. Whitehead, *Science and the Modern World*, p. 275.

Naturally, the plan of our series has led us to give the utmost freedom to the authors of the books to work out their own lines of thought, and our part has been strictly confined to the invitation to contribute, and to suggestions concerning the mode of presentation. We hope that the series will contribute something useful to the great debate on religion which is proceeding in secret in the mind of our age, and we humbly pray that their endeavours and ours may be blessed by the Spirit of Truth for the building up of Christ's Universal Church.

PREFACE

THIS is not the book which I intended to write when I accepted the Publishers' invitation to contribute a volume to this series. Its original plan was very different ; but the book has insisted on writing itself in this form. It is an attempt to state a conviction about the significance of Christ and the presentation of Christianity in its relevance to the claims and values of life, which has been slowly taking shape in my mind, in successive stages, during the last ten years. The nucleus of the essay in its present shape was a course of lectures on Christian Ethics given in 1924 to a school for clergy in the Canterbury diocese, and later on repeated in substance to the clergy of the Church of Ireland at St. Columba's College, Rathfarnham. It was the insistence of Archbishop Davidson which emboldened me to work out in book-form the ideas then tentatively suggested. It has taken six years to achieve. The conditions of my work in this period have not been favourable to consistent study. It is only by the rarest good fortune that I have one hour without interruption even during the Oxford vacation ; and coherent thinking or writing is not easy in the intervals between callers and telephone bells. Thus the work has had to be done in scraps, chiefly by sacrificing my holidays, and spread over a rather long time. Inevitably this method of composition means that various parts of the book are apt to vary in tone and quality. But the whole has been worked over this summer and brought, I hope, into something like organic unity. My thanks are due to the Publishers for their patience with my procrastination.

This essay has grown out of a friendship. The general position which it seeks to establish has been reached in years of intimate talk and companionship with my friend Mervyn Haigh, now Bishop of Coventry. Indeed, so close has been our association that I do not know which ideas and even which phrases originated in his mind and which in my own. It is as much his work as mine. But, now that " the Lord has taken away my master from my head ", meeting and conversation are seldom possible ; and for all that appears in the book as now published the writer must accept sole responsibility. Most of my recent speeches, sermons and articles have been by way of trying out certain aspects of it, and I have drawn freely on this material, some of which has appeared in *The Guardian* and is reproduced by courtesy of the Editor.

The book is designed for the " general reader ", though I realize that some sections of it must make a rather heavy demand on him. Those, however, who wish (as all sensible readers should) to skip such parts as do not appeal to them, are offered a fairly wide field of choice. The practical discussions of Part II are intended rather to illustrate a method than to be a handbook of Christian Ethics. But I hope that, so far as they go, they may not be useless. The final chapter summarizes the argument and takes it to the door of the parish church, where its contentions must be put to the test. For if what I have written is true, it seems to involve certain important consequences in preaching, worship and pastoral work and our whole conception of membership in the Church. If anything here suggested should help to re-establish the Christian religion at the heart of men's daily tasks and interests and recover its lost leadership in national life the book will not have been wasted labour, however imperfect in detail and execution.

Nobody, I imagine, can hope to trace the sources of all his ideas. I have made no show of compiling a bibliography but the borrowings of which I am conscious are acknowledged in footnotes in the text. One word of explanation may be permissible. Most of my book was already in typescript before the publication of Dean Inge's volume *The Christian Ethic and Modern Problems*, Professor A. E. Taylor's *The Faith of a Moralist* and Dr. Kenneth Kirk's Bampton Lectures. I have since made bold to insert some almost inevitable quotations from the two latter which reinforce my tentative arguments by the authority of these eminent writers. There are, however, a few almost verbal agreements with certain passages in the books named which are due to no subsequent changes on my part.

The position which I have sought to establish has thus not a few points of contact with ideas that are much in other people's minds at the moment. Yet it is exposed, as I fully realize, to damaging attacks on both flanks, and can hardly fail to incur censure from two very different schools of criticism. But I venture to believe that the centre holds, and may yet prove to be a rallying point.

The substance of the book was given as lectures in Union Theological Seminary, New York, during the Summer Session this year. It is a pleasure to associate it with the charming and generous hospitality of the President and his colleagues during our visit. I owe to a great number of friends more than I can hope to acknowledge : to the Master of Balliol—far more than he knows—for constant inspiration and guidance ; to Dr. Matthews, now Dean of Exeter, for valued criticism and stimulus ; to the Archbishop of York for all I have learnt from him ; to the Bishop of Southwark, Canon Quick and many whose names would make a long catalogue. My wife has held me to the task when I had given up hope of completing it, and has typed my illegible MS., often in several successive versions. Her insight and understanding have greatly helped in forming my judgments, and Chapter VIII could only have been written out of experience in partnership. To my parents also I owe gratitude for the peace and beauty of their home, where a good deal of the work has been done.

F. R. B.

OXFORD,
October, 1931.

CONTENTS

CHRISTIANITY AND THE NEW WORLD

PART I

CHAPTER I

THE PROBLEM OF MODERNITY

1. The Problem Stated

INCOMPARABLY the most imperious challenge which to-day confronts Christianity is the moral chaos of our generation. We cannot meet it by the repetition of formulas, however holy and however venerable. It is true, no doubt, that thousands of men and women are bewildered about the Christian creed and are asking questions which cannot be answered truly by mere citation of authorities. But there is another question, far more summary, which the whole world is asking daily, and it is calling aloud for decisive answer. In its simplest terms the question is, "Why shouldn't I?" There is no piecemeal answer to that enquiry. If we take the established rules of conduct one by one, in their traditional form, we may find ourselves hard put to it to justify them. Some, perhaps, admit no justification. What is required is less demonstration that this or that behaviour is "wrong", than a constructive philosophy of life, which candidly faces all the new factors which have entered into the moral situation to make it both more delicate and more complex, and offers genuinely positive leadership. That is the task before Christianity. We have to vindicate the moral validity and creativeness of the Christian faith when drawn to the scale of the new maps, on the twentieth-century projection of a ceaseless evolutionary process unfolding itself through the cosmic system.

The answer given must be *creative.* It is no good calling men to renewed allegiance to standards about which they remain unconvinced. No mere traditionalism can help us. We do Christianity a grave disservice if we identify the customs and conventions of an age that is now rapidly passing from us with permanent Christian moral principles. The social institutions of our predecessors were by no means all necessarily Christian. Mrs. Grundy, when all is said and done, was not a pattern of Christian conduct. And it may be that the fierce repudiation of what seem to the young her evasions and her cant is in some ways nearer to the spirit of Christ. Indeed the best among the fine qualities which characterize the rising generation is the realism and sincerity of their approach to all moral questions. The Church must meet them on their own highest level. The only authority which can be rightly claimed for any moral standards or principles is that they are genuinely responsive to the deepest and truest needs of men. An honest ethic is always an " offence ": it is always bound to challenge the weakness and the passions of the average sensual man. A " popular " ethic thereby proves its falsity. It is not one of the least of our temptations so to secularize the Christian ethic as to make it chime with the rhythm of the world. It can never offer men what they want merely at the level of their unredeemed desires. Yet no moral system can approve itself to the free critical judgment of mankind which seems to deny, frustrate or impoverish any essential needs of human personality. There have been periods of Christian history when the Church has succumbed to the theory of what has well been called the "Unnatural God".[1] It must be possible to substantiate on behalf of any ethic that claims finality that it is integrally woven into the true pattern of Man's life, able to grow with his own growth in experience, and to respond to his fundamental selfhood. This means that it must be set forth in the context of a satisfying and coherent world-view. For the question: What is the right kind of conduct? plainly presupposes another: How can we interpret the universe and Man's place and destiny within it?

It is the privilege of the Christian Church to offer the world its own interpretation, based upon its own experience of God.

The human race, from time immemorial, has asked: Where can Wisdom be found? We know the answer that has been given, not only by the Jewish-Christian Bible but by nearly all the great world-religions, that the fear of the Lord is its first principle. Is that traditional answer right or wrong? Here are the cross-roads of modern history. As we decide so the future will be. For Wisdom, in its Biblical usage, means pretty much what we call moral insight, a true discrimination of values, an understanding of what is most worth living for, and so in the end mastery in practice. That is the deepest need of civilization. And, in our industrialized society, we can appreciate the Wise Man's assertion that it cannot be purchased with gold or silver. We inherit from the struggles of our predecessors full political and social freedom: they have left us wealth, knowledge, education and the means of controlling our environment. But part of the legacy which they have bequeathed us is a desperate confusion of values. Under the pressure of democratic sentiment we have almost made a religion of mediocrity. In the modern West, as has been truly said, "everything tends to be

[1] K. E. Kirk, *The Vision of God* (Bampton Lectures), p. 213.

dragged down to the level at which it is intellectually understandable or emotionally satisfying to the man who has neither purified his perceptions, disciplined his will, nor cultivated his mind."[1] Nothing is needed more desperately than a scrutiny and revision of our standards and a valid criterion for our judgements. For centuries, almost up to living memory, it was the prerogative of the Christian Church to be the custodian of the world's values, whether moral, æsthetic or intellectual. To-day, for reasons that must be discussed later, this task has been entrusted to other hands. The most crucial function in our civilization is now discharged by novelists and critics, dramatists, editors and wireless publicists. But there is a growing dissatisfaction with the leadership of our intellectuals. It is their task to show us the path of wisdom. But the answers are as various as the voices, and few seem to speak to our condition. In the general flux of all valuations, where can we hope to find a secure standard ?

Up to about fifty years ago, at least in English-speaking countries, there would have been little doubt how to answer. It would have been taken more or less for granted that the world possesses in Christianity the final and perfect scheme of conduct, and that the decision on all moral problems is to be found within the New Testament and especially in the teaching of our Lord. But for us that answer is no longer possible. The growth of the historical sense among us (and perhaps this rather than our boasted science is the differentia of the " modern " mind), and our rightly changed attitude to Scripture make the attempt to solve modern issues by Biblical quotation invalid. Moreover that writ no longer runs. To the mind of our time that is not an argument. It involves a portentous begging of the question, which is the whole question at

[1] Laurence Hyde, *The Prospects of Humanism*, p. 16.

issue, Is the Christian reading of Man's life the true one? Are the moral standards of Christianity such that the modern conscience can endorse, or are they merely ethical traditions bound up with ways of thought and life which the lapse of time is fast making obsolete? That is precisely what has to be answered. And, as everyone knows, there is no point at which Christianity is so hard pressed. Our intellectuals tend to assume as an axiom beyond need of argument that the Christian ethic is now out of date and cannot in sincerity commend itself to the free critical judgment of our age. We cannot rely on quoting texts: we cannot postulate a Christian moral outlook. The Christian claim is what has now to be vindicated. Can Christianity come out into the open, take a survey of the various new factors, psychological, economic, sociological, and offer creative moral leadership at once more progressive and more stable than non-Christian thinking can promise? The Church stands or falls by the answer. "If the finality of the Christian ideal of personal character and the Christian rule of conduct cannot be maintained, no temporary success of the apologist in rebutting this or that ill-considered 'scientific' or 'historical' criticism can alter the fact that the Christian faith as a religion is under sentence of death."[1]

The ultimate appeal of Christianity must always be to the fruits of Christian living and their moral vitality and effectiveness. That after all is the test of its Founder. But this truth must not be misinterpreted in the way congenial to our contemporaries. Our world is quick to appreciate that test: yet it is equally prone to misapply it. Christianity *is* a way of life: ethical direction is inherent in it, and the fruits of the Spirit are and always must be the guarantee of its claim on men's allegiance. Yet it is not primarily an ethic. It has been the strength of English Christianity in some of its typical manifestations that it has grasped with

[1] A. E. Taylor, *The Faith of a Moralist*, Vol. I, p. 11.

peculiar force, sometimes to the neglect of other factors, the moral commitments of religion. In this it reflects truly the native English temper, with its instinctive flair for the practical. "Life" calls to us more than "logic"; the heights and depths of mystical experience, no less than the speculations of Theology, leave the average Englishman unmoved. The sober, duty-loving Christianity so characteristic of the national mind has about it a power and restraint which is genuinely deserving of reverence. But its very strength sometimes betrays it. The popular tendency at the present moment is to take out of the Christian religion everything distinctively religious and to call what is left "real Christianity". Thus men will assert that "real" Christianity, when stripped of its merely ornamental frillings and its doctrinal incrustations, is to put into practice the Sermon on the Mount. The Church, they think, has wrapped round this kernel a husk of largely irrelevant complexity. Hence they are impatient of Theology as of something abstract and remote from life, and ask for a "practical" presentation.

But is this "real" Christianity? Let us concede what is true in this contention. Christianity *is* a way of living: it is that before it is a theology. It is also true that the Christian Church has often tended to misplace its emphasis. It has been assumed, especially by the clergy, that when God came into the world in Christ He revealed a system of theology. But that is precisely what He did not do: He revealed Himself, at the heart of life. The Church has been fierce where Christ was gentle and complacent where He was terrifying. He made of those who sought to join His company uncompromising moral demands, but asked for no doctrinal affirmations. It has been the temptation of the Christian Church to make its first demand on disciples an assent to theological propositions, while acquiescing far too supinely in moral inertia or compromise. It is true also that in the course of centuries Christianity has become complicated and overlaid with academic erudition. There is urgent need for us to rediscover the vital simplicities of faith and to learn to speak again in the tones of Galilee. The Englishman is right in this insistence. But he is prone to forget the obvious fact that we cannot have the Christian way of living apart from the Christian religion. No doubt the tree is known by its fruits: but there cannot be any fruits without the tree. The Christian standards only apply to those who accept the Christian assumptions and seek to live in the strength of the Christian faith.

We cannot take Christ's recorded sayings and seek to "apply" them (as the phrase runs) to a life that rests on different assumptions. The prime condition of entering the Kingdom is to share the standpoint of the King; and that involves being reborn into it. Christianity, after all, is a religion: it is primarily a relationship to God which issues in distinctive ways of living and characteristic valuations on life. But the latter presuppose the former. The liberals of the late nineteenth century assumed that the Christian moral principles would always hold the allegiance of men, even though dogmatic Christianity would not survive in the climate of modernity. That genial expectation has been falsified. The slow decay of Christian faith and worship proves to have undermined the moral structure. And we cannot reconstruct Christian ethics save on the basis of Christian faith.

Thus behind our immediate question of the Christian ethic in the modern world, there stands the prior and more searching question of Christianity itself and its relevance to the world we live in. And that indicates the lines for our enquiry. The more one reflects upon the moral issues which press most heavily on the Christian Church, the more keen the recognition becomes that any discussion must be superficial if it shirks the more fundamental problem:

What do we really mean by Christianity and in what does the Christian way of life consist? We cannot solve any moral question empirically or by mere rule of thumb. That mistake has been made too often. Behind nearly all our hesitations, our perplexities and weaknesses in practice, there lie ultimate questions of Theology. The attempt to revise the Anglican Prayer Book as though it were just an "administrative" question, with no coherent philosophy behind it, nearly brought the house round our ears. That humiliating episode should serve for a warning in the sphere of morals. If Christianity is ineffective in the moral leadership of this generation, the failure lies not in its lack of zeal but in the confusion of our thinking and the poverty of our vision of God. Christ is central in our moral universe only so far as we refuse to isolate Him from the whole context of our experience.

Since I started, ten years ago, to write a volume on Christian Ethics, that recognition has been forced upon me, till what seemed at first to be quite straightforward has become a frightening and exacting task. It seems to me now that what is really needed if the Christian ethic is to be vindicated to the hearts and minds of this generation, is to re-enthrone the Christian faith in God in the only position which it can rightly occupy—at the centre of men's thinking and willing, and their interpretation of life. Short of that we are ethically powerless. In a certain sense there is no Christian ethic: there are Christian attitudes to experience. The Christian moral standard is, after all, not a code which has to be defended against the attacks of a froward generation: it is an insight to be achieved. Troeltsch was fully justified in asserting that "there is no absolute Christian ethic, rather a continual remastering of the changing materials of the world's life".[1]

[1] *Die Sozial-lehren der christlichen Kirchen*, p. 986. "Es gibt keine absolute christliche Ethik . . . sondern nur Bemeisterungen der wechselnden Weltlagen."

But the power by which this mastery is to be exercised is the Christian faith and the Christian loyalty. And the non-theological Christianity so popular in some Christian circles nowadays seems to me to be always in danger of overbalancing into sentimentalism. Admiration for "the way of Jesus" is not the centre of Christianity, nor can it carry the weight of Christian living. There are many outside any Christian affiliation who acknowledge Christ as their example and the embodiment of their best ideals, who remain confessedly agnostic about the character or existence of God. There are many inside the Christian Churches whose loyalty to Jesus Himself and realization of His companionship should put the rest of us to shame, whose faith and worship nevertheless fall short of the authentic Christian convictions. It is faith in Jesus rather than faith in God: and this is something less than the Christian religion. It is more than doubtful whether this faith can take the strain to which life subjects it. It cannot integrate our experience; for it remains dualistic in the last resort. It can scarcely possess that triumphant certainty which can withstand the acids of disillusionment or defy the relativity of history. To revere Christ's character is a precious thing; but it is not the religion of Christians. Christianity is the worship of the Father, the vision of God as revealed in Christ.

For the modern mind this is the crucial difficulty. Nearly all the forces that play upon us conspire to make belief in God difficult. In the old world everyone believed in God: that is perhaps the most signal difference between ancient and modern history. The task of the earliest Christian preachers was to persuade men who believed in God to accept Christ's interpretation of Him. The task of the Church to-day is almost the opposite; to help people who at different levels and in various degrees believe in Christ to win to conviction about God. The revival and even, it may be, the survival of Christianity in the world to-day depends on its success in this enterprise. The real question about Christian ethics is therefore to show how the Christian world-view, centred upon faith in a living God and accordingly supernatural in its emphasis, can offer itself as the interpretation of our rich and manifold experience in an ever-widening and bewildering Universe. To me, at least, that is how our task presents itself: and that is the angle from which we shall approach it.

Thus to some this book will appear "unpractical". Only towards the end shall we be occupied with detailed questions about Christian conduct. Nor shall we be directly concerned with pastoral oversight or moral counsel. Our task is preliminary to that: it is to explore the presuppositions and the adequacy of the Christian way of life in the changed conditions of a changing world. If it be objected that this is "mere theory", there is at least this partial justification: we realize a little more clearly than some preceding generations the place of thought in our religious attitudes. The conversion which is demanded by religion is in part at least an educational process, a gradual reshaping of men's thinking.

2. The Acids of Modernity

"In the long run (writes Bishop Gore) what any society is to become will depend on what it believes or disbelieves about the eternal things."[1] It is notorious that in our own day there is no one common attitude to any of the fundamental issues. Even in the domain of physical science this is a true account of our situation. No doubt we are commonly told that "science teaches" this or that statement about the Universe; and such is the modern reverence for science with its brilliant record of tangible achievement that men will believe it blindly, on authority, so agape are they at

[1] *Jesus of Nazareth*, p. 250.

the scientist's conjuring tricks. But such assertions are wholly illegitimate. There is not yet any agreed scientific position. Popular writers may invoke science to justify one or another dogmatic utterance so long as it is not a dogma about religion. But when science is true to its own genius it repudiates any such claim on its behalf. For it is, by the laws of its own logic, a resolute abstention from certainty and a ceaseless revision of hypotheses. All is quest, trial and experiment, disciplined fidelity to new facts; and therein resides both its moral grandeur and its mental exhilaration.

Thus even in the scientific field, where the modern world has achieved its greatest triumph, there is no accepted body of certain truth. When we come to the province of philosophy, which seeks to interpret the meaning of life as a whole, and religion, which is an attitude towards it, our world has admittedly lost its sense of direction. Every civilization in the past has been built upon some common world view, some attitude to life and its significance, to the powers which surround and sustain it and the context within which it is set, controlling its life and its institutions. Civilization to-day has no world view. About the eternal things it suspends judgment. Beyond that characteristic temper of mind vaguely called the scientific approach, which has impregnated the thought of our contemporaries even though they may not be conscious of it, we can hardly assume any common ground in our conception of the meaning of life, and still less in our religious attitudes, as between one modern man and another. A man's religious beliefs, we insist, are his own personal intimate concern. There is no faith that we can take for granted, no agreed standard of moral valuation. And thus, though the rhythm of modern life tends increasingly towards Collectivism, yet our civilization is not unified by any common spiritual allegiance and issues out of no inward unity. The disintegration of individual lives is thus partly cause and partly result of the disintegration in our social order. "In the Middle Ages (writes Professor Powicke) the hold of the Church was due to the fact that it could satisfy the best cravings of the whole man; his love of beauty, his desire for goodness, his endeavour after truth. In these days the demand for certainty is distracted by conflicting claims: in the Middle Ages it was not so: the divine mystery was felt to inspire a divine order in which all knowledge and all emotion could be reconciled."[1]

The moral chaos of our world is partly caused by the break up of this synthesis. We are "distracted by conflicting claims". And this is the characteristic note of modernity. Modern European history may be described, from one point of view, as the record of a widening fissure between religious faith on the one hand and the claims of civilization on the other. The culture of mediæval Christendom was reared upon an agreed metaphysic and a common relationship to the eternal order. That idealization of the Middle Ages in which some moderns try to compensate their discontent with existing conditions is perhaps rather a futile affectation. It was no golden age of peace or righteousness. In the telling phrase of Sabatier "the men of that time had all the vices except triviality, all the virtues except moderation".[2] But go as far as we will with Dr. Coulton, it remains true that mediæval Christendom had achieved a magnificent unification in which all the departments of life and all the activities of the human spirit were successfully wrought into one organic pattern, which reflected the pattern of the eternal order. God was King: Christ reigned in Heaven: and all earthly authority was "held" from God, as the knight held from his lord or the lord from his feudal suzerain. God reigned: and life in all its details was to be interpreted

[1] *The Legacy of the Middle Ages*, p. 39.

[2] *Life of St. Francis*, Introduction, p. xxv.

only by His will. Human experience had a fixed point of reference. Intellectually, the scholastic system envisaged the whole field of available knowledge, the entire sweep and range of man's activity, in the light of the one master principle. Thus " when the age of the Reformation came, economics is still a branch of ethics and ethics of theology : all human activities are treated as falling within a single scheme whose character is determined by the spiritual destiny of mankind ".[1]

It was magnificent, but it could not endure. Reality cannot be incarcerated in the syllogisms of scholastic theology. Looking back we can see clearly how inevitable it was that this mediæval system should be broken up and enlarged. " Secular " knowledge has given mankind an understanding of God's ways, a power of controlling environment, a field for research, venture and enterprise which would never have been opened to us within the circumference of that premature synthesis. Medicine supplies one speaking instance. It *had* to become conscientiously non-religious if it was to achieve its vocation. It is clear that a purely " scientific " medicine, acknowledging no religious control, has freed the race from a burden of pain and terror before which the science of Christendom stood impotent. And yet, as Dr. Rivers came to acknowledge in the light of clinical experience, the separation has injured both parties. The partnership should never have been dissolved had each respected the rights of the other.[2] That indeed has been the tragedy of the whole modern development. It was right, as it was unavoidable, that the various departments of knowledge should successfully vindicate their claim to independence of theological control. It was in truth the creative Spirit of God which was thus leading men on to explore the riches of His universe with an enterprise, a daring and

[1] Tawney, *Religion and the Rise of Capitalism*, p. 278.
[2] Rivers, *Medicine, Magic and Religion*, pp. 143, 144.

mastery beyond the imagination of their predecessors. But by a tragic and ruinous irony the price which the modern world has paid for it has been an increasing abandonment of religion and an ever-weakening sense of God at the heart and centre of our experience. Life has lost its controlling unity. The idea of progress has been dissociated from the inspiration of faith. The subsidence of the ancient framework has brought down the over-arching roof of certainty that God is regnant in the universe which, for the men of an earlier generation, gave life shelter and significance.

For us, the world is no longer a home. For " in order to be at home in this world it is not, unfortunately, sufficient to disbelieve in another ".[1] The disillusionment of this lost belief has synchronized (whether as cause or effect) with the dissolution of the social order supporting and supported by the old faith. For the greater number of modern men and women it has now become no longer possible to refer their manifold experience, with its diverse and conflicting claims, to a single principle of interpretation. There are therefore for us no ultimate obligations : each holds only within its own field. Life is for us no longer a unity : it is a number of specialized activities, parallel and largely independent, each with its own technique, its own traditions and, more and more, its own moral standards. There are thus great areas of our civilization, such as economics and sexual relationships, which seem to have broken away from any reference to Christian or even to " moral " standards. For in default of any effective synthesis each sphere and department of modern life works only to its own specifications. The " romantic " attempt to separate love from the wider context of human association, the foolish talk about " Art for art's sake ", the repudiation of all ethical reference implied in the phrase " Business is business ", are less symptoms of moral depravity than

[1] Tawney, *Equality*, p. 110.

results of this fatal dissidence in the structure of modern civilization. For, in this springing asunder of the vital stresses in the arch, religion is no longer the keystone. Religion too has become a specialization, and dwells in its own several house. Its own health, as we shall see later, is gravely imperilled by its aloofness from the vivid concerns of the surrounding world; while the world, unlit by religious guidance, either yields to "unsanctified compulsions" or plunges on blindly towards disaster. The apparent withdrawal of Christianity from any claims to effective leadership in the vast issues which press upon our society is, both for the Church and the world, the most menacing factor in our predicament.

We can hope for no fruitful appreciation of the task confronting the Christian Church without at least an attempt to understand the forces at work in contemporary life,—those so-called "acids of modernity" which have been so brilliantly analysed in Walter Lippmann's *Preface to Morals*. Since it was first introduced to English readers this book has been quoted so widely and read so avidly that reference to it has become almost hackneyed. I should be the last to underrate what we owe to this searching diagnosis. Yet Mr. Lippmann, I think, overestimates the strength of the purely intellectual solvents, at least in the great mass of the population. It is true, of course, that the traditional faith rested upon or was held to be bound up with certain beliefs about the universe and certain attitudes to religious authority into which the modern critical temper and the acids of the experimental sciences have eaten their way with destructive effect. The mediæval form of Christian society presupposes the scholastic philosophy: and those who hanker after its re-establishment must remember that the first step required of them is to re-indoctrinate the twentieth century with the metaphysic of St. Thomas Aquinas. But the hold of religion on the popular mind depends less than we commonly suppose on its rational appeal to intelligence. It is by its fruits that men will accept or reject it. People will revere a religion, despite intellectual misgivings, if it satisfies their emotional needs and proves itself in the test of moral effectiveness. The hold of the Church on people's minds in the later Middle Ages shews this clearly enough. But the attack from the intellectual side has converged in modern civilization with far stronger and more dangerous movements of profound moral dissatisfaction. And " the fact is that more men in our modern era are irreligious because religion has failed to make civilization ethical than because it has failed to maintain its intellectual respectability ".[1] The deepest causes of the lost loyalty to the Christian religion in Western Europe should, in my judgment, rather be looked for in the changed conditions of modern life and the new forms assumed by the social order.

The roots of religion are in the home and the ordered structure of society. Neither the ancient classical tradition nor the Catholic Christendom which was heir to it could conceive religion in any other context. This *is* religion in its historical sense ; and the Christian Church has preserved this tradition. We might almost say that it was the " pagan " element, rightly conserved in Catholic Christianity, which carried it on through the Middle Ages. It was, at its weakest, of the earth earthy ; at its strongest, a witness to an Incarnation. But the old social structure has crashed before the impact of economic forces. The urbanization of modern life, with its vast dormitory districts and its mechanization of the daily routine, has destroyed that sense of responsibility for the health and wealth of a man's social group which was one of religion's most secure bulwarks. A man no longer belongs where he resides ; and everywhere the modern man finds himself at the mercy of largely

[1] Reinhold Niebuhr, *Does Civilization need Religion?* (New York, Macmillan Co., 1927), p. 12.

impersonal forces. He seems, indeed, to have scarcely any foothold in the structure of our civilization. In business he is merely a unit and in politics one among many million voters. "Life to-day," as Mr. Lippmann says, "is not a social order at all as Greek city states or the feudal society was a social order. It is rather a field for careers, an arena of talent, an ordeal by trial and error and a risky speculation. No man has an established position in the modern world."[1] And all this is peculiarly inimical to any belief in an ordered universe informed by a spiritual Purpose. "It is worth remembering that the best seed-ground for superstition is a society in which the fortunes of men seem to bear practically no relation to their merits and efforts."[2] Thus now, as in the Hellenistic age, the emergence of the lonely man, homeless in a gregarious urban society, leads to the invocation of *Tyche*. "The god of the modern world is Luck."

Moreover, the application of science to the means of communication and transport has forced the world so closely together and made its relationships so much more difficult that the need for moral control and direction has become far more glaringly obvious. Yet few of the simpler prescriptions of the Christian ethic seem now to be adequate; and religion is more and more suspect because it fails to vindicate its authority in those very conditions of life which make men at once more conscious of their need for it and yet less predisposed to accept it. "Religion has been placed in such a sorry plight in fulfilling its ethical tasks in modern civilization because the mechanization of society has made an ethical life for the individual at once more necessary and more difficult and failure more obvious, than in any previous civilization."[3]

[1] *Op. cit.*, p. 247.
[2] Gilbert Murray, *Five Stages of Greek Religion*, p. 164
[3] Niebuhr, *op. cit.*, p. 13.

Christianity is thus assailed by attack on both flanks at once, both the ethical and the theological. Meanwhile contemporary life with its ceaseless movement and excitement, its concentration on what is external and increasing absorption in the mechanical, conspires to quench any vivid recognition of the spiritual aspects in our experience. How weak are the defences of spirit against the corrosion of materialism! Against the massive strength and efficiency of economic and mechanical enterprise supernatural religion seems powerless. The fundamental problem of Christian morals is not that life to-day is inherently vicious; for indeed in a great many ways it is morally finer than in the ages preceding it. It is rather that modern civilization presents itself as an enclosed system, richly endowed with much that is splendid, stored with power, resource and initiative, pregnant with still undisclosed developments, but with no seeming place or recognition for the claims of the spiritual and supernatural. It sometimes seems as though material interest were the only allegiance to which the world of our time can offer itself in whole-hearted consecration. Men have indeed found a religious substitute in devotion to the deified State as the Dispenser of economic betterment.

What is happening in Soviet Russia needs to be very profoundly considered by all representatives of the Christian ethic. That is by far the mightiest experiment of which history has any record. Its avowed aims are frankly materialistic; the Soviets have brutally repudiated all that is associated with Christianity. The Communist aims are, from the Christian standpoint, almost as satanical as their methods. Yet how lamentable is the contrast between the effectiveness of the children of this world in pursuing the ends "of their generation" and the relative helplessness of the children of light! The intense and passionate loyalties which have been called forth by that stupendous effort, fertilizing all men's convictions and organizing the life of a vast community with a single and invincible will, amount almost to religious inspiration. In face of this, the mild otherworldliness of religious teachers seems almost futile. Obviously I am not here suggesting that the spiritual interpretation of life for which Christianity stands in the world is disproved or overwhelmed by its enemies. But I do wish to suggest deep misgivings whether *our conception* of otherworldliness truly interprets the Christian genius or can hope to maintain itself successfully against the pressure of secularist forces.

The narrow dimensions of modern life, set in a purely this-world field of reference, must leave it starved and impoverished, a prey to those poisons of degeneracy which, if we read the lesson of history rightly, are endemic in all secularized societies. The task which confronts Christianity is to lift this world, so rich, yet so penurious, on to loftier planes of possibility by setting man's life against its eternal background and redeeming all its this-world concerns by the cleansing presence of the supernatural. But it cannot hope to redeem the surrounding world so long as otherworldliness is interpreted as aloofness from the world's affairs. If religion stands, as it stands at present, self-contained in its own preoccupations over against the values and interests of the world which it is commissioned to save, it will lose both the world and its own soul. Yet to identify itself unreservedly with any aims and tasks in this world of time would be to betray its charter as a religion. We must therefore enquire rather more closely into the real place of religion as a directing and redemptive force in the midst of contemporary society.

Is it true to say, as we preachers do say, that everything in life is religious? Or is religion, in its own nature, something apart, unique and incommensurable with all other activities of spirit ? In the latter case, what is its true relation to the non-religious values and attitudes—how is " religion " related to " life " ? The discussion may appear to be " academic " : but this is in truth no academic issue. It is my conviction that on our answer to it depends the whole future of Christianity as an effective force in the world's affairs. It matters pre-eminently to us in England. In this land the historic Christian Church is still entwined by countless subtle threads around the life of the realm and nation. Here, almost alone, the ideals of " Labour " and the finest social enthusiasms have not sundered themselves from Christianity. England is still at heart far more Christian than any nation of the Western tradition. Our people is readier than any—and never more so than at this moment when secular leadership fails it so disastrously—to accept a strong lead from the Christian Churches. Before English-speaking Christianity there lies such a unique opportunity as has rarely if ever before been entrusted to it. The position of our race in the coming world-order, our tutelage of emerging new nations, our weight (even in our humiliation) at Geneva and in the Council of Powers, invest with incomparable responsibility what religion may yet achieve in this country. Nothing matters more to the world and to the cause of the Divine Kingdom than that the Christian faith in England should again establish itself creatively at the heart of our people's daily life and interests.

Towards that, a theological volume may be a poverty-stricken contribution. For we must never allow ourselves to forget that, be our thought and insight never so clear into the principles of the Christian life, we may nevertheless fail disastrously in immediate practical decision, when our Christian loyalty is put to the test. Loyalty matters more even than insight ; and many an unlettered disciple can express the Christian ethic triumphantly when " to us belongeth confusion of face". But we cannot be effective in action, whether in pastoral work or in politics, till we know what it is that we are trying to do. To clarify our vision of our objectives should not be without its help in attaining them.

CHAPTER II

RELIGION AND LIFE

1. The Isolation of Religion

"We have come to take it for granted that the unifying force in society is material interest, and that spiritual conviction is a source of strife and division. Modern civilization has pushed religion and the spiritual elements in culture out of the main stream of development, so that they have lost touch with social life and become sectarianized and impoverished. But at the same time this has led to the impoverishment of our whole culture."[1]

In the last chapter we made some attempt to analyse some of those forces in modern Europe since the Renaissance which have conspired to effect this revolution. The whole direction of modern history has been away from a supernatural centre. The break-up of the philosophical synthesis which had sustained the unity of the older world has involved the abandonment or at least the weakening of the vital faith which was at the heart of it; and the changing conditions of life itself have militated more and more dangerously against a spiritual interpretation. Thus life has moved outwards away from religion, and religion has drawn back inwards upon itself. St. Thomas' mighty contribution to the culture of mediæval Catholicism was not merely that he supplied Christendom with a satisfying metaphysic. It lay still more in his discrimination between Nature and Supernature, never confused yet subtly harmonized in one rich unity of system. The actual forms of

[1] C. Dawson, *Progress and Religion*, p. 249.

the Thomist philosophy are no longer tenable by our thinking; yet it was he who made the experiment possible. For he succeeded in doing full justice to the order of nature and political life, as possessed of its own relative independence yet an integral part of the divine scheme, woven into an indiscerptible fabric of which the ultimate pattern is supernatural. But from the time of the Reformation onward there is traceable a new and disastrous tendency. The distinction of Nature and Supernature had been represented in the old system by parallel manifestations of Christian life, the "religious" and the "secular"; and the suggestion was never avoided that the former was a "higher" fulfilment of what is implied in the loyalty of a Christian. There is no need here to elaborate the abuses implicit in this conception, which indeed resulted only too easily in handing over life in the world to sub-Christian standards and obligations. The avowed aim of the Protestant reformers was to set religion free from the cloister, to deliver it from its monastic exclusiveness, to establish Christian faith and piety as the inspiration of the home and the market-place. But in fact the results of the reforming movement have worked in almost the opposite sense. The tendency ever since the Reformation, both in the Roman and the Reformed Churches, has been to think of religion in isolation, as a self-sufficient and self-sustaining activity, torn out of that many-coloured pattern of political, cultural and æsthetic interests which alone secure its virility and wholesomeness. The Christian life has accordingly been interpreted almost wholly in purely "religious" terms; and the constant danger has been to identify it either with institutional conformity or with private religious experience.

The course of this lamentable process forms a paradoxical chapter in history. Its causes lie partly in those conditions which the Reformation set itself to redress, partly in the Reformers' own background and the idiosyncrasies of their personal temperament. The magnificent evangelical appeal from the moral abuses of a corrupt Papacy to the pure standards of Scriptural Christianity led to results which were unexpected. The authority of an infallible Scripture has proved to be more sterilizing in morals than the autocracy of an infallible Pope. In their zeal for the newly discovered Scriptures, so penetrating and trenchant in challenge to moral corruption and inert conscience, the Reformers allowed themselves to become intoxicated with a crude and fanatical bibliolatry. This, in its turn, meant almost inevitably to overstress the Hebraic element in the Christian tradition and to ignore and even to seek to suppress its platonic and classical inheritance. Protestantism sought to repudiate all that was suspect of being associated with the worldly and secularized Curia. Thus in effect it broke off decisively from the humanist tradition in Christendom and attempted to preserve an undefiled faith in its austere, apocalyptic nakedness. Moreover, the still uncritical attitude of the reforming leaders to Scripture elevated the Jewish sacred books to the same level of status and inspiration as that of the Gospels and Epistles, and even at times tended to give them precedence. There is little trace in Calvin, for example, that the Scripture to which he appeals as authoritative embraces the Sermon on the Mount! This exaggerated deference to the Old Testament has left strange marks on the Anglican Prayer Book, with its passion for finding a patriarchal precedent for every detail in the life of the modern Christian. Thus, as has been said, Luther's work "amounted to a de-intellectualization of the Catholic tradition. He eliminated the philosophical and Hellenic element and accentuated everything that was Semitic and non-intellectual."[1]

The popular notion that the reforming leaders stood for religious or political liberty is impossible to square with

[1] Dawson, *op. cit.*, p. 181.

the facts. Nothing was further from their intention. It was, nevertheless, their avowed objective to bring religion into the homes of the people, to replace the aristocracy of the cloister by a new aristocracy of the market-place, to insist on the priesthood of all believers, and thus to redeem the whole range of experience by breaking down the wall of partition between life in "religion" and life in the "world". But the long-term results of the movement have, in fact, been almost the precise contrary. To speak disrespectfully and slightingly of the precious achievements won by the Reformation, as is the fashion among many clergy, betokens a real spiritual blindness. Yet it is true that in the long run faith has been brought out into the world only at the price of a virtual surrender to it. The mediæval Church had been lax in its moral demands on the individual, and had met human nature more than half-way. But it had tried (and had not failed entirely) to keep its hold on public morality and to control the conduct of groups, whether social, economic or national, by the moral demands of the Christian Commonwealth. Protestantism reversed this distinction. It has, on the whole, secured a high standard of personal conduct and religious devotion: but it has withdrawn before the challenge of Christianizing public relationships.

Formally, no doubt, the mediæval assumptions persisted both in the Reformed Churches and in that which emerged from the Council of Trent. For Luther himself no less than for Calvin the idea of a unitary society, at once Church and State, was axiomatic.[1] In Lutheran countries it becomes a State-Church, in those of the Geneva tradition it becomes a theocratic Church-State: but both alike assume the identification. Yet Protestantism in both its leading forms, and perhaps most markedly in its Lutheran version, has been prone to combine orthodoxy in belief and intense devotion in personal religion with inertia, and at

[1] Compare Troeltsch, *op. cit.*, p. 521.

times with a shameless cynicism, in the sphere of economics and politics and the great issues of public morality.

Luther insisted with splendid rightness that the essential sphere of the Christian life is in the duties of a man's "calling" (*Beruf*). Yet this insistence, which should have inspired him to think out creatively and realistically what is implied in the Christian ethic in the rapidly changing sixteenth-century world, has in fact held Lutheranism back from exerting any strong moral influence on the life of surrounding society. It has been prone to lend a religious sanction to a mere traditionalism in economics and a mere absolutism in politics.

The moral horizons of Luther himself were narrowly circumscribed and traditionalist, and his conceptions of Christian duty were confined to the immediate home circle and the undeveloped life of peasant-communities. Despite his attitude in the Peasants' Revolt, he was by origin and at heart a peasant with the peasant's rooted distrust of capital and large-scale economic enterprises.[1] He was thus altogether disqualified from offering any effective leadership in the application of Christian ethics to the new industrial life of Europe.[2] Moreover, he tended increasingly to identify obedience to the will of God with absolute acceptance of the existing order. And, as Weber observes in his fascinating monograph, "starting from this background, it was impossible for Luther to establish a new or in any way fundamental connection between worldly activity and religious principles".[3]

There was a further disqualification at the very centre of his religious position. The superb insistence on *sola fides* is the charter of evangelical religion. Yet this isolation of faith both from its expression in works and from its

[1] F. T. M. Lindsay, *History of the Reformation*, I, p. 335.
[2] Compare Tawney, *Religion and the Rise of Capitalism*, pp. 79 to 102.
[3] Max Weber, *The Protestant Ethic and the Spirit of Capitalism*, p. 85.

spiritual coefficients really destroys the psychological basis of a constructive Christian morality. For it is always exposed to the danger of allowing a private religious experience to be a substitute for the Christian task of carrying out the will of God in the world. Indeed the independence of faith—whether faith be identified with "assurance" (that is, with certain emotional states) or with theological orthodoxy—cannot but impose an invincible inhibition on the ethical expression of faith itself. The wild and almost inarticulate paradoxes of Karl Barth's Crisis Theology only give violent expression to what has been always inherent in Lutheranism. It is haunted by the spectre of having to choose between pietism and secularization. Pietism has steadfastly kept alive certain very precious religious values; it has guarded religion in its uniqueness and saved it from worldliness and exploitation. Yet it is hard to dissent from the verdict that "Lutheranism is the Protestant way of despairing of the world and of claiming victory for the religious ideal without engaging the world in combat".[1] Or, as Mr. Tawney says, less gently, "it riveted on the social thought of Protestantism a dualism which . . . emptied religion of its social content and society of its soul".

Very different both in intention and result was the system perfected by Calvinism. Here was no surrender to pietism, no handing over of Christian responsibility to the test of personal religious experience. It was theocracy in its logical essence, combining Mussolini's dictatorship with the inquisitions of Torquemada. Such a detailed and ruthless regimentation of the individual conscience by the religious group as was presupposed in the Calvinistic communities has never been known outside the walls of a monastery. So far from withdrawing before the attempt to regulate economic activity, the system aimed at economic collectivism under the rule of an omnicompetent Church. The story of

[1] Niebuhr, *op. cit.*, p. 110.

the Church in Geneva and the Puritan Settlements in New England, with the tragi-comedy of their Hebraic zealousness, has been told too often to need repetition. But history can point to no more astonishing irony than the stages by which this theocratic ideal gave birth to unrestrained individualism and threw the cloak of religious sanction over the motive of economic selfishness. It is not necessary for our purpose to do more than refer to the well-known discussions by Max Weber, Tawney and others.[1] The idea of *Beruf*, common to both movements, was invested in the Calvinist system with peculiar and ominous importance. The Lutheran isolation of faith, with its tendency to pietist subjectivity, is paralleled by the ruthless isolation of active will by the Calvinist discipline. Works were not a means of attaining salvation, but they were, as Weber observes, indispensable means for getting rid of the fear of damnation. The Calvinist does not save himself; but he does create the conditions necessary for becoming convinced of his own salvation. The stern self-control and iron discipline and the tonic bracing of the will involved in effective devotion to the Calling thus led to a new and tremendous emphasis on the activist and practical virtues. In effect, therefore, the Genevan discipline creates a new ideal of Christian character, which was accepted only too readily as the inspiration of the rising mercantile classes. "Worldly asceticism," as Weber calls it, with its sanctification of thrift, fitness and energy, preaches the gospel of Work for work's sake. "In place of the humble sinners to whom Luther promises grace if they trust themselves to God in penitent faith are bred those self-confident saints whom we can rediscover in the hard Puritan merchant of the heroic age of capitalism and in isolated instances down to the present."[2] And, as success in the

[1] For the New England developments see H. W. Schneider, *The Puritan Mind*, Constable, 1931.

[2] Weber, *op. cit.*, p. 112.

worldly calling is a manifest sign of divine election, the practical conclusion is close at hand that God helps those who help themselves, and that the amassing of business profits is the surest way of doing God's will. In this way, by an astonishing reversal of all that its founders dreamed of and stood for, Puritanism became the effective drive behind the Industrial Revolution and inspired the *laissez-faire* philosophy. Thus, though it has travelled down the opposite path from that followed by the Lutheran movement, Calvinism arrived at the same point. So completely did it identify religion with the non-religious activities of spirit that it has failed to control them effectively by spiritual and religious standards. Lutheran religion held aloof from the world, entrenched in private religious experience, and has therefore failed to redeem the world. Calvinist religion identified itself so completely with worldly activities as to find in the end that the world is too strong for it.

The Roman Church of the Counter-Reformation was admittedly far more sympathetic to the humanist and intellectual movements of the sixteenth and seventeenth centuries. The brilliant adaptability of the Jesuit order and its power of using popular thought and art as the material of Christian living is witnessed to by those Baroque churches which the taste of our time is learning again to appreciate. Yet it is impossible not to recognize that the whole aim, policy and method of the post-Tridentine Roman Catholic Church has been and remains irredeemably sectarian. It reformed itself at the Counter-Reformation: so long as purely institutional aims remain the governing principles of its Hierarchy, it cannot hope to reform the world.

Thus Christianity since the Reformation in all its main varieties of expression has less and less succeeded in permeating or bringing under religious obedience the cultural life of surrounding society. Life and Religion have gone their separate ways, and the consequences for both have been ruinous.

2. Religion and Response to Life

In ancient cities such as York or Oxford the city walls still remain standing amid the confusion of modern shops and dwelling-houses. In the past these walls encircled the city, guarding the lives of its inhabitants, defining their activities and relationships, marking out the pattern of communal life, and holding together in an organic unity its richly diverse projects and purposes. The modern city has spread beyond their boundaries. It extends for miles outside the " city " area, with its ever-expanding population, its industries constantly developing, its schools, cinemas and playing fields. The more the community develops its life the further it moves away from the centre. The ancient walls are still preserved as honoured relics of an historical past, but they no longer embrace the life of the people. The expansion, the movement, the novelty, the developing purposes and creative planning, all lie away beyond the old citadel. I have sometimes thought that this is a kind of parable of the plight of religion in the twentieth century. Religious institutions are venerated as monuments of a grand mediæval legacy, but are thought to have little direct connection with the life and movement of an expanding world. Religion is held by many of our contemporaries to be not so much untrue as irrelevant to the manifold tasks and concerns of civilization. Indeed many of the finest minds have come to believe themselves confronted with an unbelievably tragic choice. On the one side there is the Christian religion, to the claims of which they are keenly sensitive, withdrawn (as it seems) from the world, and aloof from its opportunities and enterprises. On the other side are the movement and colour, the rich gifts and exacting demands of twentieth-century civilization. The two present themselves as alternatives and men believe that they must decide between them. How can we deliver the next generation from this disastrous dilemma ?

There is probably no one who wishes to preserve the bad distinction between religious and secular. Nobody, if the issue were put to him, would deny that religion if it means anything must penetrate and hallow the whole range of life ; and the great task before Christianity is to swing back personal religion to the only place which it can properly occupy, at the redemptive centre of all experience. But this, I urge, can only be done by observing certain vital distinctions which we have been too prone to obliterate. We all agree that no living religion can accept a place on the margins of life : it must be central or it is nothing. We rightly repudiate the modern readiness to withdraw politics and economics from the religious sphere of influence, and thus in effect to assert that Christianity only applies to the more private aspects of our response to the calls which life makes on us. We rightly judge such an attitude to be blasphemy. But the way in which we express that conviction seems to need rather careful scrutiny. We commonly say in popular exhortation that of course the whole of life is religious, or that religion and life are co-extensive. But this is, I think, entirely untrue and is charged moreover with grave dangers both to religion and to morality. That nothing in life is irrelevant to religion, and that religion on its side must influence all our attitudes and activities,—so much, obviously, is beyond dispute. But that is by no means the same thing as to say that everything ought to be religious or that religion is the same as everything else : if it is, why do we need a distinct name for it ? To press to its logical conclusion what is really implied in such statements is not only to empty religion of its own unique and specific content : it is also to paralyse any creative ethic. Mediæval history warns us sufficiently against this too facile identification. At the end of the mediæval period "there is not an object nor an action, however trivial, that is not constantly correlated with Christ or salvation. All thinking tends to religious interpretation of individual things; there is an enormous unfolding of religion in daily life. This spiritual wakefulness, however, results in a dangerous state of tension, for the presupposed transcendental feelings are sometimes dormant, and whenever this is the case, all that is meant to stimulate spiritual consciousness is reduced to appalling commonplace profanity, to a startling worldliness in other-worldly guise".[1]

The truth of the matter, as I see it, rests on a razor edge position. Recent Psychology has been far too ready to talk about "religious experience" without stopping to ask what it means. Attempts are made to separate off certain privileged or enclosed areas from the whole field of human experience and to call these specifically "religious". But it is at least exceedingly questionable whether such a procedure is justified. The tendency is to equate religious experience with a certain intensity of feeling. The "Varieties" analysed by William James were in point of fact notoriously unvaried. We cannot equate the reality of religion with the emotional storms of adolescence. It is true, of course, that in more recent books such as Professor Pratt's *Religious Consciousness*, and still more in Otto's *Idea of the Holy*, this limitation of outlook is corrected. But even there the suggestion is scarcely avoided that religion *is* a peculiar kind of feeling which happens to certain people in certain circumstances. But about ninety per cent of the human race, at least in its Anglo-Saxon branches, are (to the best of my knowledge) unvisited by religious experience in this sense at all. We cannot regard religion as the monopoly of one particular constitutional temperament. Nor can we consent to expose it to the

[1] Huizinga, *The Waning of the Middle Ages*, p. 136.

chances of age, health, the state of the weather, and other quite accidental circumstances. If, on the other hand, the distinction is based on a difference, real or supposed, in the object of our experience, it is still harder for religion to sanction it. For it is surely compelled to assert that God is the ultimate Object of all experience. Religious experience cannot in fact mean anything but the life-experience of a religious man, his total response to his environment as directed and sustained by his religion.

Yet, all the same, religion *is* " different ". It is obviously not the same thing as the æsthetic or scientific or even the ethical attitude to reality: and its life depends on preserving this difference. Huizinga's study is a searching reminder that unless religion retains its proper " distance ", unless it avoids an undue " familiarity " in its intimate commerce with life, it ends in degeneracy and degradation. Religion is something unique, which cannot be equated with anything else. If it usurps the functions of ethics or of art or science or economics, it destroys them as well as killing itself. Is it not true that the moral poverty and social misery of India is due more than anything else to the unchallenged tyranny of religion, usurping the functions which should be discharged by other activities of the human spirit (the economic, for instance, or the scientific) and overwhelming this-world concerns by the unrelieved pressure of the supernatural ? Mr. Gandhi rightly desires to save India from the demoralization of spirit which accompanied our industrial revolution. But he is in danger, no less than Luther, of conferring religious sanctions on a backward-looking economic traditionalism which must in fact prove itself powerless to supply the moral needs of his people.

Thus to say that everything is religious may lead in practice to disconcerting conclusions. Religion is, in its essence, otherworldly, and if it loses that note of detachment it almost forfeits its religious character.[1] Yet if and so far as religion stands aloof, without vivid and sensitive responsiveness to the values and movements of the life which surrounds it, it can hope neither to redeem the world nor to preserve its own soul alive. For religion then becomes introverted and seeks within itself for its sustenance. Then what we call the " spiritual life " comes more and more to be interpreted in exclusively " religious " and devotional terms, with the result that the non-religious activities (which are, after all, nine-tenths of life) shrink away from religion altogether; till prayer and worship become almost inevitably " an optional epiphenomenon of the moral life, a pietistic form of self-suggestion proper only to sick souls ".[2] For religion itself is then left without content, and becomes an attitude towards an attitude, which is almost the definition of sentimentality. But there is in fact no " spiritual life " apart from those manifold occupations of thought, contemplation or conduct which are the prerogatives of spirit. These, the various non-religious values, are the raw material of religion: and religion mainly consists in relating these, through its characteristic activity of worship, to God as the supreme Source of value. It can only remain masculine and healthy in close and vitalizing contact with the spiritual soil out of which it springs. If it withdraws inward upon itself it becomes anæmic and pathological. Among people of religious temperament it becomes either a frightful preoccupation with the passing states of their own consciousness, or finds its outlet in that " churchy " chatter, more boring than anything else on earth, about the curate and his newest chasuble. For the plain man it becomes too easily satisfied with a formal and almost barren conformity. To be religious

[1] Cf. the remark of Paul Elmer More that Religion is " the union of other-worldliness with morality ". *The Christ of the New Testament*, p. 5.

[2] Kirk, *Bampton Lectures*, p. 441.

is to be "C. of E." in the well-known sense of the Army identity disk.

The rule, as expressed by von Hügel, is this. "No Grace without the substratum, the occasion, the material of Nature; and no Nature without Grace. . . . Because, without these not directly religious interests and activities, you, however slowly and unperceivedly, lose the material for Grace to work in and on."[1]

It is hard to deny that English Christianity is at present dangerously subject to some such religious introversion. Religion in this country still elicits an immense amount of loyal devotion, personal faithfulness and generosity. But its hold on national life is exceedingly tenuous. It is hard indeed to feel that the Christian Churches are playing their full and rightful part in this hour of our crisis and perplexity. It is not true that the Churches have "failed". If, in the midst of the violent forces of materialism, doubt and moral bewilderment which play on the minds of this generation, they have kept alive Christian faith and hope in millions of hearts in all sections of our community, that is not failure but rich achievement. Nor, again, is it a sign of surrender if much that used to be done by the Churches in the way of social and educational work is now carried through by State or Municipal action. That may be a sign of their triumph, in the permeation of the national conscience by Christian conceptions of duty and obligation. A tutor has not "failed" when his pupil ceases to need his detailed guidance: rather, he feels that at last his work has borne fruit. Nevertheless, despite these admissions, it is difficult to think that Christian forces are achieving anything like the effects which could and should be rightly expected of them. A political party or a social movement which possessed the finest buildings in every district, whole-time agents in every town and village, an

[1] *Letters*, p. 288.

experience gained in twelve or thirteen centuries and the appeal of a passionate conviction, would hardly feel that it was making full use of such unique and incomparable resources if it did not count more than we can claim to count in the opinions and actions of the people. Christianity does not " pull its weight " proportionately to its opportunities. This is due to no lack of zeal in the leaders or the membership of the Churches. They are not corrupt, lazy or self-seeking. They are not sunk in illiberal obscurantism. They are not insensitive to the needs of the age. The standard of integrity and devotion both among the clergy and lay people is probably higher now than it has ever been. Intellectual freedom is honoured more highly than it has been for at least many centuries. There is, at any rate in the Church of England, a growing sense of organic unity, of a common tradition and a common task. It is probably true that the Church is more " alive ", more conscious of its mission and responsibilities and more keenly anxious to serve the world, than at any time since the seventeenth century. But for all that there is some strange frustration. We are still unable to reach over the barrier. Religious life is still something apart and still breathes in an artificial atmosphere. It does not seem to spring up spontaneously out of the daily lives of the people or to be in vital relation to the forces that are moulding our future.

Out of the matrix of the world's life new events are being born daily, new forces emerging into history, laden both with incalculable peril and inexhaustible opportunity. Day by day life brings new gifts to us, sets us new tasks, teaches us new lessons. The time is astir with movement and expansion ; immense new developments are in process, laws and tendencies are being disclosed which we can still but half-understand. Almost daily enriched possibilities, new and more exacting demands, challenging or revealing disclosures, come to us out of the teeming life of the age.

It must be confessed that there is too little in the temper and spirit of the Christian Churches which can match this sense of eager expectancy, too little of such sympathetic response to the values and ambitions of our generation as would give them an acknowledged position of leadership. At times of moral doubt and perplexity the Churches seem to be unable to stand, as it were, alongside the people and show them how the Gospel which they proclaim bears upon their life situation and may help to fashion by the Christ Spirit the "changing materials of the world's life". We seem condemned to remain spectators rather than to be taking part in the game. So that the way of salvation which we offer still seems to those of our contemporaries who are engaged in the dust and heat of conflict unconvincing because so largely irrelevant. We do not suggest that the tasks and claims which fill men's and women's actual lives are themselves the direct concern of the Gospel and the material of Christian living.

Some dim, discomfiting awareness of this disabling limitation serves perhaps to account for that self-consciousness with which modern religious life is afflicted. It may not be wholly unfair to suggest that the excessive and exhausting busyness which is the bane of the Church at this moment, and that quite disproportionate concern with the speeding up of its institutional mechanism, is in truth a kind of compensation by which we seek to disguise from ourselves our own lack of mastery and effectiveness in the great concerns of surrounding civilization. A sense of strain and of rather forced activity is unmistakably present in all the Churches. It offers a most disquieting contrast with the spontaneity of the Christian spirit as it meets us in the New Testament. Indeed the danger of modern Christianity—to concern itself with secondary issues and with the preservation of its own life, forgetful of its primary task in the world—is the result of this introversion to which at present it seems to have fallen victim.

But religion is only genuinely alive if it is genuinely self-forgetful. It is less than authentic Christianity unless it is in rich and vivid response to the values and tasks of life in the world as themselves revelations of God. It can only touch with eternal significance the natural interests and tasks of every day if it breaks away from that false asceticism which it has so long and so ruinously preserved. This suggestion may well sound highly dangerous in an age so self-indulgent as ours. But it would be a complete misrepresentation of the whole position if it were to be argued that I wish to find sanction in Christianity for any hedonistic philosophy. There can be no evading the Cross. It is central in the whole Christian ethic that life can be won only by losing it ; and to obscure this heroic strain with its exacting sacrificial demands would be to abandon Christianity. It is clear moreover that in our generation a primary obligation of Christian living must be in the direction of discipline, a new willingness to endure hardship and a simplification of our standards of life. By no possibility can the Christian ethic be made to give its sanction to self-indulgence. This fructifying asceticism is ineradicable from the mind of Christ. But there is a false and barren form of asceticism which stands aloof from the values of life not in order that it may sanctify but because it fears, ignores or belittles them. This tendency to a false otherworldliness is the radical weakness of modern Christianity. Its causes lie partly in historical circumstances and partly in theological insufficiency ; so that a redirection of the Christian ethic, a recovery of freedom and spontaneity in Christian life and in pastoral practice, depend upon theological rethinking such as it is the aim of this book to suggest. But the impoverishment which results both to religion and to the life of the world from this misplaced or inadequate emphasis is unhappily not a matter of theory. We need take but one obvious illustration. We know that the Church for several centuries expended all its resources of thought and discipline in exalting the celibate ideal and suggesting that the married state was not the concern of a whole-hearted religion. We to-day are trying desperately to revive and re-establish Christian standards in the whole sphere of sex-life and marriage.

The problem before us therefore is this: How, without losing its true otherworldliness, i.e. without ceasing to be a religion, can Christianity establish itself creatively, freely and spontaneously at the heart of the actual life of the twentieth century? "I want to write a book," said Donald Hankey, "called *The Living Goodness*, analysing all the goodness and nobility inherent in plain people, and trying to show how it ought to find expression in the Church."[1] This is not the book that he would have written: but it is an attempt to follow the same clue. Now the picture of an other-worldly religion building a new society round itself, cleansing, redeeming and sustaining its values, is precisely what we can study in the New Testament. It is to this therefore that we next turn.

[1] Quoted in Budd, *The Story of Donald Hankey*, p. 127.

CHAPTER III

THE NEW TESTAMENT CONTRIBUTION

1. The Appeal to the New Testament

IN the last chapter we made some estimate of the Reformers' appeal to Scripture and some of its unexpected results. It remains true that nearly all the renewals and moral reforms within Christianity have sprung from the rediscovery of Scripture and especially the Synoptic Gospels. The moment Christianity loses touch with the inspiration of the New Testament it tends to sink to a sub-Christian level, and its moral witness is weakened or obscured. And to-day the demand of numbers of men and women, impatient of the moral compromises and secondary concerns of the Churches, is expressed in the cry : Back to the New Testament. This is a fully legitimate demand. Apart from the living springs of the New Testament the institutional life of Christianity becomes a petrified ecclesiasticism. And the sacramental system of the Church without the Gospels is blind and formal. What can it avail to share in a Life of whose character we are left in ignorance ? Nothing matters more for Christianity amid its activities and preoccupations than to study to re-learn the Mind of Christ. And if we would know what is the Mind of Christ, and recapture the authentic Spirit, to the New Testament we must always go. In this sense the demand is wholly justified.

But it is important to get our bearings true. It is right that we should start from the New Testament, but we must not start from the Gospels. The real foundation of the Christian ethic is not the " moral teaching of Jesus ". To say this invites misunderstanding which it may be well to anticipate at once. Of course it is true that everything distinctive in the Christian life now and in every age depends inseparably upon its Founder. " To understand the relation of Christianity to the social problem, the decisive factor (wrote Troeltsch) is to recognize that the teaching of Jesus and the formation of the new community is no result of any social movement. . . . ' Charity ' springs from the Christian spirit and only thereby can it maintain itself."[1] A new force came into the world which issued out of the Person of the Lord. It has no other source or explanation. Those qualities and acts and attitudes which the Christian conscience specially reveres are honoured not only and not primarily because they are seen to be good in themselves but because they derive from Him. It is not merely the beauty of his life but its specifically Christlike quality which wins veneration for St. Francis or any other of the Christian saints. We honour them as mirrors of Christ; and it is for this in them that we praise God for those who have been " vessels of His grace and lights of the world in their several generations ". Jesus Himself has set a stamp on life. He has coined an image and superscription which we recognize as of the royal mint wherever and in whomsoever found. He has invested Man with new glory. The haunting story of the Transfiguration, whatever else it may be historically, is an eternal symbol of this sovereignty. All Christian life, all Christian moral standards, all the fruits and powers of the Spirit, are in innermost relation to Jesus Christ. Nothing matters so much for the Christian as to listen to the accents of Galilee. There is no devotional substitute for the study of and meditation upon the Gospels. This cannot be said too often or too strongly.

Nevertheless it remains true that the Gospels are not

[1] *Op. cit.*, pp. 15 and 979.

the primary data for Christian ethics. For there is a moral and spiritual history behind the record of the Gospel narratives. The Life and the Sayings which expressed it had proved themselves morally creative and clothed themselves in manifold forms of moral experience and interpretation long before the records were made. The critical study of the Gospels has made the older and cruder method obsolete. It is not really possible for us to collect various isolated Sayings and transfer them to contemporary problems. We must proceed in more scientific fashion, in true line with their literary history.

(*a*) For, first, if we ask the obvious question, Why were the records made at all? the answer is: Because of the results which flowed from the incidents recorded in them. Those for whom the Gospels were first written knew Christ first as a transforming influence, a redemptive source of new moral energy: it was only later that they received a portrait. Indeed one of the startling results of the critical approach to the New Testament is to make us realize the striking difference between modern missionary methods and those of the primitive community. "Stories about the life of Jesus were no part of the original Gospel." The earliest content of the Good News we know from St. Paul's own description of what he was taught as a Christian catechumen. What he "received" from the apostolic teachers and the basis of his own evangelism was not what we should call "the Gospel story"; and certainly not the Sayings of the Master. It was that Christ died for our sins and was buried and rose again the third day (1 Cor. xv. 3, 4). That was the "good news about Jesus Christ" (Mark i. 1). It was, as it seems, the genius of John Mark which invested "Gospel" with its modern meaning, a preaching of Christ in biographical form.[1]

[1] Streeter, *The Four Gospels*, pp. 497–8. I do not wish to appear to have swallowed whole the alleged results of "Form-criticism"; nor to

Thus while the Church is founded on the Gospel, it made the Gospels, they did not make it. The converts in the first generation were not first provided with a book to read: they were gathered into a way of life, a community of the Holy Spirit, in which the authentic Spirit of the Master verified itself in changed relationships and a redirection of the inner life.

To our thinking it seems axiomatic that the primary equipment of the missionary, however limited in other resources, is at least the Gospels in the vernacular. The aim of missionary education, as the reformed Churches understood it at least for a great part of the nineteenth century, was to teach enquirers how to read so that they might appropriate the Gospels. This has given rise, incidentally, to grave social and economic difficulties. The mission schools, despite all their glorious record, have nevertheless been in danger of producing a semi-educated proletariat dissatisfied with handcraft and agriculture and intent on finding clerical employment, which in the nature of things is not available. The most recent missionary literature and the findings of various Commissions on the meaning of Christian education are fully alive to the dangers of this course. Anyone who reads the reports of the Gold Coast Government, for instance, or the Colonial Office White Paper on Tropical Education, or the official missionary records from India or from tropical Africa or from Trinity College at Kandy, will realize to what far-reaching changes the whole policy has now been committed.

But we must not allow ourselves here to diverge along this fascinating by-road. The point is this: nearly every one assumed that if you could teach a man to read the Gospels,

be able to assent to the attitude so ably represented by Sir Edwyn Hoskyns in his recent study, *The Riddle of the New Testament*. But however welcome or unwelcome, the facts given above seem indisputable. See further, Chapter IV, pp. 91 *sq.*

you had thereby possessed him of means for developing the Christian life, even though he was left in a pagan environment. And this is almost the contradictory of the methods employed by the early Church. The first converts found themselves gathered into a creative experience ; the community into which they were incorporated was a living school of Christian attitudes, and as they shared in the common life their outlook on the world and their relationships were gradually baptized into Christ. Out of that life the Gospels emerged. That was the order of spiritual logic, and we in our enquiry must follow it.

(*b*) Thus the Gospels come to us authenticated by people who had already "learned Christ": they are, that is, supported and interpreted by the moral achievements which they take for granted. But at this point we must raise a second question. Why, out of all that Christ said and did, were these particular words and deeds recorded ? If we had all the material available we might make a quite different selection. Here we must realize that the decisive factor in determining what is preserved and what has perished is not a concern for our moral guidance or the edification of posterity, but the practical moral and religious needs of the Christian groups among which the records grew up. The outstanding effect of Dr. Streeter's work is to make it possible for the modern reader to grasp far more firmly and imaginatively the organic relationship between the Gospels and the actual life of the Christian communities. Those incidents have had a survival value which were found, for various reasons, to satisfy the religious or moral needs of this or that Church. And the living traces of those men and women, their moral conflicts, questionings and answers, their spiritual searchings of heart, the intellectual problems of their faith, are still discernible upon the documents. The real evidences of Christianity are, as a great scholar has expressed it, ultimately "in men not in manuscripts ". Thus the actual forms of the records, as well as the selection of incidents, are conditioned by the moral needs, the degrees of Christian insight and experience, of the Christian life out of which they come. They make sense, as the books themselves insist, only in the light of what had happened subsequently. " After He was risen, they understood." Moreover, what is for us a crucial point, the form in which the teaching of Christ comes down to us has been shaped by attempts at Christian living. Not seldom a saying is recorded in two or more variant forms, as for example rather frequently in matter common to Matthew and Luke.[1] If we study them carefully side by side it gives us a very valuable insight into the moral life of early Christendom. We can see how two different Christian circles each gave their own interpretation to the meaning of the Master's original word. The teaching has passed through the crucible of a living Christian moral experience, has proved itself in different forms of conduct, each distinct, but both derived from Him. Behind the simple statement " Jesus said " is the story of brave and manifold ventures, some, it may be, more successful than others, at living in accordance with His Spirit. We cannot ignore the historical perspectives or treat the Gospels as a flat surface.

(*c*) So much, it seems, must be required by the smallest knowledge of literary criticism. But there is a more profound consideration: What are the grounds on which we claim " finality " for our Lord's teaching and example ? The popular modern form of apologetic has thrown an exclusive and overwhelming emphasis on the moral perfection of the historic Jesus. " Never man, we say, spake like this Man : nowhere in history is a life so perfect. He was so good that He must be what we claim for Him."

[1] E.g. the two forms of the Beatitudes ; the variant traditions on Divorce ; or the ascetic and humanist variations on the poverty *motif*. Cf. Dr. Kirk's *Bampton Lectures*, pp. 68 to 84.

But these defences are not impregnable. Indeed, the apologetic which has relied on them finds itself now in a kind of salient, a proverbially insecure position. For the actual content of the life of Jesus as presented in the Synoptics, and still more of His recorded teaching, is so drastically circumscribed by historical and other limitations that to many sincere enquirers in our day this line of argument fails to bring conviction. And it is, in my belief, exceedingly doubtful whether this familiar line of argument, by itself and without reinforcement, can take the strain which must be imposed upon it. The claim of Christians for Christ must at least have the fullest reference to the grace and truth which men have found in Him, i.e. the impression made on His contemporaries (as recorded or implied in the New Testament) and on all who since, whether by those writings or in other ways, direct or indirect, have been brought within the ambit of His influence. The final evidences of Christianity would perhaps be best preserved biographically. At least it must be recognized as fantastic to appraise the significance of Christ in abstraction from the story of Christianity. As well attempt to appraise Mahatma Gandhi apart from the last ten years of Indian history. For the ultimate significance of any man is his creativeness in the lives of others. The Christian claim for Christ is based implicitly and ought no doubt to be based more decisively on His moral and spiritual creativity in all the lives touched by His Spirit. (This will take us far beyond the circle of those who are consciously in touch with Him, even to those who may never have heard His name.) What Jesus is, is shown by what He does. "To the Hindu philosopher," writes an experienced Civil Servant, "all religions may be equally true; the administrator comparing a Christian settlement with the pariah village at its gates has good reason to know that they are not equally effective. And he will note, as more than a coincidence, the readiness of the religion which has been socially and morally most effective to submit its doctrines to the test of history and psychological experience."[1]

Thus if we would know what the secret is we must look first at the *Gesta Christi*, His moral and spiritual achievements in the lives of common men and women. This is what the New Testament can show us. Not that the New Testament could hold us with any real spiritual authority were it not supported and authenticated by personal and contemporary evidence. Yet it stands nearest to the source. And for us its witness is the more convincing in that it was never meant for our eyes. It is not deliberate or conscious argument for the guidance or conviction of posterity. It is written for the men of its own time, in the forms of their thought and language, in terms of their immediate tasks and problems. Undesignedly, un-selfconsciously, the apostolic writings allow us glimpses of the Christian groups in their daily activities, unaware of our overlooking. They permit us to see Christianity in action, building up its own way of living amongst various groups of men and women in some of the chief centres of the Roman Empire.

We have first to observe it in its effects. Then we shall find that behind the whole development there is always one and the same authentic influence, taken for granted but seldom discussed. Then when we ask what is this controlling factor we shall find our way back to the Gospels.

2. The Genius of the New Testament

Jesus lived and preached and wrought and died inside the narrow limitations, intellectual and political, of Judaism. Hence arises one of the stock objections. How can a Gospel which was first delivered to Galilean farmers and fishermen in the simple economic conditions of peasant proprietors

[1] Mayhew, *Christianity and the Government of India*, p. 14.

and village labourers and oriental fashions of life, claim to have enduring significance for industrialized Western society ? Here at once the critic encounters the paradox of Christian origins. The new religion grew out of Judaism ; it was Jewish in its form of presentation, it was committed to Jewish disciples : yet, in Harnack's oft-quoted phrase, it has never taken root in Jewish soil. The original Twelve vanish out of history (except Peter and conceivably John) almost as soon as the new Movement starts. In thirty years after the Crucifixion Palestine was already a backwater. The new faith goes, by a sort of homing instinct, to the great industrial centres of population along the trade routes of the imperial world. The first trace we have of Christianity is in such places as Antioch and Corinth, Ephesus, Thessalonica and Rome itself. From the first moment of its appearance it begins its work of social redemption. Ethical direction is inherent in it : it is faith, said St. Paul, which expresses itself in love. There were those, indeed, in the earliest communities who were for equating Christianity with what our jargon calls " religious experience " in the sense of emotional intensity. The greatest danger of the primitive Church was that inspiration by the Spirit should be thought of as something " purely spiritual ", i.e. something subjective and futile, the luxury of a certain kind of temperament. That, of course, is utterly dualistic, and ignores not only the intellect and will but also any social expression of religion. It is *par excellence* of the " sect type ". That would have been the end of the Christian movement as an effective force in the world. Against that caricature of Christ's religion St. Paul and St. John made war uncompromisingly. St. Paul insisted with tremendous emphasis that the true expression of the Christian spirit is not in private emotional delights, however rapturous and however showy, but in something less exciting but more valuable, intellectual sanity and moral fruitfulness (1 Cor. xii.

to xiv.). The fruits of the Spirit are socially creative (Gal. v. 22 f.). The first Johannine letter says the same thing ; and as for St. James he is so concerned to say it that he almost forgets his religion in his ethics.

But St. James represents a quite different standpoint : and the clash between his school and St. Paul serves to exhibit in a still clearer light how vivid was the latter's recognition of the moral dynamic inherent in the Gospel. The long-drawn and, to us, tedious controversy between St. Paul and the " Judaizers " turns essentially on this very point. It was not a merely factious opposition. It had no desire, I think, to thwart St. Paul's efforts or belittle the magnitude of his achievements. Its spokesmen might have stated their case thus. " You have done," they would have said, " a marvellous work : you have carried the good news of the Messiah half-across the breadth of civilization and gathered together a people for God's possession in most of the cities of the Empire. Now you must turn them into real Christians. Considering the material available—passionate, shifty, Levantine *déracinés*, men without a Church or a city, with no great inheritance to mould them—how can you hope to train and establish them in the moral discipline of Christ if you discard your most effective instrument, the great tradition of the Law ? That, after all, is the legacy of Israel, the ethical expression of religion. Apart from the Law faith will become mere feeling and will soon degenerate into moral anarchy."

It was, as history shows, a strong case. St. Paul himself was sensitively alive to it. He was never blind to the hardness of the task, or the moral poverty of his " babes in Christ ". But to him it seemed that to invoke the Law was to question the Spirit's all-sufficiency as the source of ethical regeneration. There was, he believed, in the faith of Christ such inherent moral vitality as would express itself in a new outlook and embody itself in a new social order. The Spirit would create a new ethic, which would be spontaneous rather than traditional, proving its moral and spiritual mastery over circumstances, as they arose. There is only one law, the law of love : its applications are infinite in number, as they are many-faceted in variety.

This superb confidence was justified. Despite all doubts and disappointments and declensions from the Christian standard, the Faith did approve itself in works. The essential and permanent result of the Pentecostal experience was the emergence of the Christian commonwealth (*Koinonia*) which was not a machinery for saving souls but the redemption of a corporate life. It was not a club for religiously minded people : it was not a society for mutual uplift : it was an integral part of the Gospel, at once the instrument of Christian living and the proclamation of God's character. To the question What does the Spirit of Christ mean ? the answer was : To share in a life like this. The Spirit " builds up itself in love ", i.e. in social life and obligation, and incorporates itself in a community which embraces and controls all relationships. It finds its true focus in the Eucharist, which is at once the climax of its worship and the organ of its economic life, the exhibition of *agape* in action, maintaining the needy from the common treasury.

The Gospel was verified in a redeemed society. It proved itself the creative nucleus which organized a new social order, assimilating all that was still vital in the culture of imperial civilization, and able to stand when the Empire fell.

Yet it was not in itself a social movement. It had indeed no programme for society. It was conscious of no mission to posterity or even to the contemporary Empire. One difficulty of the modern preacher who would recommend a " Scriptural " Christianity is the seeming remoteness of the New Testament from actual, concrete life-situations. It is hard to accept as a guide to life a library which appears to contain no reference to most of the points on which we require guidance. The New Testament seems strangely inconsistent. It makes sweeping claims for the Gospel as the satisfaction of all human need. "All things are yours," is its own superb language. Yet its positive prescriptions for living are almost pathetic in their limitation, confined as they are in their range of outlook to the obvious domestic virtues and the avoidance of the deadly sins. About the great constructive tasks of citizenship and the gifts of faith to the so-called "cultural values", it seems to have almost nothing to say. Nor are the explanations of the Commentaries adequate to explain the facts.

(*a*) The belief in an imminent Parousia was, no doubt, a contributory cause. The early Church could scarcely feel responsible for the reform of the pagan social order when that was destined so soon to perish, struck down in the Messianic cataclysm. It is true enough that St. Paul's moral judgments are at some points tinged with the colour of this belief. This is most obviously exemplified in his *obiter dicta* about Matrimony (1 Cor. vii.). But the "rigorist" note even in this passage really depends on something other than this: the expectation of the Parousia will not account for its world-denying attitude.[1] For, in general, the Parousia belief, so far from paralysing or inhibiting the moral enterprise of the community, acted, rather, as a tonic stimulus. And here we may note an interesting contrast. The millenarian dreams of the Middle Ages, and especially round about the year 1000, issued in moral stagnation and despair. The world, it was felt, was going from bad to worse: no human enterprise could salvage it: you could only wait for the coming of the Lord. *Dies irae dies illa* was the last word and the only word of efficacy. Dr. Coulton's studies of

[1] Dr. Kirk has very aptly pointed out that the main tendency of Apocalyptic is precisely the opposite of world denying: it is often almost crudely eudæmonistic. Cf. his *Bampton Lectures*, p. 63.

mediæval life show how paralysing were the effects, how morally disastrous the consequences, of this dogma of inevitable degeneracy, and how it defeated would-be reformers of ecclesiastical and monastic systems. In the New Testament period, on the other hand, to look for and to "love" the Lord's appearing had precisely the opposite effect. They did not say: "There is no more to be done, we can only sit and wait for His coming." They said: "He comes as a thief in the night, let Him not come and find us all sleeping or as foolish virgins who delayed too long. We must be ever watchful and alert, instant to put the Master's house in order so that when He cometh He may find us watching." It sharpened the edge of moral enterprise. For this faith, by projecting all issues against tremendous eternal backgrounds, lifted moral decisions high above the sphere of compromise and expediency and revealed them stark, imperative and clear cut. The inner moral dynamic of the Gospel thus issued in creative action despite the limitations and inadequacies of its earliest intellectual categories.

(*b*) We are reminded that the first converts were drawn from the slaves and the submerged classes who were not, in any case, in a position to have any influence on public life or to affect the social environment. It would therefore have been futile to urge them to feel any close responsibility for the welfare of the surrounding society. And it is, of course, entirely true that the very genius of Christianity took it especially to the outcaste people. But it is probable that we exaggerate the untouchable element in the early groups. Not many wise were called, not many noble. But it does not follow that all the first believers were ill-educated and uncivilized, with no cultural or civic heritage. One of the great difficulties at Corinth was the position of the Christian converts in the normal social life of the city (1 Cor. *passim*). Luke and Acts may have been addressed, if Dr. Streeter's "guess" can he authenticated, to the heir-apparent of the imperial throne.[1] There were a number of influential Christians at least as early as the Flavian period, as the catacombs of Domitilla witness. And St. Paul's Epistles were meant to be read aloud in the congregations to which they are addressed. They presuppose a standard of education, a sustained power of critical intelligence and appreciation of an argument, that even the Vicar of a church in Oxford would be glad to assume in those to whom he preaches.

(*c*) Nor is it accounted for by the persecutions. Everyone knows that after A.D. 64 the tone of the New Testament writers towards the Empire underwent a marked change. In the Apocalypse Rome is the Great Beast: for St. Paul it was the protecting power.[2] The scars and bitterness of persecution whether from the Jewish or the pagan side are still traceable in the Four Gospels,[3] in 1 Peter and in the Apocalypse. But this will not explain St. Paul's attitude, with which we are at the moment concerned. At the time of his missionary activity the Empire had not begun its persecution: it was Rome that had rescued him from Jewish violence. The persecution which he had experienced might have made him resentful against Jews but not indifferent to the Empire.

None of these explanations is satisfying. The real reason for St. Paul's attitude and that of the New Testament as a whole is to be sought on a far deeper level; and the search will take us near the heart of the matter. Surely it is an arresting paradox which primitive Christianity displays to us. It is set in the midst of the Roman Empire, the most ambitious political experiment, the most grandiose

[1] *The Four Gospels*, pp. 534 ff.

[2] Cf. ὁ κατέχων in 2 Thessalonians ii. 7; Romans xiii; also Acts *passim*.

[3] Cf. Mark xiii. and parallels and indeed the whole of Mark (see Rawlinson's Commentary, Introduction, pp. xv. *sq.*); cf. also Matthew x. 16 ff, and xxiii.; John viii., etc.

cultural tradition in the whole range of recorded history. The Church believes that it is the salt, the antiseptic which saves the world from decay. Yet it appears to be quite unconcerned with the civilization which surrounds it. For the strength and grandeur of the Roman genius and the brilliant legacy of Hellenism it shows no signs of real appreciation. St. Paul, no doubt, like all other preachers, manœuvred for a favourable position when he began to speak, as at Athens. But he had about him no true touch of Hellenism. He remains pertinaciously provincial and incurably, ineradicably a Jew. We need only to refer his famous judgment written among the teachers of art in Corinth: they turned the glory of the invisible God into the statue (εἰκών) of a corruptible man (Rom. iii. 23). That means, in effect, the Hermes of Praxiteles. For all that the Empire stood or might stand for, the New Testament as a whole cares nothing at all. Towards the urgent problems that confronted it, moral, political and economic, it appears to present a complete indifference. Civil obedience is no doubt enjoined and carried (as it may seem to us) too far, since Nero's government were the "powers that be".[1] But this is motived by expediency, not by the sense of any constructive mission to the sickness of imperial society. St. Paul's legitimate gratitude for his *civitas* is mainly because of its help to him as a missionary. (He could get about the mission field easily and had no difficulties about passports.)

The Church as revealed in the New Testament is normally conceived as a closed society sharply distinct from the surrounding world. Within is light and the world without is darkness. The Christians are as a "colony of heaven" (Phil. iii. 20) in the midst of an alien tradition. They would live at peace with their neighbours "if it may be": but they stand ultimately in opposition to the kingdoms of the

[1] Romans xiii. 1; cf. 1 Peter ii. 13 ff.

world and the glory of them. The very word "saints" is charged with omen of the coming collision between the Church and Cæsar. The Christians are a people apart. Even Roman justice is "ungodly" (1 Cor. vi. 1 to 7). The Church has no concern with the world.

Nor is this merely a Pauline attitude, bound up with the dominance of one man's character. The Johannine school takes the same standpoint. Despite the prologue of the Fourth Gospel, which is the very justification of Humanism, despite the great evangelic utterance that God sent His Son to save the world, it warns the faithful not to love the world, for the world lies in the power of the Evil One. This tension of unreconciled opposites is in the grain of primitive Christian thinking. This is the paradox of the whole New Testament. Never has there been a stronger emphasis on the ethical implications of religion. Yet its actual ethical directions appear to us to be almost obscurantist. St. Paul's moral judgments about marriage or even about the master-and-slave relation might be said truly to fall below the level of the best contemporary pagan sentiment.[1] If a copy of the New Testament had been delivered to Marcus Aurelius as it is to our Kings at their coronation, he might have indulged in outspoken comments. He might have complained that it shed no clear light on the duties and problems of statesmanship, and was merely concerned with a *prava superstitio*. Christians would have had no cause for resentment at what would have been a perfectly sound criticism. The objections raised against it on this score are the measure of its strength. It is not a book about ethics but a book about the Christian religion. The New Testament *is* an other-worldly book: its primary concern is not with social duty: it is with sin, forgiveness and atonement and the

[1] Dr. Kirk, *op. cit.*, p. 78, goes so far as to speak of St. Paul's moral inertia. This may be thought to be exaggeration: but the phrase does strikingly call attention to a vital factor in the whole case.

source of spiritual regeneration in the redemptive love of God the Father. "The darkness is past and the true light now shineth." Its eyes are so dazzled by the light that it seems to move uncertainly and gropingly among the shadows in the cave of the world. It is pressed down with an exceeding weight of glory. The primary mission of Christianity was not to elaborate a "social Gospel" but to proclaim the vision of God in Christ. It cannot think of this life as real at all, save as faith in the true God is at the centre of it.[1] On other terms it is "vanity" and illusion. But Christians have "entered into life" as the Spirit of Christ has laid hold upon them. By contrast nothing else is quite real. And the Holy Spirit is, for the New Testament, the endowment and prerogative of the Church. Not that any Christian thought would have denied that whatever in the world is good and true is the creation of the divine Spirit. St. Paul concedes that by implication (Rom. ii.), and the Fourth Gospel states it more explicitly. But the true life of fellowship with God through the Spirit of Christ in men's hearts is something known to Christians alone. All other experience of God is, as it were, secondary and derivative.

However much later speculation, thinking in terms of validity and order, may have perverted this great intuition it is central in the New Testament conviction. It does not involve despair of the world: it does not spring from any false dualism or oriental distrust of life. The other-worldliness of the early Church is rather a massive concentration on the one thing which the world needed most. The Church had bought the pearl of great price, and it had sold all it had to buy it: for minor expenditure it had a poor eye. If the New Testament seems to us unsatisfying, it may be because we are asking the wrong questions. It may be that what seems superficially to be a failure in its range of sympathy,

[1] Cf. the Johannine use of ἀληθής and ἀληθέια by contrast with the "unreal" κοσμός.

a starved outlook over the width of life, is in fact a miracle of concentration on the one thing which the world really needs of it. It is not concerned with life in its detail but with life in its core of worth and significance. It is offering the one pearl of great price by which all precious pearls are appraised. It is, after all, a book about God and Christ's revelation of the Father. It is not because it tells us how to behave in this or that particular situation that we invest it with eternal value : it is rather as the victorious expression of the innermost meaning of life itself, stripped of all its contingent circumstances. In the language of one of its own writers, it draws aside the veil from the holy of holies and discloses there, not what Titus found but something in itself so rich and hallowing that everything in life is transformed by it. It shews us God " in the face of Christ ", a new vision of the divine glory, a new faith in human possibility. In other words it offers the world access to the ultimate standards of valuation, the eternal sources of holiness and power.

The prime concern of the preaching of the Gospel and the essential function of the Church was to give what men most desperately needed, for lack of which the old world was dying. It took to the world a God whom men could trust and a new conception of Man's life, revealed in the light of an eternal destiny. That laid down an enduring foundation on which civilization could be built : it was the source of a truly vital ethic. The root failure of the pagan ethic, even at its noblest and finest, was the narrow reading of human life, circumscribed by temporal horizons. Now it was seen against eternal backgrounds. There was more in life than had been supposed. As the Bishop of Oxford wrote many years ago : " It is on the basis of a new life introduced and active in the world that all Christian ethical theory is erected. The human life that is under discussion is a fuller thing than had been supposed before, the area of human action is enlarged so as to take in the whole spiritual world, and a new certainty and clearness of meaning has been given to it."[1]

That was the secret of the Christian ethic. It took some time, naturally enough, for the Church to work out in detail the ethical implications of faith and its application in terms of social duty. At first, as in the New Testament period, its concrete ethical prescriptions are still largely formal and traditional. It is possible, as Dr. Kirk has argued, that the catalogues of virtues and vices so characteristic of St. Paul's letters are coloured by the conventional Stoic lists. The *Two Ways* of the early Christian literature are almost stock literary material. And the first systematic treatise on Christian ethics, that of St. Ambrose, is built on Cicero's volume *De Officiis* and was even published under the same title. But this, after all, is what we should expect. Ethics cannot live " in the air ". An ethic which stands in no relation to the moral traditions of its age and time is only another name for fanaticism. The demand for complete " originality " in the teaching of Christ or the Apostles is really a sign of very shallow thinking. The moral creativeness of Christ Himself is not shown in discussing conduct in different language from that of the Rabbis, but in the new temper and insight which He brought to bear on existing material and the common stock of moral reflexion. On other terms it would have been almost meaningless and almost devoid of constructive power. And the same will hold of the apostolic teaching. The ethical application was all to come, and in each Christian generation that demands new effort of heart and brain and new ways of actual expression. The concern of the Church was with the life in itself ; and that is what is " new " in the New Testament, the source of moral and spiritual vitality which is the authentic spirit of the Master. Its primary task when the Movement started was

[1] T. B. Strong, *Christian Ethics* (Bampton Lectures), p. 68.

not so much detailed moral guidance as the assumptions of the Christian life. "Make the tree good," as He said Himself: "a good tree cannot bring forth evil fruit nor can a corrupt tree bring forth good fruit." It was Troeltsch's great contribution that he so massively stressed this central truth, that the social ethic of Christianity issues out of the Christian religion.[1]

But when this seemingly other-worldly Gospel goes out into the Graeco-Roman world it evokes creative response to life over the whole field of human interest.

3. The Redemption of Paganism

In that great philosophy of history which St. Paul first sketched out in *Romans* he sees the Gospel as the redemptive answer to the bankruptcy of human moral effort, both in Judaism and in the pagan world. For the purpose of our present enquiry it is the latter with which we are most concerned. It was not only among the chosen people that men looked and longed for a Deliverer. Paganism too awaited its Messiah. In saying this I am not thinking chiefly of the so-called "Messianic" Eclogue or of the queer popular expectation "that people coming out of Judæa would be the masters of the world",[2] but of all that was implied and never realized by classical civilization at its best. For what we see in imperial society at the time when Christianity comes into it may be described as the nemesis of naturalism. And there seems to be a law in the moral order that what is natural tends to become unnatural unless redeemed by what is supernatural.[3] The fate which overtook the Hellenic genius, so keen, so radiant and world-

[1] "Diese sozial-ethischen Gedanken und Kräfte quellen aus der christlichen Religiosität," *op. cit.*, p. 979.

[2] "Ut ex Judaea profecti orbi terrarum imperarent," Suetonius *vit. Vesp.* iv. 5.

[3] Cf. G. K. Chesterton's *St. Francis*, Chapter II.

affirming, is the crucial exhibition of it. The Hebrew mythology was entirely right. A snake always gets into the garden : the tree of knowledge yields but Dead Sea apples. All the best things in life " go bad on us " unless referred to a transcendent standard. If religious history has any lesson it is that no religion of pure immanentism can support the weight that men try to make it carry. It collapses in paralysing scepticism or in moral chaos and degeneration. This is what had befallen the Hellenistic culture.

Hellenism had made claims on life which could be satisfied only by something which Hellenism itself could not provide. It presupposed a confidence in life, a sense of inner security and freedom which has in fact no basis in experience save in the strength of spiritual conviction that at the heart and core of Reality is a mind and will to whom mankind is dear and in whose image it is made. The Hebraic gifts of the Christian Church were necessary to make possible the Hellenic valuations. The idea of personality, as has been said, was the gift of the Church to classical philosophy.[1] That depended upon its faith in God who is not the God of the dead but of the living, the God to whom persons are dear. And that was precisely what the Greek world-view conspicuously and disastrously lacked. The Greek temper of mind at its best was clear-sighted, gracious and "humane", incredibly enterprising and constructive. But a sort of suspicion lay upon the heart of it. It could never really trust life with abandon. It was always looking over its shoulder lest the avenger punish its presumption. Even in the hour of its triumph its maxim was " to think mortal thoughts ". Thus though its whole attitude was humanist (or as we had better say, humanitarian) it could never believe genuinely in Man because it believed in nothing which is more than Man. Aristotle (Ethics X) tries to escape : but his intellectualist idea of God really leads him to the same impasse. The

[1] Cf. Strong, *op. cit.*, p. 129.

moral life can have no eternal basis, for only pure reason is divine. Ethics therefore can be discussed only on an empirical and pragmatic level, where it can never possibly do justice to the needs of spiritual personality. It was this humanitarian presupposition which led to decay and disillusionment. Underneath the highly polished surface there was always lurking a treachery and cruelty which broke out horribly at notorious moments. And the cult of light, knowledge and *vertu* could never successfully discipline or sublimate the elemental instincts and impulses.[1]

The Olympian worships, which the conquering race superimposed upon the indigenous cults, were the idealisation of Hellenism. Apollo, who came nearest of the Pantheon to the status of a national deity, stands for the conquest of the Hellenic spirit over the " beastly devices of the heathen ". But Olympianism was hardly established before it began to exhibit signs of decay. This was due less than we suppose to moral criticism of its mythology ; for there is often no very close connection between a people's mythology and its religion. Socrates did more than anyone else to discredit the Homeric mythology : but his dying words were a gesture of conformity. And the same apparent inconsistency is found in the later sceptical philosophers. The essential weakness of the Olympian cult is traceable to more deep-seated causes. It ignored large elements in human nature. It did not reckon with the instinctive life, and it sought to avert its eyes from death. This, perhaps, is why throughout Greek literature there is always the haunting undertone of melancholy, a sense of frustration and unfulfilment. There is no sadness in the art of the world like the sadness of the Greek Anthology. Before the onslaughts of the tiger within us and the decisive challenge of death the Olympian world-view was dumb and powerless. " The Olympian gods," says

[1] For an estimate, which is a refreshing antidote to the " sweetness and light " of popular panegyric, see Earp, *The Way of the Greeks*.

Professor Murray, " knew themselves at heart to be but metaphors."[1] Even in their noblest presentations they remained aspirations unrealized. They expressed a glorious confidence in Man but gave no ultimate ground for believing in him. Hence even in the golden age men were doubting their own cardinal assumptions. Hellenism had nothing to sustain it. There have probably been very few religions less religious than the Olympian cultus. The buried " Pelasgian " cults came to the surface (for religions do not die, they are transformed) and the indigenous Aegean worships began to influence or to supplant their conquerors.

The decline and fall of the Olympian gods synchronized with the failure of Hellenism. For in incidents such as the Corcyrean massacre Hellenism seemed to have betrayed itself. After the disaster of Aegospotami Hellenism failed with the failure of Athens. The Hellenic world-view appeared to be discredited. Men were assailed by those qualms of conscience, that scepticism about human nature, which we have experienced since the world war and describe self-consciously as the " modern temper ". The faith and philosophy of the fourth century seem to reflect a defeatist attitude. Life seemed to have betrayed its favourites, and growing fear and distrust of life broods over the Hellenistic age.

That world was reaching one of those periods when the will to live seems to be inhibited and vital forces to be atrophied.[2] And this may be the inevitable result of a purely immanentist world-view. Humanitarianism, as we shall see later, is never more than a short stage from Naturalism. And, as has been profoundly said, to make the elements of Nature-religion human is inevitably to make them vicious.[3]

[1] *Five stages of Greek Religion*, p. 100.

[2] Cf. Statistics of population given in Tarn: *Hellenistic Civilisation*, pp. 86 *seq*. Is it more than a chance coincidence that the same phenomenon can be traced now among some of the tribes of tropical Africa ?

[3] G. Murray, *op. cit.*, p. 90.

Nowhere is the contrast more striking between the Christian and the pagan outlook than in this point of their attitude to Nature. St. Paul summarizes the whole difference when he asserts that the pagan world-view failed to distinguish "creation" from "creator".[1] That is to say its faith was naturalistic and consequently "Nature" betrayed it. If there is one place before all others where the modern Englishman feels he is near to God it is when he is enjoying his garden. "'Tis very sure God walks in mine." But that certainty is a Christian gift. For pagan thought nature is never *safe*: it is terror by night and sickness of soul at noonday. We put a bath for birds in our gardens, or a della Robbia Madonna: in the Graeco-Roman gardens stood Priapus.

Popular writers still exploit the contrast between the "grey" breath of the Galilean and the sunshine confidence of paganism. But this is exactly the opposite of the truth, so far, at least, as concerns the Hellenistic age. Its typical and characteristic development, till Christianity came to deliver it, was a neo-Platonist or Gnostic dualism, a profound and radical unbelief in life. The splendid aspirations of Hellenism seemed to have withered away in disillusionment. Rome's superb political experiment had not fulfilled the ambitions of its subjects. Momentarily the accession of Augustus had seemed to inaugurate an era of peace after the long carnage of civil war. The high hopes which hailed his accession are reflected in Vergil's poetry and in the worship of the genius of Augustus which arose spontaneously in the eastern provinces. But these, too, had proved to be delusory. "In the fifteenth year of the reign of Tiberius Cæsar" the destiny of the world was held in the hands of a sadist pervert poring over entrails among his astrologers at Capri.

This despair lay heavily on men's hearts, and life itself

[1] Romans i. 25.

had come to appear inexplicable. The confidence of the Hellenic springtime, which had thought to possess all wisdom and all knowledge, had ended in a paralysis of enterprise. Indeed the mind had wellnigh surrendered any attempt to explain the universe. Philosophy had narrowed its field to practical preoccupation with conduct: how to live tolerably and well in a capricious, terrifying universe ruled by the implacable destiny of the stars and the "world rulers of this darkness". The "city of gods and men" seemed far distant. There was no such living metaphysic as could invest life with a creative unity or lend it a vital sense of direction. The donnish inhumanity of the Stoics, which admittedly did make a system of life, made it something so theoretical that it could have no meaning for the plain man when his head was bowed as well as bloody "beneath the bludgeonings of chance". "Without hope and without God in the world": all in all, it is not an exaggeration.

Thus religion offered itself to the world as a haven and refuge from the storm, no longer as a creative intuition. It appealed to men as a way of escape from life, not as a way of mastery over it. The world was oppressed with a longing for redemption: the feeling grew, since Plato had expressed it, that only by way of some divine disclosure coming into life from outside it could men find the way of truth and freedom. But the distance between God and man seemed now to be so vast and unbridgeable that no direct communion could be expected. So strangely had the "humanist" religion cancelled itself out in its development. There was no hope of finding Reality except through the endless hierarchy of "mediators" who intervened between God and man, and then only by magical procedure. This demand was met on a certain level by the oriental mystery religions which were now flooding across the Western Empire. The Mysteries did offer to sick souls at least some hope of emotional release, some sense of contact with the supernatural, a *viaticum* for the dread, final journey. But the Mysteries were, when all is said, little more than a solemn pretence, a projection into cultus and symbolism of the unfulfilled longings of broken hearts. Their central figures were frankly mythological; they could not cure the hurt of the people. Hence one may trace throughout the whole period a drying up of creative forces, whether in thought or in art or conduct. For "no one can set his mind and will to work with a broken spirit".

There was only one way for that world to confidence and hope and renewal: it must recover its faith in life. And that could be only by winning a conviction of a righteous Will which could be trusted, and with which men can have communion, at the living centre of the universe. Just that was the gift of Christianity. "Blessed be God and the Father of our Lord Jesus Christ"; there sounds a new note across that wan society. It made personal religion possible. It gave men a God they could believe in, and so they were able again to trust life. Its inmost sanctities were now safe. Men who had sought to humanize experience, to make the world a home for man's spirit, and had thus made it alien and terrifying, could now be truly "at home" in the world. For once God has found us as Redeemer, the Father and Sanctifier of our spirits, we can dare to trust Him as Creator, and move out freely over the fields of life without moral misgivings or disaster.

Hence this Judaic, other-worldly Gospel which presented itself to the critical mind as folly, goes out into the Graeco-Roman world and at once awakens a vivid response to life along all the lines of interest and activity. Joy and peace are the notes of the New Testament and these spring out of a vital way of living. There is far less fear of life in the New Testament than there is in Plato's *Republic*. There is even less of the Puritanic spirit. Plato, let us remember, had proposed not merely a moral censorship of literature, but to exclude all poetry and drama from the confines of his ideal polity. We cannot suppose that men who wrote such poetry as the " Praises of Agape " in 1 Cor. xiii. would have supported so ruthless a programme. For while we have stressed, as the facts necessitate, the rigorist note in the New Testament, it is equally possible to refer to passages which are quite as strikingly humanist in their emphasis. " The fruits of the Spirit " breathe the air of humanism, so does the great passage about " values " (Phil. iv. 4 to 9), and the prologue to the Fourth Gospel. And—though such judgments must remain undemonstrable—will anyone question that the Beatitudes breathe in a spiritual climate which might have seemed native to Sophocles ?

Here we meet the authentic Christian genius. Christianity *is* otherworldly, essentially and relentlessly religious. Yet it reveals itself from the first not only as a redemptive antiseptic, the salt that saves the world from decay, but as a vital and transforming force within the movements of this-world history. It exhibits itself as the creative nucleus of a rich and transfigured social order. Its most typical effects are ethical and are manifested in redirected character. It evokes new qualities from human nature, new possibilities, new range and width, and raises it to new heights of heroism. It evolves its own ideal of character and thus its own unique scales of value. " Roman philosophy ", says Mr. Bailey, " had become the search for the ideal type of character." If we take the finest expression of the pagan ideal of character and put it beside the authentic Christian saint, Socrates for example beside St. Francis, at once we are conscious of a distinction, indefinable but yet decisive. Among those that are born of women, as Christ might quite easily have said, there hath not arisen a greater than Socrates : but he that is least in the Kingdom of Heaven is greater than he. The beginnings of that transfiguring process are visible within the New Testament ; and this is the essence of Christianity. Life is being transfigured from within. If we ask the secret of that transformation, that is what the New Testament takes for granted: "the servants which drew the water knew".

Iesu, spes paenitentibus,
Quam pius es petentibus,
Quam bonus te quaerentibus;
Sed quid invenientibus?

That is the very shrine of the Christian ethic.

But it would be a starved interpretation which confined the fruits of the Spirit to merely moral forms of expression. Virtue after all is not the whole of life. It can rightly be claimed for the Christian spirit that it has penetrated and transformed the intellectual and æsthetic values. Because, if God is the Father of Jesus Christ, and if man is made for fellowship with God, then men's whole approach to nature and to beauty must be transfigured. The spirit of scientific enquiry will normally flourish best in Christian soil: though Christians have been too frequently blind to this. It is clearly true also that Christianity soon began to build up its own art, gradually creating its own forms distinct from those of the Hellenistic convention. The new content made its own forms. The new wine was poured into new bottles.

This development lay in the future, and outside the New Testament period. But there is even in this period a signal and unsurpassed example to which too little attention has been given as an exhibition of the Christian genius. I mean the New Testament itself. Christianity is the one religion which has really believed in the common man. And Christianity was the first society which took the broken illiterate vernacular, the κοινή of the Mediterranean seaports, which no scholar would ever have dreamed of using as a literary medium, and made it the organ of a supreme literature. Here is something which takes us deep into the sources of Christian inspiration. It was the Church, let it be always remembered, which first wrote great poetry in vernacular.

As soon as that is written one realizes that it carries us back behind the Christian Church. Behind the Church stands a village Poet, the sheer beauty of whose tales and sayings still haunts the world's imagination.

So we pass, in the order of Christian logic, behind the developments which we have been studying to see what is the secret presupposed in them. By this way we come to the Gospels.

CHAPTER IV

THE ETHIC OF JESUS

1. The Teaching and its Truth

THE Christian movement cannot be accounted for in any terms of the natural climax of tendencies at work in the ancient world. It is true that Jewish and oriental influences were rapidly penetrating the West. But the normal development of that process, had it not been deflected by other forces, can be seen in the wild surmises of Gnosticism, the various forms of Hellenistic syncretism, or the cult established by the Emperor Julian. But these were in fact merely freaks and throw-backs. The main line of advance was totally different and was due to the arrival of a new force. "It cannot be too strongly insisted that the victory of the Church in the fourth century was not, as so many modern critics would have us believe, the natural culmination of the religious evolution of the ancient world. It was, on the contrary, a violent interruption of that process, which forced European civilization out of its old orbit into a path which it would never have followed by its own momentum."[1] As Schweitzer remarked, the logical conclusion of the *religions-geschichtlich* criticism is to make it almost immaterial whether Jesus of Nazareth ever lived. He hardly affected the situation. But this school is now hopelessly discredited. No interpretation of Christ can be true which fails to account for Christianity. And conversely no account of Christianity can be regarded as anything but fantastic which makes Christ Himself unimportant to it. A new

[1] Dawson, *Progress and Religion*, p. 157.

thing had come into the world, born out of His mind and person. A new life and spirit are made manifest, expressing themselves creatively and spontaneously in manifold and diverse forms of activity, all stamped with the same authentic character, all instinct with the same essential quality. What in itself was this new thing? What was the original source of the new Christian way of life?

In the previous chapter we made some study of the Spirit in action in the *Koinonia*. We recognized the comparative insufficiency of the ethical teaching in the New Testament. Yet we saw that a new moral dynamic is always assumed at the living heart of it, and brings forth the characteristic fruits of the Spirit in a new sense of ethical direction, new ranges of insight and imagination, new capacities for moral heroism, new depth and quality in living. Something, we saw, was taken for granted in the Christian confidence and enterprise; and this, which is silently assumed, so spontaneously and un-selfconsciously, is what constitutes Christianity. We have now to ask how the historic Life controls and animates these developments, incarnated in new ways of living. In what sense is the Founder of Christianity also the source of the Christian ethic? Can we find in the records of His life and teaching authoritative moral guidance for the Christian life in the twentieth century?

Only those who have reflected a little or have some acquaintance with New Testament criticism will realize that this is a problem at all. For the old-fashioned believer and perhaps still for most modern Englishmen the recorded sayings of Jesus are to be revered as infallible guides to right living, were we but brave enough to carry them out. And we more sophisticated disciples cannot too often remind ourselves that Christ Jesus is offered to the world not as a "problem" to be debated about but as the answer to its moral neediness. Nevertheless, as we have already insisted, we cannot rightly regard the Christian ethic as founded upon the moral teaching of Christ. For so soon as ever we seriously think about it, that suggestion is seen to be exposed to a number of invincible difficulties.

(*a*) There are among Christ's recorded sayings injunctions which, if obeyed literally by all who seek to be loyal followers, must prove definitely incompatible with the continuance of society. Is it possible to claim for such sayings that they offer trustworthy moral guidance ? If we are to regard the teaching of Jesus as legislation about Christian conduct, then the only way to escape from this impasse is by the theory of the double standard, the Precepts binding upon all Christians in the rough and tumble of " secular " life and the Counsels offered to those who would be perfect, which means in effect to live as " religious ". That, as we know, was the mediæval compromise. And if we start out from these premisses the conclusion is as inevitable in logic as it is unjustifiable in ethics. If an ideal is impracticable, it is no doubt better that it should be realized in some social medium, however artificial, than that it should be suspended in the thin air of religious sentiments and be realized only in subjective experience.[1] The two-standard theory has this justification. But what are we to say of a moral principle which is such that it is not merely hard but impossible to carry it out under the conditions of life as we have to live it ? Nor is it easy to venerate a standard which is not merely merciful to failure but actually *content* with the second best. Yet if the " I say unto you " of the paradoxes in the Great Sermon means " You, followers in later ages, are to behave as I now enjoin ", then are we driven into these false positions. It must therefore be that the premiss is wrong. And it has to be realized as a first condition of rightly understanding our Lord's teaching, that these words of grace were not spoken to us, nor intended consciously for our ears at all.

[1] Niebuhr, *op. cit.*, p. 122.

Blessed are our eyes for they see and our ears for they hear: but the audience whom our Lord had in mind and to whose thoughts and circumstances He addressed Himself were not twentieth-century Europeans. He spoke to the people actually before Him. And He was not, like modern religious teachers, speaking to the Press or a microphone, in generalizations for a " wide public ". He was speaking to people actually before Him, different people on different occasions, needing therefore different kinds of advice and relative insistence on different principles. Instructions issued to the Twelve as they set forth on a missionary journey in the special circumstances of a vocation that demanded " neither scrip nor gold nor shoes " are not to be taken as law universal for Christian householders in England. Out of the sayings recorded in the Gospels Christ speaks inexhaustibly to the deepest needs of men in all times. But they only disclose their eternal significance if they are first studied and understood in the limitations of their original context.

I do not wish to be tiresomely obvious. But one still meets Christians so frequently who suppose that Christ in some way " foresaw " the circumstances of their lives or the moral issues of western Europe and intended His teaching to apply to these, that it seems necessary to be quite definite in setting aside that point of view. The first law of sound exegesis is studiously to avoid reading back into first-century documents attitudes and ideas that belong to the twentieth. This applies as much to the sayings of Jesus as to any other document of the period. We must not, for example, allow ourselves to import into the parable of the mustard seed assumptions about evolution. Still less can we look in the parable of the labourers for light on the conditions of modern industry, the minimum wage demand, for example, or the rights and duties of employers.

Any discussion of Christian ethics starts, therefore, from mistaken premisses if it begins, as so many discussions do, by collecting the sayings in the Synoptic Gospels, grouping them under various headings and then proceeding to "apply" them to contemporary moral perplexities. Because, frankly, they will not apply. They belong to His world, not to ours. Now to accept this no doubt involves us in certain difficulties of a new kind. But it rescues us from absurdities of the old kind. It emancipates us from juggling with texts. Whatever fresh heart-searchings it may imply for us, at least it delivers us from the futility of that useless verbal debating which thinks to solve questions of Christian ethics by quoting some chance phrase He used, some saying about a sword for instance, as though it disposed of the case for pacificism. We shall never be inwardly free in our attempt to interpret the mind of Christ till we have disclaimed once for all this obsolete bibliolatry.

(*b*) There is a further question to face. This is, indeed, inseparably bound up with the whole Christian belief in an Incarnation. A real incarnation in history involves real historical limitations. It involves at the least that the thought-forms He used and the materials for His thinking and teaching are those proper to Palestine in A.D. 30.

Can we believe both in a real incarnation and in the universal authority which Christians claim for His moral principles? Nothing was more remote from the mind of Christ than the assumptions of European liberalism. Nothing is more entirely absent from His thought or His presuppositions than the humanism of the twentieth century. He was not a modern leader of social movements, but a Jew of the first century. One of the few "assured results" of critical scholarship working on the Gospels is to put it beyond all dispute that Christian thought was conditioned and controlled not by such ideas as we take for granted, but by those rather which we find more difficult, the unique, inalienable Jewish tradition of a living and transcendent God, revealed and mediated in Scripture.[1] Jesus conceived His mission and carried it through victoriously in terms of the Messianic expectation. All was conditioned by His own time and place. If, then, He was always speaking to His contemporaries in those terms and against that background, how is His moral teaching valid for us ? To claim that He was laying down rules for His followers in some later age threatens us with the tyranny of Mohammedanism, permanently fettered to standards which reflect the political and moral conditions of Arabian society in the sixth century. But however Christianity be defined it is at the least a creative life : it is never static and never completed. Such metaphors as those of the Vine represent as the living essence of it a growth derived from a living source. And this means that the very claim for the universality of Christ involves continued reinterpretation of His teaching and of the framework of His thinking, even of the Messianic idea itself. To recognize this may carry us a long journey, further than some Christians are ready to venture. At least it is fatal to the glib notion that the moral teaching of Jesus is, as it stands, a sufficient guide for problems of conduct amid the perplexities of the modern era.

(*c*) Quite independently of the New Testament there is also this inherent difficulty. How could Jesus or anybody else lay down in advance directions how the good man ought to behave in circumstances which had not then arisen ? There cannot be acts which are right independently of all circumstances. According as the conditions vary so will the acts which express the good will ; and by consequence morally good actions will seem to be contrary to

[1] This is re-emphasized almost brutally in Sir Clement Hoskyns' *Riddle of the New Testament.* It is carried there, however, so far that the personal character of Jesus and the quality of His Spirit hardly seem to matter to Christianity. It is quite vital to my position that we cannot leave the question where he leaves it. See below, pp. 98 *sq.*

one another in the context of varying situations.[1] For indeed, as was recognized long ago by Plato, to equate goodness with specific actions leads to moral confusion and futility: it will make the just man into a "kind of thief". And in fact we find that our Lord commends conduct which appears to be inconsistent and contradictory. One man is enjoined peremptorily to silence: another is to proclaim the good news. It is wrong to keep back from parents by the legal fiction of Corban what filial obligation owes to them. Yet it is right to *hate* father and mother. The good life will utter itself spontaneously in apparently incompatible forms of action, as may be demanded by varying contingencies. Thus we can never decide what is right in this or that actual situation by any mere quoting of sayings. He was not concerned with advice about conduct, but with the exposure of motive, penetrating the inner heart's secrets with the two-edged sword of His inescapable insight. As He said Himself: Make the tree good. The holy will and the redeemed judgment are equally manifest in all actions, that is, in every response to circumstances of a mind so trained and a will so hallowed. The circumstances are simply "given" material: the way a man handles such material, be the occasion trivial or momentous, is what exhibits the quality of his spirit. So it is too with the quality of the insight which is revealed in our moral judgments. The circumstances are more or less unimportant. What matters is the integrity and the insight which inspire the judgment brought to bear on them. That was our Lord's concern in His teaching; and that is what gives the teaching itself significance. For the circumstances on which He passed judgment, the moral issues which He was asked to clarify,

[1] Cf. "No one knows in advance what particular line of conduct will in some unrehearsed contingency most surely conform to God's will or keep a man's honour bright. That is precisely what you can only discover when the contingency is upon you." A. E. Taylor, *Faith of a Moralist*, I, p. 83.

were, after all, not of His choosing. He was not selecting examples for a textbook but answering actual questions put to Him, whether by life itself or by enquirers. They are particular, temporary or local: what is eternal and universal is the Spirit which lives in the answers.[1]

This is of quite crucial importance. For some of the best and most sincere minds among the younger generation are admittedly disappointed and disillusioned by what seems to them the limitation and inadequacy of Christ's moral teaching. They had been told that in the Lord's sayings they would find the clue through the maze of moral perplexity. They have taken us at our word and searched the Scriptures thinking that in them they would find eternal life. But they have not found what they had been led to expect. Two-thirds of their ethical questions seem to be not merely unmentioned but not even contemplated in His teaching. He does not seem to have guidance to offer them. Christians have claimed more than they can substantiate. And thus they conclude, sadly but quite definitely, that this is not "he that was to come", and that they must look for another.

But are they perhaps asking the wrong questions? For, if our position is sound, then it follows that the eternal value of the recorded sayings of Jesus is not as telling us how we ought to behave, but as telling us about Him, mediating to us His spirit and revealing His fundamental attitudes. The material about which He spoke was "given" by His life-situation and that of those to whom He was speaking. It is of their time, not of ours. But Jesus Himself is in His response to it, in the perfect mastery of His touch, the holy quality of His thought and feeling. His words are all perfectly characteristic: through all of them His Spirit speaks to us: through them we know the mind that was in

[1] For this paragraph cf. an admirable chapter in Canon Hodgson's *And was made Man*, pp. 13 to 30.

Christ Jesus. The significance of a creative artist is not to be sought in his subject-matter. He may paint a yellow chair like Van Gogh or a " Last Judgment " like Michael Angelo : all that matters about the " subject " is its adequacy as a medium to express what the artist wishes to say. But what makes the artist himself great or small is the ultimate quality of his imagination as revealed through the medium he works upon. It is even so with the artist in living. We shall find more of detailed moral advice in Plato or Seneca, for instance, than we shall find in the Synoptic Gospels. Seneca had an answer for every question. But is that what we claim for the Gospels ? " If Christianity," said Blake, " was morals, then Socrates was the Saviour."[1] It is true that St. James and St. Matthew think of the Gospel as the " royal law ", the Torah of the new Israel. It is true also that our Lord's mission connected itself directly and immediately with John's preaching of ethical reformation, and that He conceived the function of the Messiah primarily as that of the Teacher, an idea which is without precedent in Judaism. He stands in the prophetic tradition. The whole colour of His thought and teaching is essentially ethical, not eschatological. But as to the content of the teaching, the Gospels do not suggest any such body of articulated moral principles as admit of being worked out consistently into an " ethic " for the modern Christian.

All His thinking is ethical through and through, but His chief concern is not with ethics. He has changed the world's moral standards, but He was not primarily a teacher of morals. A collection of the sayings of Jesus is earlier than the first written Gospel. But it is noteworthy that Mark is concerned less with Christian morals than with Christian doctrine, with the significance of Jesus Himself. And that is the genius of these records. The Gospels confront us with a Person whom to face honestly must be decisive in a man's

[1] Oxford edition, p. 430. I owe the reference to M. G. H.

whole commerce with life. Their burden is not how we ought to behave but to portray for us His disclosure of the meaning of goodness itself, the innermost quality at the heart of life. They reveal to us heights and depths in moral and spiritual possibility which " had never entered into the heart of man " and unexplored ranges of valuation. They thus awaken in men responsive attitudes and lead them out to new moral ventures. But the things which they will inspire men to do are not the things which Jesus Himself did. Nor did He leave us ethical directions to which we can appeal to solve our difficulties. The eternal value of His sayings is primarily the witness they bear to the quality of His thoughts and intuitions. They are precious because they manifest Him, in His characteristic self-revelations. They are the expression of His spirit, and are thus normative for the Christian life. But rather by way of redeeming our attitudes and lifting us into a world of new insights, than by giving us positive guidance in detail about the moral demands of Christian living.

2. The Life and its Limitations

Our minds should now be prepared for the next stage in our attempted interpretation. Once we have grasped the historical limitations imposed upon a disclosure of God at a definite point of space and time, in a definite social and economic context, a result follows which sounds disconcerting. It is clear that for the great majority of Christian disciples in later ages there can be no literal *imitatio Christi*. Yet that " Christ left us an example that we should follow in His steps " must be utterly central in discipleship. How is this paradox to be understood ? We must be humble and reverent here. Yet we must think candidly and courageously. For it is hard to resist the impression that much popular apologetic for the unique claims which Christians make for Him has been built upon foundations which will not carry the weight. The modern attack on the Christian position concerns less its truth than its relevance. That Jesus lives, that grace and truth shone forth from Him, that He has been the greatest of the Torch-bearers lighting mankind upon its way, all this the modern temper concedes thankfully. But are Christians justified in going beyond that? Do they not assert more than can be substantiated in claiming for Him uniqueness and finality? It is not probable, our age suspects, that a revelation given so long ago, framed in a setting of the first century, can be the final and "definitive" disclosure of the way of life for men in the twentieth century. Now the test of this claim must lie in the sphere of ethics. Can it be successfully established that what is revealed in the life of Christ is finally and completely adequate to the claims, tasks and interests of life in our complex forms of civilization? Christians bravely assert that it can. And St. Paul's superb phrase "All things are yours" is the true voice of Christian experience. But the world studies the recorded Life in its seeming remoteness and its limitations, and it is precisely this claim which it denies, respectfully yet decisively. So the real issue is set. But, in my judgment, the paramount question is commonly asked, and answered, in false terms.

We labour to prove, as seems to be demanded of us, that all the elements in the good life are present in the Life portrayed in the Gospels. We allow ourselves to affirm in popular preaching that all the values prized and sought after by the twentieth century are fulfilled in Him. But anyone can disprove this assertion, which indeed is quite obviously untrue. There are many elements in the good life, many legitimate and worthy interests, which find no place in His thinking or activity. Once this has been pressed home upon us the Christian case is supposed to have failed. But surely these arguments and counter-arguments rest on mistaken assumptions. They assume that a perfect disclosure of goodness will embrace all forms and species of what is good. That would mean, in the end, that the best man is the man who has done the greatest number of good things, that is to say, has responded to life along the widest conceivable front. That assumption is radically false. What gives a man his place in history is not the number of things he has done but the quality of his response to life. The Stoic ideal of the balanced life, or a character such as that of Goethe, lacks just that intensiveness of quality which makes it creative in the lives of others. It is not those who have done something of everything who have most set men's hearts on fire, but those who have done something supremely well.[1] This is where the Christian claim for Christ centres. He was not an Admirable Crichton. He did not do everything good that can be done. He revealed the meaning of goodness in itself. And the claim that this disclosure is final should be based not on the diversity of the elements embraced in His acts and His experience but on the supreme quality of His will.

Not, of course, that He was an " unbalanced " character. We can hardly exaggerate, for example, the magnificent intellectual energy which lies behind the simplicity of His utterances. Yet it was not intellectual research in which His glory was to be manifested. He rejoiced in the lilies of the field, and saw the whole drama of men and women with an artist's appreciation. But His orientation to life

[1] This section was written four years ago. I feel, therefore, strongly reinforced by this extract from Professor Taylor. " Mere dispersion is the characteristic moral condition of the amateur in living, as mere concentration on the partial is that of the fanatic. That is why I cannot but feel that, when all is said, the life of a man like Goethe, with its manifold but imperfectly co-ordinate and hierarchized responses to so many aspects of the total human environment, must be pronounced second-rate by comparison with the life of a man like Socrates. It is not merely the specifically saintly man who can truly say of himself '*one* thing have I desired of the Lord" .' *Op. cit.*, I, p. 104.

was not chiefly or primarily æsthetic. So again, as Canon Streeter rightly points out, all the traits and excellencies of character are present potentially in the Gospel portrait.[1] But not thus, by methods of analysis and re-synthesis of factors, can we portray the inexhaustible Christ. He was not a generalized goodness but an entirely individual man. And what He is, is the focus and constellation of all these sentiments and attraits in that utterly unique expression, that incomparable richness of response, which is characteristically His own. His life was a supreme concentration on the one pearl of great price—the phrase is surely a fragment of self-portraiture—which was the secret of His vocation. That was what made Him the man He was. There, too, is the secret and source of that moral and spiritual creativity which He has exercised and ever exercises on all who are brought within the sphere of His influence. It is on this that the Christian claim should be based.

We may be helped to a true approach here by a suggestive Christian analogy. Let us try to enter into the secret of the Mirror of Christ, St. Francis of Assisi. There is probably no one figure in Christian history who exercises anything like such influence or holds such a compelling fascination over the mind and heart of the modern world. No milder phrase will do than to say that he "haunts" us. He has become for us the personal symbol in which we objectify our recognition that a secret has faded out of life which it would be worth all progress to recapture. He is probably the one official Saint whom the Twentieth Century would canonize. Yet this appeal, if we come to analyse it, is so strange as to be almost paradoxical. For Francis had no interest whatever in most of the things which for us give life its value. We are immensely concerned with physical health, with the claims of intellectual research and with justice in economic distribution. Of all these the saint was

[1] *Reality*, pp. 206 *sq.*

contemptuous. He ill-treated his body, "brother ass", to death and lived in a manner we should regard as beastly; he sternly forbade books to his disciples; and as for economic redress his one desire was to show complete contempt for it. It is as the Poverello that we think of him. That, as we know, was the manner of his life and the tendency of his recorded teaching. But the inspiration which has gone forth from Francis has expressed itself in ways strangely diverse.

It is easy to sing Dr. Coulton's tunes and torture ourselves with the thought of the perversion of the Founder's vision by his followers. We think of the suppression of the Testament, the successive modifications of the Rule. We recall that, within a few years of the Founder's death, disciples were expelled from the Order for wishing to take his precepts literally. It is right for us to keep these facts in mind, for no Christian can face without misgivings the challenge of the implied parallel. But we must carry our thought a step further. Francis himself died of a broken heart, feeling that all his work had ended in failure. But it is the real pang of that tragedy that the institutionalizing of the brotherhood and the new expression of the original impulses were *inevitable* if they were to survive at all. Despite all the insistence of its Founder, the Order quickly applied itself to learning, and produced its Grossetete and its Roger Bacon. It was he who inspired the magnificent Basilica in which (with significant irony) his bones rest, and gave a new birth to Umbrian painting; and his spirit chiefly verifies itself among us in plans for social and economic reform. Francis embraced lepers, and changed clothes with unwashed beggars. We should condemn both of these actions: we try, instead, to banish poverty and extirpate the curse of leprosy. But this is in the authentic tradition. We should have no such keen social conscience had not the heroic spirit of Francis dared these heights of exalted dedication. It is he who has set a pricking in men's consciences. But what is required by a true Franciscan spirit from men and women in the twentieth century is, very frequently, a kind of action which Francis himself would perhaps not recognize.

Francis is thus a creative moral force, but is not exactly and strictly our "example". It is rather that he achieved a certain tone in his response to the claims of life which sounds on unforgettably. What makes him a moral and spiritual leader whose fire still burns in the most unlikely hearts, for great numbers of modern men and women the one "real Christian" they have heard of, is not the *width* of his response to life so much as its quality and intensity. It is not because St. Francis realized and embodied all those values which our world applauds that he became a pattern in the art of living. As we have seen, he embodied none of them. His was a soul deliberately emptied of nearly all those positive aims and values which we regard as lending life significance, in order to be the focus and incarnation of that passionate self-consecration to the love of God and the brethren which makes his life a creative inspiration. In other words, it was not what he did but the spirit in which he responded to life—the precious quality of character which expressed itself in his choices and reactions, that crowns him with moral and spiritual leadership.

This well illustrates our contention, that what makes a man truly "great" is not the number of things he has achieved or the range of values he has realized. Francis triumphantly refutes that fallacy. Put him side by side with the classic "humanists", with Goethe or Cicero or Dr. Johnson. They were far more "balanced" characters, who realized a far wider range of values, and exhibit, in one way, a more complete ethic. But nobody would describe them as "haunting". Or, again, we might contrast St. Paul with Seneca, or William Blake with the virtuous Mrs.

Hemans—an "example", surely, for any Christian home. It is not in his omnicompetence as an artist that the greatness of Michael Angelo resides: it is rather that he never wholly "succeeded". It lies in that superb intuition which could never find fully adequate expression. All these illustrations support the main point that what makes a man a creative force is not how much he appropriates from experience and environment, but the unique, distinctive, personal way in which he experiences life and lives it. The materials on which he must work, the particular context and situation which define the form of his vocation, are tasks assigned to him by the facts of life. The man himself is what he makes of them. It is the quality of character determining his acts and valuations which claims our homage and lays its spell upon us. His significance lies in his personal reactions: not in the number of things he has achieved, but in what he has most intensely realized. And the greater the man, the more personal in quality, the more "characteristic" are his words and acts.

A man who tries to "realize all values" is normally an ineffective amateur, like the House of Lords in Gilbert and Sullivan. This law seems to hold good of the higher reaches of spiritual achievement, as well as of technical and professional skill. The Saints do little and are much. Yet in every age there are thousands of Christian saints who remain unrecognized by the Church because their manner of life does not conform to the typical pattern of canonized Sainthood.

Now this bears closely upon our main enquiry. Since the death of Francis the whole world has changed, mentally as well as in outward ways. The whole context of our thoughts and feelings, as well as the content of our moral duty, is as different as can be from his. To seek for moral authority from St. Francis, in the sense of taking him for our example and trying to live exactly as he lived, would not be true discipleship at all, but only a foolish antiquarianism. Franciscanism does not mean "copying Francis": it means translating his spirit into action in our own entirely different circumstances. It is circumstances that define vocation. The spirit of Francis lives in men and women, acting in ways he would not understand, achieving aims he deliberately eschewed. Yet in all these rings the authentic Franciscan note. We might take men so varied and so diverse as Brother Leo (the "little sheep of God"), Roger Bacon and Giotto, Father Damien and Paul Sabatier; and in all of them St. Francis lives on. They are in the true line of the tradition, and we know the spirit of Francis partly through them. In this sense, but only in this sense, we could call him the "founder of Franciscan ethics".

I would urge that this is a pregnant analogy. We find, all the way down the Christian story, the thoughts and lives of men and women and children controlled and enriched by a new creative spirit, consecrating them to new valuations, evoking from them new qualities of character. In different circumstances and with varying aptitudes they have responded in their various ways to the claims which the situation made upon them. Their lives look as unlike as possible; the content of what they conceive to be their duty—that is to say, their conception of Christian ethics—has been as varied as their varying circumstances. But in all great Christians, in every time and place, we detect one unchanging characteristic, unmistakable and convincing. It is that which the New Testament calls Agape, the unique, distinctive Christian quality—what Christianity essentially *is*. Through their utterances there rings a tone which all fellow-disciples recognize: on their characters are moulded lineaments which we can trace to the authentic Portrait; a spirit breathes through all their acts and attitudes which we hail as that which draws from Galilee. They are all fruits from the authentic tree: and the tree is known by its fruits.

Now it is here that we find the true basis of the claim that this is a " final " disclosure, incomparably and supremely adequate to all our moral and spiritual needs. Jesus gives life a new direction, inspiring men and women throughout history to bring the new scales of valuation, that penetration and delicacy of insight which He alone has made possible, into countless tasks and life-situations of which He had no direct cognizance.

This is the real point of His " sinlessness " which we commonly rob of half its glory by presenting it in negative terms. It is not the fact that He never committed sin which is the secret of His redemptive influence. He redeems us rather by His matchless insight into the ultimate meaning of goodness, His interpretation of what love may be, the new avenues of possibility in spiritual achievement which He opens to us. In His presence our highest and best seems tainted. It is the unmatched quality of spirit, the unfathomably new and rich content in the significance He has given to life, which makes Him for us the Lord universal, Saviour and Sovereign of our hearts. Thus He is, in Von Hügel's phrase, " not *extensively* but *intensively* inexhaustible, since the truths and laws He showed and lived for us with especial profundity and power are themselves inexhaustible, and can and do combine with every conceivable growth and trial of man, giving them their fullest fruitfulness ".[1]

These are the lines along which to meet the objection alluded to in an earlier paragraph. It has been asserted in popular Christian preaching that the acts of Jesus are the perfect criterion to set before us in all moral choices. Men have been advised to face each decision in the light of the question : What did Jesus do ? The implied suggestion in all teaching of this kind is that the life of the historic Jesus is commensurate and coextensive with our modern problems.

[1] *Letters* (to C. J. Webb), p. 160.

And if not, it may seem to the superficial judgment scarcely relevant to the issues before us. Our moral tasks and perplexities are conditioned by the calls of family life, education, patriotism, economic effort, art, science, citizenship and so forth. It is for these that we need a Christian ethic. Yet, when men study the Life in the Gospels, they find that few of their interests have a place in it. As with His teaching, so with His life. There are great tracts of human life and interest, with the duties and opportunities involved in them, with which He seems to have been unconcerned. Much that for us constitutes the material on which the moral will must be exercised seems not to have touched His experience. He was celibate: at that point of life where for most modern men and women the moral pressure is felt most urgently He seems to have been untouched by our infirmities. His method of life made Him independent of the so-called economic nexus, with its clashes of duty and responsibility. His thought was not perturbed or dismayed by the complexities of our modern knowledge. Questions of peace and war and national policy do not seem to have weighed on His mind. The social problem was outside His horizons. All in all, His life was so limited, so circumscribed in its outlook and experience, so narrow in its range of response, that it seems to many almost irrelevant to the ethical issues of the twentieth century, and indeed scarcely adequate as the medium of a revelation that claims to be final.

There is real insight in this implied criticism: but it does not see quite far enough. If people confess themselves disappointed, as many do, with the Portrait put before them, may it be that, again, they are looking for the wrong thing? It is here as we found it to be in the story of Francis. Our Lord's life *was* drastically limited: but the limitation was deliberate. There are many fields of interest and activity, many varieties of moral experience, with which He willed to remain unconcerned. His life was a massive concentration, setting aside all that was subsidiary. "How was He straitened till it was accomplished." He was not as it were a connoisseur collecting pearls of wisdom and beauty from a wide, entrancing range of values. For His vocation's sake He "emptied Himself" in a sense other than St. Paul intended. Life, for Him, was deliberately emptied of much that for us rightly constitutes the positive content of its worth and value, that it might be the supreme and perfect focus of spirit in its relation to God's holiness.

It is here, as Von Hügel insisted, that we find the true uniqueness of Christ. "I think our answer will have to consist in an increased discrimination between the *religious* sense and even the moral instinct, and in showing if we can, and I think we really can do so, that our Lord had this sense in the supremest degree known to us anywhere. It is this religious sense that lights up His world, and it is a world which, apart from that still living light, is in great part as dead as the moon: this is an exaggerated image of what I believe to be the case here."[1]

This is an arresting formulation of what appears to me to be the right standpoint. Our Lord's task was not to provide mankind with an improved system of ethics. It was to reveal new depths of meaning in moral and spiritual attitudes, to disclose the ultimate quality of spirit in communion with the Holy and Eternal. In other words the concern of Jesus was not primarily with conduct at all. It was not so much to affect the relationships of men and women to one another: rather it was to redeem the relationship of all men and women to God. His was essentially a religious vocation. His whole life moves in the sphere of the Supernatural. The whole burden of His thought and action is that life's true centre of gravity is not to be sought in this world at all. Beneath all His lovely "humanity"

[1] *Letters*, pp. 159 to 160.

always sounds the relentless ascetic note. It has been the great achievement of modern scholarship to rediscover the central position of the Kingdom of God in His life and teaching. But the Kingdom is no "good time coming" as the consequence of reforming movements, still less as the climax of evolving processes. It is utterly supernatural and transcendent, the *gift* of the Father's good pleasure. It demands detachment and concentration. It belongs to eternity, not to the world of time. It is God's overwhelming reality pressing upon the unreal desires, the false values, the confused thinking, the feverish hopes and despairs of earth. It is what the Fourth Gospel calls "Truth", the absolute moral and spiritual standard before which all men's values must be summoned. "This is the judgment," as St. John says: "light is come into the world and men loved darkness rather than light." There is no escaping from this tremendous emphasis except by distorting the evidence of the Gospels. To soften these otherworldly stresses is to make nonsense of the whole story.

Our Lord's function as He conceived it was not directly the reformation of morals. It was to reveal God's holy will. That was His mediatorial prerogative. "No man knoweth the Father but the Son and he to whom the Son will reveal Him." That was His vocation as He conceived it. And this defines, colours and controls the whole course of His ministry and passion; setting those iron limitations to the range of His activity and interests and summoning Him to the destiny of the Cross.

This is involved in the "Messianic" consciousness as uniquely interpreted by Him and His reading of the Messiah's task. What rich chances of leadership and service are deliberately excluded from it! He was the Messiah, the climax of history, the inaugurator of the new age, bearer and agent of the divine purpose. Manifold and urgent were the voices calling to one who was to discharge this function. Splendid open avenues of leadership were offered by the conditions of life in Palestine in the fifteenth year of the reign of Tiberius Cæsar. There was the burning issue of Jewish nationalism over against the imperial sovereignty, baffling to diplomacy on both sides. There was the question of economic justice, the gulf between the Roman millionaires amid the palm-beaches of Tiberias and the poverty of the cottagers in Capernaum. There was, too, the cultural issue, the whole problem of right adjustment between the Palestinian tradition and the Hellenistic world movements. There were these and many like issues, political, social and economic, all calling for supreme insight, inspired leadership and moral heroism. If One so gifted and endowed had given Himself to these or similar causes, He would have led the people towards a new world and presided over a golden age in history. He could pass through any of these open gateways to brilliant and redemptive achievement. Jesus was not deaf to these voices. But they were, for Him, the voice of Satan. He was keenly sensitive to the appeal of them ; that is perhaps the meaning of the Temptation. But when He heard them they were repudiated. Not because these were not legitimate and needful contributions to human welfare, but because they were not embraced in His vocation. Not such a Messiah was He to be. His vocation was to redeem the world at its point of ultimate need and destitution. It was through and through a supernatural task, to reveal God's spiritual holiness as the central reality of life. He would be a Messiah who was a teacher. He would go to the world and take in His hands nothing but the offer of truth and spiritual freedom. He would be Himself the instrument of the Kingdom, the incarnation of the divine will. Where He was, there it should be present, the Kingdom, the power and the glory. And, thus deciding, Jesus willed Calvary. The ruthless foreshortening of His life in time to which

He then gave inward assent involves the conviction that His significance lay in the eternal and supernatural order.

3. The Messiah and His Destiny

The interpretation which I have been suggesting is open to a dangerous misconstruction. To insist so strongly on the " religious " note may expose one to the charge of wishing to minimize the moral content of our Lord's life and the moral sovereignty of His teaching. And there are schools of thought in the Christian Church to which such a conclusion would not be unwelcome. Recent criticism of the New Testament makes it perfectly clear that the Gospel narratives are intended rather as sermons than records. That is to say, they are coloured at many points with the ethical and doctrinal interests of the Christian groups out of which they emerge. The conclusion, amongst the more radical scholars, is that the Gospels are first-class documents for the early chapters of the Christian movement, but have little objectively reliable to tell us about the Jesus of history. The corollary is not hard to supply. For this may be made to buttress the claim of the most rigid form of institutionalism. For, on this showing, we know nothing about the Founder of Christianity other than what the early Church thought about Him. Right or wrong this is our sole evidence. The conclusion does not lie far away that the Jesus of history is but a shadowy figure about whom we have scanty information, and that the sole fountain of authority whether ethical or theological resides in institutional Christianity. So, by the bold if perilous manœuvre of accepting gifts from the enemy, the results of the most destructive criticism have been turned into a victory for conservatism. As Newman's theory of development, by its underestimate of historical origins, was made to serve the ends of reactionaries, so the most drastic trends in modern scholarship have been pressed into the service of rigorism. Modernism in its Roman form, prepared to "accept with natural piety" what has emerged, that is, the Roman Church, can make that Church in its present-day form the sole arbiter of truth and the sole source of authority in morals. There is a group of brilliant Anglican scholars who seem to be working towards the same result. It is, in my judgment, dangerously misleading. And that makes it imperative to define more closely the critical assumptions of my position.

It is well known that this school of Modernism is preoccupied with the dramatic form in which the Gospel narratives are presented. We touch here the question of eschatology. It is certainly true (as we shall see presently) that realistic New Testament criticism has annihilated the "liberal" position, which sought to depict our Lord almost exclusively as the teacher of a simple ethic of God's fatherhood and human brotherhood. That interpretation is no longer tenable. It has been destroyed by more searching study of the structure and content of the Gospels. But the eschatological school of criticism which has shown us the way to a more historical portrait, so far minimizes the ethical content in the life and teaching of Jesus that, if it is right, then everything in this volume is not merely mistaken but meaningless. This imposes upon us the obligation to examine its contentions more narrowly.

For the "eschatological" interpretation our Lord was not a teacher at all. He was the Herald of the coming Kingdom. His whole thought and action were determined by the conviction that presently, immediately, before the standing harvest had ripened (Matt. ix. 37), God would strike in to break the back of history and roll up the existing world order. Then, by sheer catastrophic intervention, would dawn the new age of the Messiah in which Jesus Himself would reign as Son of Man. Thus there could, in the nature of things, be no real concern with ethical questions. The social order was under sentence of death. His task was to rouse men to believe in the Kingdom, to hasten its coming by faith and repentance.

At first His preaching was hailed with enthusiasm: "the Kingdom of God was being preached and men were willingly pressing into it". Soon suspicion and hatred closed round Him. The Kingdom tarried and God's arm was shortened. At the last, alone with His secret, He forced the hands of the Jewish authorities and devoted Himself to the Cross that so He might release God's activity and enable the Kingdom to be established. This, His last obedience, would be His triumph. He believed that by accepting the Cross His Messianic glory would be fulfilled and the Son of Man would come on the clouds of heaven. He died with the great cry of disillusionment.

This exegesis, as everyone knows, was worked out by Weiss and Schweitzer with relentless force and magnificent passion. In the form in which Schweitzer presented it we can only regard it as fantastic. If this were the true account of the matter then it seems wellnigh impossible to account for the existence of Christianity. The result, moreover, could only be reached by violent treatment of the available evidence. There are very few scholars now living who would accept Schweitzer's position in his own extreme and paradoxical version.[1]

But this does not and should not imply that the eschatological standpoint is false. It comes at least far nearer the truth than the portrait of the Jesus of history drawn by the critics of the Harnack tradition. For them, the eschatological emphasis which is present so strongly in the Synoptic Gospels, and the whole belief of the primitive Church in the

[1] Dr. Warschauer describes his book, *The Historical Life of Jesus*, as "the life of Jesus which Schweitzer did not write".

imminent Coming of Christ, is the result of misunderstanding. The original sayings have passed through the crucible of the Jewish mind and Jewish expectations. They have thus been coloured and misrepresented by the presuppositions of their hearers. They reach us not in the form which He gave them but in that imposed upon them by the disciples. All that serves Schweitzer for evidence is thus in truth secondary material and must be eliminated by criticism. The primary and authentic material exhibits Christ as the preacher of righteousness and the evangelist of God's Fatherhood. The overlay has distorted the true portrait.

Now we do not and cannot hope to know in detail what exactly Jesus Himself believed concerning the nature of the Kingdom or the manner of its coming, or His place in it. For we cannot determine with sufficient accuracy the ideas held by the first disciples or by the various groups of believers through whose minds the traditions have passed, to be sure how much allowance to make for what they may have read into His sayings. We can never be certain what He thought about it. Yet it seems to be scarcely disputable that the expectation of the primitive Church is based upon some authentic element in the Master's own thought and teaching. Nor, I think, can it reasonably be doubted that it was His belief that in the Father's purpose His death was the determined condition for the coming of the Kingdom of God, and that by His voluntary acceptance He would pass into Messianic glory. Whether or not He believed the Kingdom to be about to dawn in the imminent future it is perhaps impossible to decide. One school of critics tends to cut out all evidence that seems to confirm this ; the other, all that tends to disprove it. But neither procedure is justifiable. Both suggestions are traceable to Himself. But, in any case, the Kingdom of God whether it be distant or near is a totally different conception from that of the so-called " end of the world" ; and both again must be distinguished from that of the " coming of the Son of Man ".

The proofs offered on both sides of this controversy are falsified by this radical confusion of ideas that ought to be kept clearly separate. And the helpless chaos of popular Christian thinking about what is commonly called the Second Advent (a phrase which has no New Testament justification) is due in large measure to the same confusion. The real facts are, I believe, as follows. Our Lord worked with three distinct notions which subsequent thought has quite wrongly identified. There was, first, the Kingdom of God which He described both as now present and as yet to be fulfilled. But of its exact " when and where " He declared Himself to be ignorant. (Mark xiii. 32.) This double conception of presence and futurity is, it is clear, necessarily applicable to all God's gifts and disclosures. (" It is not yet revealed what we shall be : but we know . . .") It is this idea of the Reign of God, presented by Him in pictorial, Jewish terms which is re-translated by the Ephesian school in the more " inward " language of life eternal, known now as a present reality, hereafter to be possessed in fuller fruition. Secondly, there was the climax of history, the Consummation of the Age, when the wheat and tares should be finally separated, and Good and Evil stand out in their naked reality. Such a conception is plainly inherent in the moral government of the universe. There are, thirdly, the mysterious assertions about the Coming of the Son of Man : and this, in the earliest tradition, is spoken of as something immediate. It was to become true " from this time onwards ". It was to be the consequence of the Passion. It was on this latter conception that the Parousia expectation rested.

The confusion in which the debate has become involved springs partly from a mistranslation, partly from treating as though they were identical ideas which originally were quite distinct. The Authorised Version uses the phrase "the end of the world" to render συντέλεια τοῦ αἰῶνος—the Consummation of the Age; and popular thought identifies this conception both with the fulfilment of God's Kingdom and with the Coming of the Son of Man. Hence the "second coming" of Christ is identified with the end of the world, in its crude, astronomical sense; and the ghastly pulpit speculations follow, despite the Master's definite disavowal of them.[1]

But He spoke of the Coming as immediate. There is nothing in the authentic tradition about a deferred and distant Parousia, such as we describe as the "Second Advent". The New Testament speaks about a Coming, which it expects in the immediate future. And this runs back to the teaching of Jesus. Where the early Church was mistaken was not in expecting the Coming too soon but in failing to see that it had occurred already as the precondition of Christianity and the living source of its own Christian experience. That recognition was not to be long delayed. The probable development of St. Paul's thought finds its climax in the Fourth Gospel. And here, the Coming of the Son of Man as the triumphant consequence of the Passion is identified, explicitly and emphatically, with the gift of the Spirit in the hearts of believers. "It is expedient that I go away: if I go not away the Comforter will not come to you. . . . I will not leave you orphans: I am coming to you." Thus the ethical transformation wrought on the world by the Spirit of Christ is intimately and directly related to that element in the thought of Christ which He Himself in the days of His flesh expressed in the symbolism of eschatology. It is of the greatest importance to recognize this. Because, as it seems to me, the whole controversy of ethical *versus* eschato-

[1] It is well known to students that the procedure is already traceable in the "little apocalypse" embedded in St. Mark xiii. and parallels (cf. Matt. xxiv. 3, "of thy coming and of the end of the world").

logical is really debated round a false antithesis. The two terms are in no sense exclusive.

From the standpoint of historical criticism the eschatological interpretation is much nearer to the Jesus of history than the traditional portrait of liberalism. It is also essential to emphasize the immensely important religious contribution which we owe to the apocalyptic school. It has driven the proverbial coach and horses through the threadbare canvas of the Victorian picture. It was the assumption of liberal Protestantism that His whole activity is to be interpreted primarily as that of an ethical teacher. And its leaders were no less prone than the eschatologists to ignore or delete such documentary evidence as would not easily square with their preconceptions. But the mutilated portrait which they constructed was a worse caricature than that of Schweitzer. In their desire to make Him "sympathetic," to modernize His outlook and teaching, they succeeded in making Him utterly insignificant. They rightly insisted upon that humanity which the Gospels themselves never called in question. But they so interpreted "perfect Man" as to mean a depressingly ordinary person. Thus whatever our standards cannot measure must be either legendary or misreported. Nothing is true which we cannot understand. If He was Man, He was just like one of us.

But this is a defeatist theology. It merely retreats before its difficulties. For, even if the apocalyptic elements in the Gospels as we have them now are the reflexion of a later age, rather than actual records of His words, would such sublimely imaginative language and the exalted emotion it expresses ever have grown round one whom men had known as the mere teacher of a bourgeois ethic? That is the failure and blindness of liberalism. It attempts, very rightly, to set the Master free from the unreality of the old tradition, which made Him a theological lay-figure in a half-mechanical scheme of salvation, rather than a real man among men. But it brings to its subject too defective an insight. Consequently it has scaled down His imperial mind, with its stupendous vision and experience, to the measure of a well-meaning Sunday School teacher. But in truth, if this were an authentic portrait, there would never have been such a thing as Christianity. What has happened, we ask, to the majesty and terror, the fascination and mystery, which invest Him in the Gospel narratives ? " They were afraid " : He was too great for them. The whole story moves in an atmosphere of wonder, fringed, as it were, with a " numinous " corona whose flames leap up in immeasurable splendour into spaces which we cannot chart. We cannot tear it out of that setting. Apart from it, there is no story to tell. And it is the triumph of the eschatologists to have recovered that atmosphere. Thus, while discarding the metaphysical " mystery " which clings too often round conciliar orthodoxy, they have yet preserved the essential religious values which liberal Protestantism allowed to perish. They compel us to face the Hero of the Gospels as one whom we can never " understand ", who outsoars the range of our imaginations and our poor reach of spiritual insight, and dwells upon heights that our minds can never scale. And that is a very great contribution. However much we may wish to disagree either with their methods or with their conclusions, at least they have given us a Prince and Saviour (Acts v. 31) girt about with majesty and awe.

It seemed but just to make this acknowledgment, which may also serve (I hope), incidentally, to explain more clearly the critical standpoint which lies behind the discussion in this chapter. But, when it comes to an attempt to estimate the central emphasis of our Lord's Sayings, then the position of the eschatologists seems to me to be definitely mistaken. If we were forced to accept a barren antithesis, and choose between " ethical " and " apocalyptic "—without hesitation we decide for " ethical " as less misleading than the alternative. He was, we should hold, essentially a Teacher, and His emphasis throughout was ethical rather than eschatological. The choice that determined the method of His mission is surely made clear in the Temptation story.

The imperial reach of His imagination, rejecting all the kingdoms of the world and the glory of them as inadequate to His conception of what He had come to be, reveals itself later in His mysterious vision of the Son of Man riding upon the clouds. But the choice He made in the wilderness is sufficiently plain from the sequel. There were many short-cuts, any of which would lead to a brilliant and immediate "success". He flung behind Him all these possibilities. He chose the way which demands so much more faith in the strength of God and in human nature—the slow, disappointing method of the Teacher. He would be the Sower going forth to sow, baffled and limited at every step by the receptivity of the human soil. And when we scrutinize the recorded teaching, it can hardly be doubted that our Lord stood in the true line of the *prophetic* succession. What affects a man's standing with his God is essentially his moral attitude. It is "from within out of the heart of man" that the decisive factors issue. It is not in ceremonial observance but in the secret chambers of the heart that the meaning of true religion is found. Communion with the Father depends utterly on the singleness of men's desires and thoughts and the direction of their wills. (The Temptation shows the cost to Himself of mediating the divine knowledge.) For whereas the creeds of Christendom conceived God mainly in terms of metaphysical essence, our Lord conceived Him in terms of moral attributes. Hence to "love" God means to love one's neighbour. The prerequisites for the Sovereignty of God He conceived and described as moral, through and through. The Beatitudes describe the type of character, the tone and temper and quality of spirit, which makes for the coming of the Kingdom.

In all this we acclaim the tradition of the prophets ; and if this is not rightly called " ethical " teaching, it is hard to say what that word can mean.

But, having established this, we must go further. This ethical teaching is not merely ethical : it is essentially *religious*. Faith in God is the very nerve of it : cut that nerve, and we shall have nothing left. It is only as seen against its proper background in His own religious intuitions that the teaching can claim its enduring significance. If He is wrong at the core of His thinking, if man is not made for eternity, if the centre of gravity for this life is not to be sought in a supernatural order—then the ethics of the Sermon on the Mount must be confessed to be gravely misleading.

The uniqueness of our Lord's moral insight depends upon this religious orientation. It is " ethics thought from a new centre ". We must be merciful *because God is merciful*, that is His tremendous imperative, and perfect as the Father is perfect. The " ethic of Jesus " means the realization here in spatio-temporal experience of the qualities of the Divine Life. It is finite life centred in the Infinite. It is this essentially " otherworldly " note, the sense of God's transcendent reality as the meaning of life and the Good for man, which is witnessed to by the dramatic symbolism of the traditional Jewish apocalyptic.[1]

[1] But this is a moment in our Lord's experience which is not patient of modernization. It is bound up with the Messianic consciousness. It remains opaque to our ways of thinking. It is not, indeed, altogether impossible to trace certain contributory factors which may have been present in His expectation of His coming as Son of Man. On the one hand He was Messiah, the Inaugurator of the New Age. As such He was God's anointed representative, the agent of the Divine redemptive purpose. That purpose, because it was God's, must prevail. On the other hand it was certain beyond argument that His mission would end in failure and rejection. His thought was always utterly realistic, unclouded by comforting illusions. Here, then, were two groups of facts to both of which He must remain loyal, as the price of His own inward integrity. It was, perhaps, out of this conflict that the crucial expectation took shape. He was Messiah, but not yet. He was Messiah, but still to be revealed. Here, He was a fugitive

Precisely what our Lord expected to happen when He thus made use of apocalyptic language is beyond any possible conjecture. The forms of His thinking and expectation are conditioned by historical limitations. His experience is incommunicable; His insight into spiritual reality is His own, magisterial and certain. But the thought-forms in which He must formulate those intuitions and innermost experiences to His conscious mind and to His disciples are those of a Jew at that point of time. The whole Messianic category is of His world and not ours, a world frankly as dead as the moon. We must accept it realistically as simply "given" and non-rationalizable. It is the form of a unique experience. Then we must have the insight to understand that it is, after all, the frame, not the picture; to see the light of the sun shining through it, and acclaim there the reality of God. *Sic dilexit Deus mundum.*

Yet the Messianic form of His thinking is not something which can be painted out to leave a more "human" and "sympathetic" portrait. It is integral to the Christ of history. For, as we have already contended, it is the permanent, irreducible evidence of that transcendental range in His consciousness without which the story makes nonsense. It is also the inevitably right expression, inevitable as a great artistic creation, of the claim which He made on the future. The Kingdom which it was for Him to inaugurate is a Kingdom not of this world: yet it was to be realized in this world. It is the invasion of human history by the sovereign holiness of the living God.

and a failure, the Servant of rulers whom Kings despised. As a lamb He would be led to the slaughter. But was it not written that thus it must be? This, too, was a part of Messiah's mission, the path by which He must enter upon His glory. Hence the Messiah-to-be must be stricken, smitten of God and tormented; but through death, out and on the other side of death, He would "come", Messiah in deed and truth, victorious, vindicated and invincible. "From that moment there shall be the Son of Man, seated at the right hand of the Power and coming in the clouds of heaven."

It was, eternally, but it was yet to be. By His death it would become actualized. And so it was, when (as St. Paul said), He was " designated as Messiah by His resurrection from the dead " (Rom. i. 4), and the spirit of glory and the spirit of God was released by Him into the hearts of men. Pentecost was the Messianic victory ; the inauguration of the Kingdom of God ; the transvaluation of ethical values, so that the last is first and the first last.

The vision of God's holy love, seen through the windows of Christ's mind and mediated by His spirit, is the differentia of the Christian ethic. The prudential and self-contained ethic of the Aristotelian or the Stoic rests on one conception of God ; that of Christianity on another. They could not say, as He said : " the hairs of your head are all numbered ". For Aristotle's God cannot know the existence of our sublunar world. The Stoics could not say : " There is joy in heaven over one sinner that repenteth " ; for virtue is a man's own achievement,[1] and repentance an unmanly emotion. Nor could God be concerned with sinners.[2] The Gospel of Christ shatters our complacency by the vision of God's unapproachable holiness mirrored for us in the face of Christ. It exhibits the inmost essence of that holiness as a going forth in redemptive love. Thus it leads us to look out on life and to respond to it from a new centre. As men are possessed by the Holy Spirit a " new heart " comes to be fashioned in them : they are made " partakers of the divine nature ". All the distinctively Christian claims and insights, with their ethical revaluations and their new range both of humility and heroism, spring from that supernatural source.

[1] Cf. Juvenal's " Monstro quod ipse tibi possis dare."

[2] " Heine once said that he too might have died to save men, had he not shrewdly suspected that they were not worth saving ; and this remark, by displaying the absolute contrast and antithesis of the attitude of Jesus, makes that attitude more luminously clear." Barbour, *A Philosophical Study of Christian Ethics*, p. 97.

But our Lord did not travel through Palestine discoursing upon a " new idea of God ". His thought of God was never defined. And indeed the highest cannot be spoken. It can be experienced and done. The only way whereby in the last resort such spiritual intuitions can be outwardly expressed is through the symbolisms of art and the acted convictions of living. He gave them symbolic expression by means of the stock pictorial imagery of Scripture, and the popular books of devotion. He suggested in parable and aphorism aspects, analogies and illustrations of the central certainties in His own experience. He described in the Beatitudes, for example, the qualities of temper and spirit characteristic of the true life in which the Father's will should be sovereign. Language was his artistic medium, and He used it with unapproached mastery to set forth the truth in His soul. But essentially by His life and death He uttered the divine revelation and manifested forth His glory. He is Himself the truth which He knew. His cross was the final manifestation of the ultimate quality of the Divine Will. "Truly this man was the Son of God." He that had seen Him had seen the Father. The life of Christ, and His death and resurrection, made the holy God of the Old Testament a transfiguring and redemptive reality in men's moral and religious experience.

The Gospel went to the Graeco-Roman world. It seemed to that world at its first impact an alien thing, hopelessly irrelevant to the hopes and claims of a humanist civilization. To the Greeks folly, there was nothing in it ; it appeared to them as a Gospel of death. It proved itself, as we have already seen, the creative nucleus of a new society, sustaining, redeeming and transvaluing all that was vital in the surrounding culture. What the Hellenistic civilisation was to the primitive Christian movement, that the philosophy and the social order based on the concept of evolution are to contemporary Christianity.

NOTE

It is only fair to acknowledge that the point of view set forth in part of this chapter was elaborated by Dr. Boyd Scott in his volume, *Christ the Wisdom of Man* (Hodder & Stoughton, 1928). The book never became widely known and the author's rather unfortunate terminology perhaps stood between him and his readers. But it was very nearly the only book which had " seen the point " about the Ethic of Jesus.

It has also been pointed out to me that a striking passage in Moberly's *Atonement and Personality*, pp. 147–148, serves partly as confirmation, partly as corrective, of some things which I have said in this chapter.

CHAPTER V

HUMANISM AND THE GOSPEL

1. What is Humanism?

THE tradition dies hard that Christianity is in some sense inimical to the arts. "What has Christ to do with Apollo?" "When put on its mettle," says Professor Grierson, "the Christian Church has always distrusted and must always distrust the arts, for in them the free spirit of man will endeavour to express itself uncurbed and in its entirety."[1] Why should it not? If the Christian life is, as St. Paul claimed, an emancipation, is there any factor in the Christian attitude which regards such free expression with disapproval? That there is such an element is the firm conviction of nearly all the exponents of Humanism. John Addington Symonds, for example, in his classic work *The Renaissance in Italy*, is at once exultant and rather shocked by the development which he has to study. His treatment is, no doubt, in some ways obsolete, yet in essentials his point of view coincides with that of Professor Grierson. "The spirit of Christianity and the spirit of figurative art are opposed, not because such art is immoral, but because it cannot free itself from sensuous associations. It is always bringing us back to the dear life of earth, from which the faith would sever us. It is always reminding us of the body, which piety bids us forget. . . . When the worshipper would fain ascend on wings of ecstasy to God, the infinite, ineffable, unrealized, how can he endure

[1] *Cross Currents in English Literature of the Seventeenth Century*, p. 19. I refer again to this stimulating study in the next chapter, pp 135–136

the contact of those splendid forms in which the lust of the eye and the pride of life, professing to subserve devotion, remind him crudely of the goodliness of sensual existence? As displayed in its most perfect phases, in Greek sculpture or Venetian painting, art dignifies the actual mundane life of man ; but Christ, in the language of uncompromising piety, means everything most alien to the mundane life.[1]

There is much in that passage that invites criticism. The result of the whole enquiry in this book will, I hope, make sufficiently clear how mistaken (in my view) this position is. We may take it here as a well-known expression of an idea which is still widely circulated, and need not, therefore, concern ourselves with details—the strange ambiguity, for instance, between the words sensuous and sensual. Broadly stated, it contains a half-truth. It is certainly not true that Christianity is at all distrustful of the arts as such. After all, it was founded by a Poet who tamed the hearts of men by His beauty. The Orpheus symbolism in the catacombs seems, no doubt, to say more to us than was consciously intended by the painters. At least, let us remember that it is there ; a religion which felt that the arts were anti-Christian would hardly have made its burying places bright with stucco and fresco like the pagan dwelling-houses. The idea that the early Church was afraid of art is a fallacy which should have been exploded by the better historical knowledge now available.[2]

The one exception—its outlawry of Drama—was due to its inability to countenance the lubricity and idolatry involved in it. It was not the art it feared but the paganism. To the art itself there was no hostility. As was suggested in a previous chapter, it had quickly begun to develop an art of its own, especially the supreme art of architecture. Yet we must admit a strain in Christianity of which the state-

[1] *Renaissance in Italy*, Vol. III, *The Fine Arts*, pp. 18–19.
[2] Cf. " Art (Christian) " in E.R.E., and Dearmer, *The Necessity of Art*.

ments quoted would be justified. Puritanism (in the popular sense) is no product of the Reformation. Apart from the hermits and the Stylite saints and other products of that fierce asceticism which soon crept into the Church from alien sources, it has always lived within the Great Church. We have only to think of Leo the Iconoclast, of the Cistercians or of Savonarola, to appreciate the strength of this tradition. There are indeed two strains in Christianity as there are in the fabric of European culture—the world-affirming strain and the world-denying. " In the civilization of the European peoples the Hebrew and the Greek traditions have entered into combination, but their mutual adjustment still raises questions on which men are not agreed. Both in the Jewish community and in the Christian community to-day there is an opposition between traditionalist and modernist, orthodox and liberal, which really springs from the old difficulty how to harmonize the claims of the God of Israel with the claims of intellectual culture —an opposition which exists not merely between man and man but often within the individual himself."[1] There are certain crucial points in history when the two seem to be specially in conflict, or one or the other to be gaining mastery. The theme has been magnificently worked out in Merejkowski's novel, *The Forerunner*, based on the note-books of Leonardo da Vinci. In that stormy, enigmatic soul there are two faiths struggling to be born—the Hellenic (we may say) and the Jewish-Christian, the faith in Man, free, self-directive, lifting himself up towards divinity, and the faith in God, redemptive, self-disclosing, stooping to clothe Himself in Humanity. It is, to use Dostoiefsky's phrase, " the struggle between two mighty opposites, the God-Man and the Man-God, between Christ and the Belvedere Apollo ". It is only to put this in different language if we say that here, focused in one life, is the issue between the

[1] E. Bevan in *The Legacy of Israel*, p. 42.

world of the Renaissance and the mediæval world of the Christian legacy. In the Renaissance and the Reformation the two strains, Hellenic and Hebraic, confronted one another for a moment in apparently unrelieved opposition. There is obviously nothing more essential for the Christian ethic in the world we live in than to define its attitude to the problem.

Possibly the best account that can be given is to say that in all genuine religion there are and always must be two stresses, that on Transcendence and that on Immanence, which have to be kept balanced and proportioned. If either is misplaced or neglected, then life becomes ignoble or unstable. Christianity claims to see and to make life whole by keeping the two in right poise and perspective. It may be true that in the Byzantine and mediæval forms of Christianity the stress upon Transcendence was exaggerated. The Byzantine Art would certainly suggest that. The "humanism" of Renaissance painting was not, after all, a mere technical improvement, the necessary line of advance and progress from the limitations of Byzantine artists, as Addington Symonds apparently assumed. It was not, surely, that the Byzantine craftsmen were unable to draw the human form correctly. It was, much rather, that they did not wish to. They stand for a different attitude entirely. They do not assume that a humanistic art is the right way to express the Christian faith. They do not think of God as within Man, but as the King, immortal, invisible, dwelling in unapproachable light. Conventional, mysterious, distant symbolisms are the only means of conveying such suggestions. The Renaissance paintings became more "natural", not merely because the artists could draw better (though that no doubt is true so far as it goes) but because they expressed a different philosophy. The Renaissance (if we may use the text-book label) is in fact the reaction towards Immanence as the central doctrine of religious faith, and therefore inevitably expressed itself in a "Humanist" response to life.

But it would be quite untrue to argue that the Humanism of Renaissance circles was a movement away from Christianity. Savonarola may have so regarded it, and its legacy in the modern world has shown a violent swing in that direction. But in itself the Humanist movement was of legitimate Christian descent. Erasmus and Colet were among the Humanists, and the Reformation, if they had achieved their aims, would have taken the form of a Christian Renaissance. They were not conscious of any opposition. Nor can we suppose that the Renaissance suddenly burst on a sleeping world by a kind of spontaneous generation. It had a long ancestry behind it, and it was of the authentic Christian lineage. What was new in the so-called Renaissance was the rediscovery of Greek culture, and that was only in the fifteenth century, after the fall of Constantinople. The Renaissance proper had begun much earlier, and within the fold of the Catholic Church: the age of Dante and St. Thomas and of the great Cathedral builders can hardly be described as a "dark" age. The fact is rather that the Christian spirit, with its vivid interest in Man as the organ of the divine mind, had long previously been fertilizing the sterile tradition of Byzantinism. The whole ethos of Byzantine culture drew from essentially oriental influences: it was a culture of the "archaic" type,—static, immobile, and unprogressive. But a new life had long ago been stirring in it and was manifest in signal creations of art, literature and philosophy. To employ a distinction used by H. G. Wells, there had been a largely Christian "renascence" for centuries before the Renaissance. The naturalism of quatrocentrist art, and the new interest in the human form characteristic of Renaissance painting, probably owed a very great deal more to the influence of St. Francis of Assisi, than to any other single cause. Indeed, had it not been for Christianity, both the Humanism of the Renaissance and its remains in what the modern world has agreed to call the Humanist philosophy would have been quite different from what they are. The question is whether whatever is true and vital in the Humanism of the twentieth century can survive the subsidence of its Christian bases.

This is the question which we must now examine. But the answer depends in part on terminology. One rises bewildered from much current argument to ask exhaustedly, "But what *is* Humanism?"

Humanism is an ambiguous word, and much misunderstanding and confusion spring from the various distinct senses in which this over-worked noun is used. The Humanism which is in debate in most modern argument and controversy means, of course, something quite different from what it meant to Colet or Erasmus. But if we ask precisely what it does mean, the answer is not so simple as might be wished. At the present moment in the United States, which is the citadel and shrine of Humanism, discussion about the meaning of this word is developing into a new religious war in which the rival sects outlaw heretics and exterminate them without pity. But the issues at stake are still obscure, since the true faith remains undefined.[1]

But at least these different senses are distinguishable. (*a*) It is used in the traditional "Oxford" sense of *literae humaniores*—that is to say, a liberal education based upon a literary culture. That was what it meant for the Renaissance humanists, and I am not aware of any Christian principles which would make "Greats" a sinful self-indulgence. I quote an authoritative definition. "Ancient Latin writers used the word *humanitas* to denote the civilizing

[1] The curious may find the nearest approach to an orthodox definition in Prof. Irving Babbitt's "Essay in Definition" in the volume, *Humanism and America*.

influence of polite letters and of the liberal arts; and they also applied the epithet *humanus* to a character which had received that influence. The Italian scholars of the Renaissance, to whom the Classical literature of antiquity was not merely a model but a culture and indeed a life, found it natural to employ a phrase not used by the Ancients and to speak of *literae humaniores*, meaning by the comparative not 'secular rather than theological' but 'distinctively humane'."[1]

(*b*) But as the Renaissance movement developed, this contrast came to be accentuated. The sense of freedom and emancipation, the thrill of discovery and widening knowledge, the new confidence in Man himself, his endowments, his gifts and his capacities, led naturally toward the conclusion that Man is master in his own universe and could mould his destiny to his own will. The sense of creatureliness and dependence before the might and mystery of things seemed to give way before the advance of Science, and thus the religious approach to life came to seem increasingly unnecessary even if not positively harmful. The whole tendency of the modern age has been to eliminate the supernatural. It has sought to "humanize" our experience, bringing nature under our control and making it intelligible to man. Man, not God, has been its pole of vision. The almost necessary result of this is the so-called "religion of humanity". It is only in this sense that Humanism means anything antagonistic to Christianity. We might avoid considerable confusion if it were called Humanitarianism.

(*c*) But this philosophy, as we shall see shortly, degenerates almost inevitably into a naturalistic attitude. We shall have to explore the causes of this paradox. For the sheer fact is that this buoyant attitude which built its confidence on belief in Man, certain that he needed God no longer, has

[1] R. C. Jebb in *Cambridge Modern History*, Vol. I, p. 538.

ended in such a disbelief in Man, such radical distrust of human nature, that the world is half-paralysed by reason of it. It has tried to believe in Man instead of in God, and now it can " put no confidence in man ". The " debunking " fashion in biography is but one symptom of a mortal sickness. The eroticism of " advanced " literature is a desperate confession of disbelief in that very human nature which it sets out to explore and glorify. We have tried to humanize our experience, to take Man as the measure of all things, and now we are fast losing faith in Man. The whole struggle of the post-war age in our " devaluated " civilization is to maintain the distinctive human values against the pressure of merely " natural " forces (the lusts and passions of our pre-human ancestry) and the mechanization of our ways of living. Nearly all the forces of our society are inimical to personality. It is this that constitutes the situation faced by the new American school of Humanism. Since the older humanist and romantic movement leads—as they see clearly—to sheer Naturalism, repudiating all human values, these writers urge an acceptance of " Humanism ", by which is meant a philosophy of life which will face seriously and frankly Man's moral and spiritual dignity and his place and destiny within the universe.

So far, it is obvious, Christianity and Humanism seem to be natural allies. But this is not the full account of the matter. For one school—and that the most popular—of the Humanism current in the United States (and that which has most influence in England) seeks to combine this humanist moral philosophy with a non-theistic and " critical " attitude in its interpretation of the universe. It is, in a phrase which excellently describes it, " a naturalism in metaphysics and a pure humanism in ethics ".[1] It is, indeed, a desperate effort to establish a belief in human values on a purely naturalistic basis. And this, as we were

[1] Quoted by Horton, *Theism and the Modern Mood*, p. 44.

taught years ago by the eloquence of Bertrand Russell, can but lead to despair and disillusionment. For this latest down-to-date novelty is but an astonishingly naïve and unsophisticated version of that lie in the modern philosophic soul—the attempted divorce between " fact " and " value ".[1] But we cannot genuinely believe in Man or the excellence of Man's prerogatives unless we also believe in something more than Man. We cannot combine the Christian valuations with a non-Christian metaphysic. Humanism will soon have to choose.

The following passage represents fairly one trend in contemporary Humanism.

" It is a constructive social suggestion that we endeavour to give up . . . the quest for companionship with a being behind or within the fleeting aspect of nature ; . . . that we acknowledge ourselves to be adrift in infinite space on our little earth, the sole custodians of our ideals . . . that we may then turn from the recognition of our cosmic isolation to a new sense of human togetherness and so discover in a growing human solidarity . . . the goal we have all along blindly sought, and build on earth the fair city we have looked for in a compensatory world beyond."[2]

This is, in effect, what Mr. Lippmann offers us as the " high religion " of the twentieth century. His point of view will occupy us later on. But meantime, I quote two freezing sentences as a commentary on this position. " Ours (says Mr. Krutch) is a lost cause, and there is no place for us in the natural universe, but we are not, for all that, sorry to be human. We would rather die as men than live as animals."[3] One might have supposed that a Humanist

[1] See below Chapter VII, pp. 182–185.

[2] Quoted from Max Otto in *Theism and the Modern Mood*, p. 44.

[3] Joseph Wood Krutch, *The Modern Temper*, p. 249, last sentence of the book. Cf. his chapter on " The Paradox of Humanism " in the same volume.

philosophy would have asked itself the question : What is Man ? But this apparently has been overlooked.

(*d*) There is, however, another school widely known as " literary Humanism " led by those two highly distinguished authors, Dr. Paul Elmer More of Princeton, and Professor Irving Babbitt of Harvard. This is, in its essence, a neo-classicism in literary and artistic criticism, by way of reaction from the " romantic " movement, to the influence of which these writers trace all that they deplore in modern tendencies. (It is said in America that Professor Babbitt is so hag-ridden by his fear of Rousseau that he looks under his bed every evening lest the shade of Jean Jacques should be lurking there.) It is an appeal from emotional eccentricity back upon a centre and a norm ; an attempt to recover the sense of form and " fitness ", to set forth the distinctively human life in firm contours and clear-cut lines, as neither fully divine nor merely animal. This attitude has now developed into a systematic philosophy embracing art, morals and politics. Its central principle is the sense of form, and so in morality of the " inner check ", happily described as the *frein vital*. About this there is a good deal to be said, and it is, in my view, open to strong criticism. But here and now all that is necessary to complete this " outline " of modern Humanism is to notice that the metaphysics of these eminent " literary " humanists is not naturalist or humanitarian. Dr. P. E. More is a professing Christian and an important theological writer. Irving Babbitt has long suspended judgment on the ultimate and religious issues ; but in his latest utterance he declares himself " unhesitatingly on the side of the supernaturalists ".[1] And though this is, as the context makes clear, a long way this side of a Christian *credo*, it draws some of the sting from the criticisms of Mr. Hyde and Mr. T. S. Eliot.[2]

[1] *Humanism and America*, p. 39.

[2] L. Hyde, *The Prospects of Humanism*, pp. 79–96. T. S. Eliot, " The Humanism of Irving Babbitt " in *For Launcelot Andrewes*, pp. 120–142.

"Humanism" is thus intended by this school almost in the sense of the Renaissance scholars.

(*e*) It is rather in this sense than in the former, that it is used by most English writers. Here, it is, for the most part, quite untechnical and commonly connotes wide human interests, a rich and genial appreciation of human nature and its manifold works, and the fascinating lights and shadows of character. It means to love people more than theories; to enjoy the rich movement and colour of the ever-moving drama of human life; to be sensitive to all true forms of value, to discriminate the real from the counterfeit; to practise historical imagination; in a word, to be truly educated. This is its use in English writing, and this is surely authentic Christianity. *Nihil humani alienum puto:* it really takes a Christian to say that. But within the circumference of Christianity humanism is sustained and disciplined by the supernatural faith which is at its centre. The Christian temper can move out freely over the wide fields of human interest and the range of art, literature and history, and find in these vivifying contacts with a purifying and life-giving Spirit. We shall see that where such a faith is lacking, there the humanist approach to life cannot support the weight of its own demands. For without this centre of redemptive reference, Humanism becomes human-all-too-human. It degenerates quickly into a *mere* humanism—humanitarianism, as we have called it—which loses touch with what is most human in us, and at last surrenders to the animal.

We have already seen, in bare outline, how this process worked out in Paganism. But the implications of this whole philosophy, and the results to which it appears to lead, can best, I think, be set forth in a study of the European Romantic Movement, of which our age is the spiritual offspring. What follows will appear to be mainly critical. But, lest the reader should lose the thread of the argument, let me say again, quite clearly and definitely, that there are essential values in Humanism—however much we criticize some expressions of it—which are quite vital to Christianity. That is what we are concerned to establish. The following critique of Romanticism is intended only to clear the ground for consolidating a fully Christian Humanism, built round a supernatural centre.

2. Humanism and Naturalism

There came, as we know, at the end of the eighteenth century, such another movement of expansion as is popularly ascribed to the Renaissance. It came largely by way of revolt against established faiths and institutions. This, of course, is no modern phenomenon : but it broke through then with catastrophic force. The desires of men are always in conflict with the limitations imposed by their own finitude. Man, as has been said, is a creature seeking finite gratifications for infinite desires. Religion is perfect and successful when it presents the Transcendent and Unconditioned as that which does not merely frustrate and limit, but completely satisfies these aspirations : then we can say " In His will is our peace ". Such, we may claim, is Christianity at its best and its most authentic. But this presupposes of religion that it shall eagerly welcome and consecrate the expansive desires and impulses of men. This expansiveness and the desire to grow, to achieve a condition better than the present, whether economic, political or spiritual, is after all, the condition of life at all. When religion fails to achieve this, and presents itself as a merely limiting force or—still worse—as mere convention, then whatever is on the side of progress is morally compelled to repudiate it. It is then men think that belief in the gods is what frustrates the fulfilment of human happiness. Priests are classed with tyrants and deceivers.

On a different level the same should be true of political and social institutions. It is, in the very nature of things, impossible for men to find peace or satisfaction out of the stuff of their own desires alone, like so many spiders spinning their own webs. They can find it only in mystic loyalty to something strictly superhuman,—at the present stage we must not say more than that—something which transcends and yet objectifies, filling with significance and content the individual's self-transcending impulses. Ideally, they can find such stability through active membership in a social group, which " means " all that they feel themselves to mean, and invests the life of the individual with a power and value richer than his own. To whatever extent this may be achieved, society is both stable and progressive : where it is not, where there is disharmony or the social order disappoints men's hopes, there either society stagnates or free men are in revolt against it. For a brief period after the Restoration some such stability seemed to have been achieved. The legacy of the classical revival was a sense of form, an eye for what is central, a distrust of eccentricity and effusiveness —a concern with men less for what divides them than for the great things that they have in common. It may be suggested that our Augustan literature, and perhaps Georgian domestic architecture, are true manifestations of this spirit. But by the end of the eighteenth century this stable order was collapsing. It had rested on too narrow a social basis. " Form " decayed into mere social " good form ". Faith in God as the Source of Order degenerated into a barren Deism. " Reason ", in life, in morals and in the arts, became a merely conventional good taste. None of them had any life in themselves. So that when the spring of the new life came—borne largely on breezes from Geneva —it presented itself in its first florescence as anti-social and anti-Christian. That at least was what its critics believed, and that it should have appeared to take this form is a judgment on the religion of that period and a warning to modern Christianity. For most of the English romanticists at least were profoundly religious men. Shelley no doubt called himself an atheist and fluttered the pious dovecotes of his time: but he was a spirit drunk with adoration. What seemed to him a kind of obscene tyranny was the lifeless caricature of Christianity which passed current for belief in God. "I would rather be damned with Plato," he remarked, "than go to heaven with Archdeacon Paley"; and many a modern Christian would agree with him. For then, as had been two hundred years before, and was again a hundred years later, the Christian Church was blind to its opportunity. What might have been, if a living faith in God had availed to supply the spiritual leadership of that new tumult of developing life! The world to-day would not be the world we know. These things are written for our warning. For the whole story of the next two centuries is the story of a gigantic disillusionment. Men were driven into the false position of having to choose between Christianity and what seemed to them the line of hope and progress; till in our time to believe the Christian faith is held to betoken either a third-rate mind or an irreformable obscuranticism. The last two centuries have seen the efforts of what was in itself a fine fighting faith to build a nobler order of society on a purely humanitarian basis. The world has tried for the last two hundred years to order its affairs on the assumption that the life of man and the tasks of civilization are self-explanatory and self-sustaining. It has been urgently brought home to us (as over and over again it forced itself on the high souls watching this movement and fondly hoping that they would witness the world's great age beginning anew) that this is a faith with no constructive power in it. What Mr. Crane Brinton says of Byron might be said of almost any prophet of this new religion without God, from Rousseau himself to Mr. Bernard

Shaw. " Faith in Nature is perhaps not enough. If we have learnt anything from Byron in his writings, Nature is not even justified by her works."[1]

Faith in Nature was the dynamic both of the Revolution and the Romantic Movement. That in itself is no trivial creed. If Nature means what it meant to Aristotle or the moral philosophers of Stoicism—the end or purpose for which a thing exists—such a faith would not be far from the Kingdom of God. For " to follow Nature " then means to give ourselves to the ultimate Power and Purpose of the world, disciplining our unredeemed desires to find peace and freedom in conforming to it. In that case, what is natural to Man is what brings him most near to God. But to Rousseauism it means no such thing. Whatever was meant by " Nature " in intention, in fact what is natural came to be equated with what is least specifically human, least rational and least disciplined. It comes to mean often emotional effusiveness—rather akin to what " inspiration " meant to some of St. Paul's converts in Corinth (cf. 1 Cor. xii). And that moves below the level of Christianity. For if we take Nature in this sense and if we accept the Christian valuations, then Man is not part of the natural order. To humanize Nature is one thing, and a quite legitimate artistic fancy: to naturalize Man is quite another and is indeed spiritual treason.

" Man is born free and everywhere he is in chains." The Romantic creed is frighteningly simple. All that is good lies in Man's desires, all that is evil in his environment. Man is naturally good: and Man in his essence, in what is " natural " to him by contrast with the " artificial " barriers imposed by religion and society (priests and tyrants as the idiom went), is spontaneous impulse and feeling. If men's naturally good impulses are prevented from coming to fruition the inference is that failure is due to the corruption

[1] *Political Ideas of the English Romanticists*, p. 163.

of external circumstances.[1] It is therefore these artificial barriers, which meant in effect existing forms of government and the moral standards of respectability, which must be destroyed if freedom is to be won. Heaven will arrive if all men are free to indulge and express their naturally good impulses. Hence, as we know, the doctrine "Follow Nature" came to mean a surrender of the will and reason in a carnival of sentimentalism and an uncontrolled facility of emotion. One impulse from the vernal wood was prized above all the wisdom of experience.

It is not hard to realize in retrospect with what fatal ease such an attitude degenerates into a mere Naturalism. This indeed is the charge which has been levelled against the Romantic theory of life in Professor Irving Babbitt's weighty criticism as set forth in his *Rousseau and Romanticism*. It is not merely that the sentimentalism inherent in the romantic position is at times too little appreciative of truth and tends to measure the worth of any experience in terms of mere emotional intensity. There are many forms of popular religion which would be deserving of the same censure. It is, rather, that the whole assumption underlying romantic art and literature is the complete surrender of a standard. It is an expansion, but from no centre other than the feelings of the individual. Classical art—to use the text-book jargon—looks out on life from an acknowledged centre, a point of reference common to all concerned, an agreed interpretation of the universe and of Man's place and destiny in the scheme of it. Romanticism is the exact reverse of this. It is the abandonment of any intention to interpret anything objectively—"the doctrine that the only art which was of value was art which expressed the artist's personal reactions as an individual man".[2]

[1] *Op.* Brinton, *op. cit.*, p. 178.

[2] Wilenski, *Miniature History of European Art*, p. 43, where he regards Rembrandt as the founder of the romantic movement in art.

" Expression " thus becomes an end in itself regardless of what it is that is expressed. Self-expression justifies everything. When to such a theory is added distrust of artificial " reason ", a dogmatic faith in naturally good impulses, a belief that whatever is primitive is good, certain results are almost bound to follow, if not in creed, at any rate in behaviour. In our time the new stress on instinct, derived in part from Bergson's philosophy and in part from Freudian psychology, again tends to exalt what is primitive, subrational and indeed merely animal to a primacy to which it has no true claim. Some of the " nasty " books of modern coteries are, so it is easy enough to say, the results of attempting to follow Nature. Hence the neo-classical school of Humanists, and Mr. Lippman from his own angle, call on us to repudiate romanticism, its indiscipline and self-indulgence, and take a real Humanism seriously. Man, with all his rational prerogatives and his high spiritual capacities, must be the measure of his own values, the guardian and guide of his own destiny.

But is Humanism in any better case ? For that, after all, is what " Follow Nature " meant to all serious thinkers of that period. It is quite unfair to dismiss the theory because of the moral irregularity of Rousseau himself or Byron or Shelley. Religion can hardly afford to use that argument !

Nature, to such a man as Wordsworth, means the source of health, truth and holiness, of what is real, creative, and ennobling. He would have said that the voice of Nature is none other than the voice of God. It is that which gives meaning to man's life. It was Nature, he believed, that inspired men with that impulse to freedom, peace and righteousness, which made it for him joy to be alive. We know the story of his disappointment and how he settled down in his old age into diehard political reactionism. Hazlitt rather unkindly said of him that he had lost his way in Utopia and found himself in Old Sarum. "For if the revolution in ideas meant the natural goodness of man, the revolution in fact meant the supremacy of an ill-educated middle class.[1]

In England, the doctrine of natural goodness coalescing, oddly enough, with Calvinistic predestinarianism, was the drive behind the Industrial Revolution. It spelt, in effect, the right of the successful to uncontrolled economic exploitation. It became the philosophy of *laissez faire.* Thus following Nature was found to lead, on the Continent, to the orgies of the Terror and the fury of democratic nationalism, in England to the domestic rights of Englishmen and the miseries of Rochdale and Peterloo.

It might have been thought sufficiently disillusioning. Yet Shelley and Byron in that generation are again protesting in the name of Nature against the very conventions and iniquities to which belief in Nature had given rise. They, too, believe in Man's natural goodness, if a false and artificial social order were no longer to have dominion over him. The Victorians kept that faith still undefiled, though they protected themselves against its consequences by a code of bourgeois respectability and loyalty to established institutions.

Even this much is enough to make it clear that belief in Nature and in natural goodness is in fact the Humanitarian philosophy. It is the faith that there is that in Man, once set free from unfavourable circumstances, which has the power to rise triumphantly to a new and more splendid social order. And this, despite the religious language and the doubtless sincere religious feeling with which its prophets and priests have invested it, cannot be held to be genuinely religious. It is in effect the belief that human life is self-sustaining and self-redeeming.

In the nineteenth century this attitude received over-

[1] Brinton, *op. cit.*, pp. 95, 59.

whelming reinforcement from the so-called evolutionary hypothesis. The theory which was popularized by Darwin's writings—though it is in itself as old as Greek thought—of man's descent from sub-human ancestry, seemed in the shock of its first impact to be the death-blow to Christianity. But it soon became a religion in its own right. For if the Golden Age is not behind us, if the story of Man's life on earth has not been one of such disastrous failure, falling away from a realized perfection, but rather one of a gradual ascent leaving ape and tiger far behind, then the Golden Age must be before us, in a grander future yet to be achieved. It is hard perhaps for us to realize the sense of freedom and emancipation brought by this faith to a generation nurtured on a conventional evangelicalism. It appeared, no doubt, to discredit Theism. For the doctrine of Natural Selection, as developed at least by Darwin's disciples—Darwin himself remained a professing Christian—threw the whole weight upon environment and seemed to suggest that life was a process wholly conditioned by external circumstances. Amongst the more philosophically minded this seemed to lead to scientific naturalism. But this was not its effect on popular thought. Diffused in a vague and half-unconscious fashion through the thinking of that generation, it appeared mightily to reinforce the legacy of belief in natural goodness. Man, after all, is not a fallen creature: he is a creature working towards perfection. Prostituted though it was by Prussianism and by certain economists in England to support the idea that might is right, the net result of the theory of evolution was to diffuse an optimistic temper and to inculcate in the popular mind a faith in progress as something "natural", which meant in effect almost automatic. The Dean of St. Paul's has pulverized this phantasy. There is no such thing as automatic progress; we have learned this truth in drastic experience. The bourgeois Tennysonian Utopias, the confident hopes of

1851, the Manchester doctrine of economics, hardly survived 1914.

It would, however, be a profound misreading of all that is strongest in the thought of our time if we assumed that faith in evolution has been discredited by the war or the even greater disillusionment of the peace. Rather it must be recognized as dominant in the whole outlook of the present age.

Men's minds are full of the thought of an open Universe—a creative process, not a created fact, a movement whose life is within itself, out of which new events, new values, new and undisclosed possibilities ceaselessly emerge into present fact. It is self-contained and yet it is self-transcending, bringing and ever to bring forth new treasures. This world-view is not mechanistic nor is it anti-religious in tendency. By writers such as Professor Julian Huxley, it is imbued with a rich religious colouring. It is the religion of the man in the street—the real rival of Christianity. Science supplies it with its sacred scriptures: a great host of literary scientists serve it as prophets and evangelists; the astounding, tangible "results" of Natural Science are its miraculous proofs; the formula "science teaches" is its ritual. (For there is that about the modern Englishman. There is nothing he suspects more than cleverness. Yet so successfully has he been indoctrinated with the infallibility of scientists, that if only you start by saying "Science teaches", he will gladly assent to almost any nonsense.) It is the religion of popularized science: the romantic faith in Nature made more convincing and enriched with moral and religious sanctions. If, as every morning's paper demonstrates, man can now control his own environment, wringing the secrets out of the natural order, issuing his decrees to air and sea, shaping circumstances to his will, then the last barriers are down. We may have failed often in the past through our sins as well as our negligences and ignorances: but now at last our feet are on the highway. We are entering now (and this is wholly true) upon that new stage of evolution, the era of conscious control. We are now responsible for our own destiny. Give us time and we will make ourselves perfect.

This is indeed the characteristic utterance of the romantic legacy in belief and conduct. "We place perfection where it should not be—on this human plane. As we are painfully aware that nothing *actual* can be *perfect*, we imagine perfection to be not where we are, but some distance along one of the roads. This is the essence of all Romanticism. Most frequently, in literature at any rate, we imagine an impossible perfection along the road of sex; but anyone can name other roads for himself. The abolition of some discipline or restriction would enable us, we imagine, to progress along one of these roads. The fundamental error is that of placing perfection in Humanity."[1]

It is no doubt a fundamental error; but it is the creed of some 50 per cent of the more seriously minded moderns. It means, at its best, a belief in education and the ennobling influences of culture, a friendliness to all kinds of uplift, a disinterested social service, an encouragement of philanthropic effort, a support of peace movements and the like, and sincere respect for religious institutions. Professor Julian Huxley, for instance, describes his creed as "Scientific Humanism". It often uses Christian-sounding language, though as a rule contemptuously rejecting the Christian theological assumptions. It has no concern with what is "supernatural". It rests on the strictly humanist assumption (using the word in its theological sense) that there are within the sources of civilization creative and regenerative forces adequate to respond to its own demands and carry it forward to a more splendid future. Poverty, disease, crime and ignorance are within our power to eliminate, and

[1] T. E. Hulme, *Speculations*, p. 33, a furious book, furiously stimulating.

scientists will eradicate the Old Adam; education, travel and economic betterment will enable us to put on the New Man.

This is the creed of Western Civilization in its twentieth-century expression. Under the tutelage of the West it is fast being adopted by the Orient, and by those rising nationalities which are now stepping out into history. It is becoming a world-wide religion—the one live alternative, indeed the one serious rival to Christianity. The choice between these two views of life is obviously the crucial decision on which the future of civilization rests. Can we still hold to a "supernatural" faith, to the old belief in a transcendent God, unchanging and unconditioned in perfection, the inexhaustible Giver of all good, the Source and Sustainer of our aspirations? Or is our trust wholly within this life and the temporal emergent process in what is ever changing and developing and so in the end transitory and perishable? The latter faith has had a fair trial: it is being tried out on a grandiose scale over the whole field of human enterprise. And, as I have been eager to claim, it has achieved much that deserves our gratitude. But now, at the very threshold of its triumph, in the hour of its most spectacular achievements, the world is paralysed through lack of faith in it. It has set Man on the world's vacant throne: but it can no longer worship its idol. Self-worship is seldom successful.

This is the scepticism that is destroying us. Beneath the noise and clamour of civilization a new note is making itself heard, a cry of wistful and poignant disillusionment. The prophets of the last generation are ceasing to be prophetic for us. We know too well that we cannot mould and control the materials of our outward environment till we have learnt to master ourselves. And that is the secret that we have forgotten. Hence the scepticism and despair which is eating at the heart of our generation. Under the garish, flamboyant surface of contemporary Western culture, is a growing distrust of life itself. The only obvious way of escaping from it is the attempt to achieve perpetual motion, to " have another drink " and a " good time ". But the more serious and reflective spirits are weighed down with a sense of frustration, through the lack of any standard of values. " The consciousness that something in life is *sacred*—worth living for and worth dying for—is one of man's moral indispensables." But the average man of to-day has no real standard by which to test the values of his desires or the relative worth which is implicit in them. Ethics, says Lippmann, becomes a traffic-code, a way to enable as many desires as possible to reach their goal as quickly as possible. It is impossible, as we have discovered, to build " humanist " ideals in ethics on a naturalistic theory of the universe. If we pride ourselves on being merely human, we shall soon cease to be even that.

3. Christian Humanism

Thus the " romantic " attitude to life falls more and more into discredit. The question for us is : What is the alternative ? Must it be by way of reaction, a limit set to our faith in human nature, a reduction of the claim we make on life, a swing back towards absolutist government, as is happening in disillusioned Europe ? This is what seems to some well-known writers and especially to the " literary humanists " to be the only possible solution. Thus in France M. Maritain would call us back to the Thomist philosophy, as the only faith that can integrate experience and give society an enduring basis. That enterprise would appear to be as hopeful as it would be to reconstruct ethics on the basis of the Song of Deborah. The Thomist system, in its original form, is beyond artificial respiration. We have noted earlier the immense gratitude which Christian morals owe to St. Thomas. But a mere glance at a diagram of the universe, as Dante or St. Thomas conceived it, is enough to show that no modern world-view can be built upon the scholastic philosophy. Experimental science has shattered it. No attitude which is based on that position can hope to bring back the Christian faith into the centre of the modern outlook, and the ways of life and forms of experience which express our evolutionary philosophy.

M. Julien Benda urges detachment, to which he seems to assign an absolute value ; but he advances no constructive view of life to invest it either with quality or direction. Yet true detachment must be the correlative of attachment to something real, as it is in Plato for example, and (still more) in the Synoptic Gospels. Unless controlled by positive valuations upon the meaning and worth of our experience, it is little more than the Epicurean scepticism. The same weakness would appear to vitiate the prescriptions of literary humanism. Thus Professor Babbitt and his school propose a return to " classical " criteria as well in morals as in art and literature. This means characteristically a sense of " form ", a recovery of proportion and normality, an attempt to see life whole from a centre, by way of reaction from the eccentricity of the more recent experiments in living. But what *is* the norm, and where is the " centre " ? For, despite the assertion I have quoted, it is quite certain that Mr. Babbitt seeks it, not in a supernatural order, or in any pole that eternally abides, but within the confines of " humanism ". His ultimate law-giver and moral sanction is the principle of the " inner check "—the *frein vital*, as he himself describes it, to stress his disagreement with Bergsonianism—putting the brake on our instinctive impulses. But this is intolerable intellectualism. It ignores, or proposes to eliminate, two-thirds of the human constitution, and is thus a purely negative morality. Indeed, he himself makes this admission, and comes down on the side of mere rigorism. " A purely affirmative morality," he writes, " is almost necessarily an emotional morality."[1] And thus, I suggest, he gives his own case away. No Christian, at least, with the Gospels in front of him, could subscribe to so relentless a verdict. It is simply to despair of human nature. For the nature of man can never be fulfilled in any purely rational scheme of conduct. The good which is to unify his life and organize the diverse claims and impulses of personality round a true centre, must be such as to give full scope and satisfaction to all the powers and faculties within us. It must be that through conformity to which we can rise to the full height of personality. And that can never be found within ourselves. So long as we seek within mankind itself for our standards, or for our salvation, we are looking for something which is not there to find. The centre which can give life poise and unity lies, says religion, in the will of God. It is there only that Man can find peace.

What Mr. Lippmann offers his contemporaries as the " high religion " of the twentieth century is a popular version of the same philosophy, though Professor Babbitt has criticized him fiercely for his " flagrant misuse " of the humanist ticket. We must not ask life for more than it can yield us. As we grow " mature " and " disinterested " we shall discover that it is not possible to have everything that we desire; so we shall learn to discipline ourselves and to desire only what is possible. Regardless of Aristotle's protest, we must learn to think only mortal thoughts, awake to the limits of Man's capacity, knowing just how much life can offer us, and accepting it with tranquil resignation. This is " wisdom for them that be mature "—even if not quite St. Paul's version of it. But what is to be done to help the " babes " when tortured by the conflicts of passion or weighed down by unbearable calamity, this " high " religion does not appear to specify.

But this is only Stoicism in plus-fours. It is no doubt

[1] *Rousseau and Romanticism*, p. 180.

admirable worldly wisdom, but to call it "religion" is to talk nonsense. It is "bear and forbear"—the dreary maxim of Marcus Aurelius' meditations: but that is scarcely a dynamic faith. No conviction or creative enterprise can spring from such a negative attitude. It is in the end but noble despair.

Neither of these humanitarian creeds can be the living soul or inspiration of a genuinely humanist ethic. And this has been the debacle of Humanism—to end in despair of human nature, because it has shirked the question What is Man? or if it has asked it, has been unable to return the exultant answer of Christianity. But this is not the only alternative. There is a real Christian form of Humanism which sings its way through the New Testament, especially the Epistle to the Ephesians. It offers all that romanticism stands for—the ample vista of Man's potentialities, a far-flung reach and range of aspiration, a claim on life that has scarcely any limit to it—but all sustained, disciplined and fructified by a burning conviction about God and the vision of His transcendent love and holiness. This is the "humanism" of the Gospel. If we read the life of Temple Gairdner[1] or recall that of the late Archbishop Davidson, we can see this attitude personified. We find it there in individual lives—vivid interest in all that is interesting, gladness in all the good things of life, a reverence for and trust in human nature, hallowed and controlled at the core of selfhood by faith, hope, love and consecration enkindled by the vision of God in Christ. This is a faith which is built on foundations. Christianity, when it is true to its own genius, is able to believe in Man recklessly, despite all that saddens and discourages, because it has seen the vision of God, the eternal source of all worth and wonder—lifting us up to become sons of God.

That is the spring of all creative effort, sureness of touch

[1] *Gairdner of Cairo*, by Constance Padwick, S.C.M.

and mastery in life. On the whole and in the long run those men and women have been most effective in changing and remodelling the present world, who have realized that goodness, in whatever form, is not in the end something that we produce, but something that claims us and is imparted to us by the eternal and unchanging Goodness. The vision of God is the spring of moral fruitfulness. The source of all creative conviction is the vision of One who is " Faithful and True ", unchanged in underived perfection. The real lesson of the present age is not that faith in a living God is obsolete, but rather that we have made too small a claim on the glory and majesty of the Lord. The irreligiousness of our contemporaries is in fact a standing rebuke to the poverty of the Church's thought of God.

That is the tragedy of the last three centuries. When the new knowledge flooded in, new desires were struggling for expression and a new power was put into man's hands to mould the order of nature to his will, the official Church was found on the wrong side. It offered the modern world a false choice—between belief in God, as it understood Him, and what seemed to be belief in Progress and the hopefulness and wonder of Man's life. Its vision of God was too poor and sterile to inspire and direct all that new knowledge and the enterprise and confidence engendered by it. That sets Christianity its task to-day. What may not yet be if we have grace to rise to it—if across the confusion of the world, outwardly secure and self-indulgent, inwardly blinded by doubt and self-distrust, we could show the light of that compelling vision! That, indeed, is the theme of this volume. Faced with the colour, interest and movement and fascination of the life around us, in what way can the Christian faith in God redeem it from corroding triviality, enrich everything that is of worth in it, cleanse, direct, sustain and sanctify its manifold enterprises and activities?

"Humanitarianism (it has been said) is the peculiar possession of a people who have worshipped for centuries the Divine Humanity, apart from all that even our humanism would have been other than it is. It is from this Christian moral tradition that both the older Deist movement and the new movement of evolutionary vitalism have derived whatever positive religious value they possess. . . . Either Europe must abandon the Christian tradition, and with it the faith in progress and humanity, or it must return consciously to the religious foundation on which these ideas were based. . . . It must be recognized that our faith in progress and in the unique value of human experience rests on religious foundations, and that they cannot be severed from historical religion and used as a substitute for it."[1]

Christianity is a religion of redemption. The heart and life of the Christian ethic is the redemption of our desires and wills, the transfiguration of our values, by God's power and presence in Christ Jesus. Nothing short of that can be called Christian, however friendly to the Christian spirit. That is our inevitable emphasis, the basis of even the most meagre study of the Christian ethic in the modern world. The question is, how to relate this Gospel to the tasks and claims of life as a whole. How can we set the Gospel of Christianity where, if anywhere, our world can see its relevance—in the context of emergent evolution, and of those claims, tasks and opportunities, so rich, so fascinating and so complex which are the actual stuff of life and morality?

We have already outlined in principle the line of approach by which we shall seek the answer. It is to believe in God as well as in Christ. Creator and Redeemer are one God. He meets us in Christ as the Father of our spirits, in the gifts and discipline of life itself as the Creator of a living Universe. His manifestations in the "natural" order are other than

[1] Dawson, *Progress and Religion*, pp. 242–244.

His work as Holy Spirit ; but the same divine Spirit is at work in them. The meaning of Man's life at all its levels, in all its varied and manifold concerns, is to be found in doing God's will—not as merely pious aspiration, but as sharing in an eternal life.

That is our subject in the next chapter.

CHAPTER VI

DOING THE WILL OF GOD

1. Ethics and the Supernatural

IN the last chapter we paid some attention to the ramifications of modern Humanism. We saw that through all its various forms and developments there runs one constant conviction—a firm and even defiant belief in Man, and his resources, endowments and capacities. This conviction, it is to be noticed, is massively and uniquely emphasized in the Bible and the Christian tradition. There, however, it rests on a further conviction—the tenacious faith in a holy and living God as the Determiner of destiny, the Source of spiritual values and the Guarantor of the human prerogative. Our contention was that apart from this faith Humanism has no secure basis. As we watched the stages of the romantic movement we observed in it a fatal tendency to slide back towards a mere Naturalism and thus, like all philosophies of pure immanence, to let the snake get into the garden. Allied with popular Evolutionism and increasingly tending to substitute belief in Man's immanent resources as the sufficient source of salvation for the traditional faith in a living God, by whose gift Man can partake in life eternal, it has met the same fate as befell the Hellenic Humanism. Seeking to humanize Man's experience and to make the world a home for his spirit, it has left him homeless and disillusioned and is less and less able to justify his distinctively human prerogatives. We saw, too, that the neo-classic Humanism advocated by leading American thinkers is too much vitiated by intellectualism and far too negative in its central insistence to supply any enduring foundation for a full and vivid belief in Man, or a satisfying basis for ethics. No revival of pagan humanitarianism can meet the needs of thought or of life in the circumstances of our civilization. The line of advance along that road is impassable. Yet we have been eager to claim that there are values in Romanticism and the Hellenic tradition of Humanism which are vital to modern Christianity. We have urged that religion can only be fresh and vital, a spring of spontaneous inspiration such as can redeem, direct and fertilize the manifold life and interests of the world, if it is in vivid and sympathetic response to the fascinating values and opportunities, the rich and ever-widening claims and tasks of our absorbing and many-coloured society. The Humanism that loves all things human must, we suggested, be re-established in the heart of an over-ascetic Christianity. Humanism itself in its widest ranges can rest only upon a Christian foundation: while the Christian faith cannot issue in its characteristic and most creative achievements save as wedded to the "humane" outlook.[1] What we need is a revived Christian Humanism.

This is of course no novel suggestion. Christian thought at nearly all periods has preserved some traces of this intention. There have always been those who, like Clement and Origen, the Oxford Reformers, Westcott, Church or von Hügel, have sought to build up such a Christian philosophy as would enable the Christian religion to justify, direct and enrich the best gifts that thought and life offer us. That tradition has never entirely perished. And it may be suggested without undue arrogance that the historical legacy of Anglicanism lays on that Church special obligations and endows it with special aptitudes for reviving it in contemporary religious life. For this was the justification

[1] Cf. T. S. Eliot on "Religion without Humanism" in *Humanism and America*, pp. 105–112.

of Anglicanism in the controversies of the seventeenth century.

The struggle between the Church and the Puritans was not merely between proud prelates and plain men seeking religious liberty. It was between two views of Christianity —as Baxter and his friends were eager to emphasize. And however lacking in sympathy and insight may have been the method adopted by the Churchmen, the truth on the whole was on their side. They stood for a richer conception of human nature and a more humanist version of Christianity. "There is no doubt that to the humanist mind some of the sweetest spots in the tormented life of that stormy century are due to the influence of the Church of Hooker and Andrewes and Laud and Taylor,—the recovery of the idea of beauty as an element in religious architecture and worship, the revival of discipline in the Universities, the rebuilding and redecoration of Colleges and Chapels: great scholars like Selden: gentle, quaint students and antiquarians like Burton and Sir Thomas Browne and John Earle and Isaac Walton."[1] English Christianity was at that period confronted with two dangers at once. On the one hand the Puritan presentation meant, in effect, to isolate religion from nearly all its humanist values—to present it indeed in its essence and its strength but as a faith almost entirely negative in its attitude towards the surrounding civilization.

On the other hand the new speculations in the natural and social sciences were, under the influence of Hobbes and the new atomic and mechanistic theories, increasingly rationalist in tendency; and the art and drama of the Restoration had become what they inevitably became since the Puritans refused to redeem them.

This was the problem before the Anglican Church, and it called for clear insight and strong restraint. Its leaders

[1] Grierson, *op. cit.*, Chap. VI, on Humanism and the Churches, p. 210.

might have become merely worldly: they might simply have accepted the confused values of their period and said roundly: "This is what religion means." (It was discovered a hundred years later how fast a "reasonable" Christianity slips into worldliness and barren Deism.) Or they might, alive to the danger on this side, have steered their course towards a "pure" Church, uncontaminated by the world, and come to port as a self-contained sect. But both these disasters were avoided—then at least, if not always subsequently. The firm trust in reason and experience and the broad sweep of tendencies in history so characteristic of judicious Hooker is the note of all that is best and greatest in the Anglican leaders of the seventeenth century. Seen in the large, despite all its limitations and all its failures in statesmanship and humility, the Church at least made the attempt to clothe itself in and thereby transfigure the strong, rich fabric of national thought and life.

More recently, as we have already suggested, this great tradition has been forgotten; and the Church has shrunk away from the life of the nation. The task which awaits Christianity in our time is to revive and re-establish this magnificent Humanist legacy amid the new conditions of a new world. This task involves for its successful achievement the reconstruction and consolidation of a firm theological basis. In particular it involves a fresh understanding of what we mean by doing the will of God—a phrase which gives us the key to the whole position. For in God's will *all* values are consummated.

The modern mind tends to suppose that ethical problems can be resolved by the same methods as those of natural science—that is to say by induction and analysis, by the correlation of data and the observation of results. It is assumed in the questionnaire method that to ask what sufficiently many people believe, will give us the truth about the question at issue. It is a somewhat precarious assumption. No doubt this empirical approach has its value for the Christian moralist. It is at least concerned with real issues and faces actual life-situations ; whereas the treatises on Christian ethics move, too often, so high in the realm of theory as to leave the facts of life far below them. Yet to confine ourselves to such methods is, in effect, to abandon Christian principles. For modern thinking, as for Aristotle, Ethics is a branch of natural science : for the great Christian tradition it is a province of Theology.[1] That at once defines its essential character. It is rooted, for us, in a supernatural faith, inspired by supernatural resources. Its values are absolute and not merely relative. It insists, of course, that the " good for man " is not to be sought in any such abstract principle as would do violence to human nature—it was on that ground that we found fault with the " Humanists " —but in something which " can be done or possessed by man ".[2] But it affirms that this must be sought in nothing intrinsic to human nature, but in the sharing of a divine life —which derivatively and by God's " grace " may be realized in human experience.[3] It lies in perfect self-consecration to communion with the Heavenly Father. For Christianity that is the " end " of Man—to glorify God and enjoy Him for ever. Hence the insistence of Christianity on its own specific ideal of character. It is not the mere achievement of virtue, however consistent and however noble, which will satisfy the Christian demand on character. That is only to be fulfilled in *holiness*, in the heart and mind offered to the Father and transfigured by the Spirit of Christ. The Christian is a man called to holiness—to detachment from the world's values and consecration to the divine will. " Be

[1] Wicksteed, *Reactions between Dogma and Philosophy*, pp. 481–483.

[2] Aristotle, *Ethics*, I, vi. 13.

[3] Cf. " The inmost meaning of the moral life of man [is] an endeavour towards an eternal good made by a creature who, in so far as he achieves the end of his endeavour, achieves also a derivative or communicated Eternity." A. E. Taylor, *The Faith of a Moralist*, I, 118.

not shaped to the pattern of this world, but transfigured by the renewing of your minds." Saintliness is the goal of Christian conduct.

This, no doubt, suggests an otherworldliness which would seem for that reason incapable of providing the basis of a constructive ethic. And there have been phases and interpretations in the moral history of Christianity in which such a criticism has seemed to be justified. Monasticism rested on the assumption that the full Christian vocation could not be realized in the actual world of society. The Reformers attempted to substitute the ideal of a "secular" form of saintliness, to be realized in the tasks of a Calling. But the world seems to be no place for saints: we in England have had some experience of what the rule of the saints means in practice, and we have no desire to repeat it. Englishmen are suspicious of saints. Thus when modern Christians hear the words about "rejoicing in the Saints' fellowship and following their good examples" they are left with a certain feeling of uneasiness. They are hard put to it to understand how this is a practicable aim. What precisely are they meant to do? Are they to sell all and give to the poor, while their families are transported to the workhouse? or to try to grill themselves on gridirons? or to spend their days in unremunerated contemplation? If that is what the Christian life asks of them, then its ideal must plainly be false. If all men were to be saints, it is suggested, the work of the world would never be done.

But in point of fact the Christian ideal may be otherwise interpreted. It may mean that there is in life a richness of content which will never disclose itself to mere common sense, that there are depths and delicacies of insight which are open only to the single eye, and ranges of heroic consecration which only a life that is lived with God can sustain. It does not mean that it is demanded of all of us that this should be manifested in the same forms. I do not know of a better statement of what is involved in the Christian standpoint than the following extract from Professor Paton :

> "To accept the ideal of the saintly life as the highest expression of the moral will is not to say that all men should be saints. Religious genius . . . is rare, and even apart from that the work of the world must be carried on. . . . If he demands that all men should be saints and nothing but saints he would seem, at least in the eyes of common sense, not only to be a menace to society but also to be in danger of narrowing and emptying the moral life itself. The world requires all sorts of people for the development of the coherent good life and it is a narrow point of view which would ignore the necessity of having good doctors and good poets and even good engineers. . . . None the less if we accept saintliness as an ideal we set up a standard by which all our acts are to be judged, and we recognize at least the possibility of a higher type of coherence even in our human society. What the saint actually does may belong to himself alone, but the spirit in which he does it should be manifested in a different way in all the various avocations and pursuits of men. In that sense the saint does demand, and rightly demand, that all men should be saints. If he be genuinely understood and accepted as a standard or ideal, then to fall away from this ideal is to be conscious of unworthiness. . . . The saint demands, not that we should be like him but that we should co-operate with him in his holy task. And here as always genuine co-operation means a willing in the same spirit, even although we are leading a totally different kind of life."[1]

This long quotation may, I hope, be justified as giving admirably clear expression to the point of view which seems

[1] W. Paton, *The Good Will*, pp. 434, 435.

to me to be true. It is one of the great dangers of clergy and other teachers of Christian ethics that they should expect Christians of all kinds to express the Christian faith in the same way, and predominantly in that way to which their own training has accustomed them, in certain devotional habits and aptitudes. This, I feel sure, must be profoundly mistaken. It means, in effect, as Canon Quick has observed, trying to turn into second-rate mystics people who are really intended by God to express their religion in quite different fashion. We need, it would seem, a more careful investigation of what is implied in the idea of " holiness ", if we are to protect the Christian ideal either from an overstrained pietism or (on the other hand) from barren formalism.

All moral philosophers from Plato onward have recognized that the Good for Man must reside in that which most completely harmonizes and most nearly brings to full fruition all his powers, capacities and endowments. That is the norm or centre of equipoise which is presupposed by the neo-classicists in their ideal of the " balanced " life. But within Man himself it is not to be found. Mere introspection will not discover it. If there is one clear lesson from Psychology it is that the way of peace, freedom and power is never to be discovered by introversion: that is the path to frustration and conflict. A man can only find true fulfilment by issuing out of the prison-house of self, identifying his desires and interests with some end or purpose other than his own, in realizing which he will " find " himself. That is what Christianity has always said: only in losing the soul can a man find it. It claims therefore that true personal fulfilment lies in doing the will of God—in the identification of self with the Purpose informing the universe and Man's finite strivings within it. And this is indeed the presupposition of all psychological poise and adjustment. Psychology is emphatic in its advice against the danger of seeking harmony on too elementary a level of experience. Moral philosophy reinforces the warning. For the soul—as Professor Taylor observes :

> " will only have a real and not merely an ideal inner unity of personality when its good is one and all embracing, a real and living single good which is the source of all goodness and leaves nothing of good outside itself. That is to say unity of personality and interest will only be attained, if at all, by a soul which has come to find its principal good in God. If God—the concrete unity of all good or its one Source—is not real, the complete unification of personality in ourselves . . . cannot be real either, and the supreme purpose of the moral life will be a self-baffling purpose."[1]

Thus the achievement of Man's good presupposes the supernatural. It is of the very nature of Ethics that it passes into religion. For if our moral life is a ceaseless striving towards that which ever eludes us as we approach it, then it is for ever frustrated and fragmentary, thwarted by contradiction at the heart of us. In some sense or other the good must be *possessed*, as that which gives life its meaning and significance, even while we seek to achieve it. Just in so far therefore as the " good " life is realized it means that we are partaking in the supernatural. Conversely, life will fail of its richness if lived on a *merely* " moral " level. For if Man is made for communion with God there is that in him which is denied its fulfilment, till he enters upon that relationship. He cannot be " saved "—that is, he cannot realize the full possibilities of his manhood—on a lower level of experience. The moral standards of Christianity, with their otherworldly demands and stresses, turn on this cardinal assumption about the nature and destiny of Man and the character of his final good. And this ascetic, otherworldly emphasis is wholly indispensable to the Christian ethic. To

[1] *Op. cit.*, I, 101.

obscure it or minimize it is treason. Christianity offers itself as the true way of life—i.e. the way to realize that good in which alone Man's life can be completed, both in this world and in the " world to come ". Hence, as we have seen, its claim on character can never be fully described or satisfied in terms of a " categorical imperative " : it is never merely " doing our duty ' (cf, Luke xvii. 10). It is a sharing of the Father's will. This is not to say that a duty-loving life, with no conscious supernatural reference, is not—so far as it goes —a true expression of the perfect goodness of God. To say that would be something like blasphemy. But it does and must imply the assertion that such a life falls short of its full possibilities. The good which it realizes is a true good : but the life itself remains thwarted and impoverished within these constricted horizons. And thus, conversely, a life of " service " which conceives the good that it seeks to achieve for its neighbours wholly in terms of this-worldly ends—health, comfort, justice and so forth—renders to that extent less than perfect service. They are the best servants of their fellow-men who seek for them first the kingdom of God and righteousness.

Thus, as von Hügel used to insist with almost wearisome repetition, there is inherent in the life of the Christian a certain " costly " duality and tension. And it is only within Christianity that there is achieved a true poise and balance between the claim of religion and that of morality. The Platonic tradition emphasized magnificently the absolute claim of the eternal values. But it, and the oriental philosophies with which it has such close inward kinship, have never succeeded in doing justice to the claims of what is temporal and contingent. They have never found a secure place for history. Their whole outlook leads them away from it. For this world of action, change and time—and this is implied in the very idea of will—is for them never quite genuinely real. Such a philosophy is irreconcilable with the Christian doctrine of Incarnation. And it has certainly been the fatal tendency for this type of profoundly religious thinking to sit loosely to the claim of morality. Notoriously the ancient faiths of India have proved themselves relatively ineffective in moral and social regeneration. So keen is their thirst for the true and abiding that they have never faced seriously and searchingly the obligations of life in time. But this is to cut the nerve of ethics. For if we shirk this and that claim, and evade the demands of successive duties, of this and that and the other actual choice, we reduce the good life to an insubstantial day-dream.

On the other hand, much contemporary philosophy, drenched as it is in " evolutionary " thought, seems to fail for precisely the opposite reason. It does full justice to the notion of Time, and at this point comes closer to Christianity. But it lacks just that which is safeguarded by Platonism. It tends to regard process in time as the only reality there is. And thus, while it gives full recognition to the good will active here and now in the realization of actual forms of goodness, yet it allows no place in its system to any absolute or eternal good. Hence, despite its religious language, it does in fact rule out religion by depriving it of a real Object ; so that the good which is the goal of Man's life becomes but the successive realization of impermanent and transitory values. Thus the moral life itself remains, in the last resort, self-contradictory.

It is in the Christian reading of Man's life, based as it is on faith in an Incarnation, that the seeming contradiction is reconciled. In the Christian world-view the supernatural is conceived as manifested within what is natural, yet as self-complete and transcendent. And Man's task and destiny is interpreted neither wholly within the time-process, nor as an escape from this world of time, with its fragmentary goods and conflicting duties, to the more real heaven of eternity ; but as the realization here in time of a divine and eternal goodness in the sharing of which he is fulfilled. The Kingdom is present, and it is yet to come. The " good " life means so to live and labour as to realize here in this world of time the perfect goodness which we already possess—that the supernatural Kingdom of God may come on earth as it is in heaven.

This metaphysical position is utterly central to the Christian world-view. The Christian ethic cannot be maintained by any purely ethical arguments. It presupposes God and eternal life. We cannot commend the Christian ethic unless we can re-establish conviction in an eternal and living God. But contemporary intellectual movements seem to conspire against such a conviction. It is therefore to this question that we must turn before our enquiry can move towards its conclusion.

2. Evolution and the Will of God

For Christian thinking Man's goal and fulfilment consists in " doing the will of God ". No ethic that rests merely on " evolution " can justify its own obligations. How absurd is the attempt to give moral guidance without any ultimate and transcendent standards may be gathered from the rows of small books which offer practical principles for conduct " without discussing any of those vexed questions which belong to religion and philosophy "—that is to say without making up their minds what Man is, and what is his goal and destiny! No mere description of an evolving process can throw real light on problems of conduct: it is bound to break up in moral scepticism. " Whatever emerges must be accepted " is a formula equally empty of moral content with the cynical phrase " whatever is, is best ". It contains no constructive principle for ethics. We can only find decisive conviction by asking what is the meaning of the universe? What is its purpose and whither its tendency?

What Christians mean by the will of God is the Christian answer to that question.

But this faith maintains a precarious existence in our intellectual climate. In the traditional Christian philosophy the will of God has been conceived and interpreted at least as relatively a static principle. But for the thought of our time there is nothing static. It is doubtful whether official Christian teachers yet realize at all sufficiently the immeasurably far-reaching changes in the whole interpretation of the universe, the whole width and range of our thinking, involved in the evolutionary philosophy. It involves a far more drastic revolution than the astronomical theories of Copernicus. The real challenge to the Christian thinker is not the revision of his myths and symbols to suit a heliocentric astronomy in place of the old geocentric scheme. It is a demand far bigger than that. The question is not whether our little system of planets and satellites is heliocentric or whether the earth is the centre of its gravity: that little system and the life it cherishes is after all but an evanescent moment in the infinite depths of stellar space and time, fading out into new forms of energy. The real question that has to be faced is whether God is the centre of the universe—whether indeed there is anything fixed about it. That is the issue which is raised by the tendencies ruling in current thought. We do not even begin to do justice to it by sad attempts to adjust the myths in Genesis to some sort of terms with evolution. Something far more is demanded of us—to think ourselves sincerely and courageously into the world-view which is now taking shape under the influence of evolution and to set our creed in this new cosmic context. The theistic emphasis can no longer be laid on God as a personified Creator, anthropomorphically conceived and pictured, who is the centre of Biblical religion: it must be on the immanent, creative Spirit revealing Himself in the life of the whole universe in all its manifold, stupendous processes. But the question is whether this necessity is fatal to a supernatural faith and rules out belief in a "personal" God.

Christian thought has from the beginning been able to welcome the theory of development. Its whole system of apologetic, the Messianic claim made for Christ, rests firmly upon the idea of a Purpose developing through history, reaching its climax in the Incarnation. And even now there is nothing more impressive, nothing that speaks so clearly and decisively of a Purpose operative in the course of history, than this moral miracle of Israel and of that Holy Thing that was born out of it. I do not suggest that the old apologetic has here lost any of its force. The convergence of the lines of causation—of nature, of history, of grace—on that one corner of the Roman Empire, on that one incident in Man's experience, is still, to my mind, overwhelmingly significant. But hitherto this line of thought has presupposed development within a fixed scheme—within a universe relatively fluid but yet ordered by an Eternal Law—a stream of movement which is (as it were) canalized. It is these containing banks which have now been thrown down. The traditional Christian philosophy of history which has hitherto formed the background of the Gospel seems now to be dwarfed into relative insignificance on the vast stage of an emergent universe.

But this is assumed, in much current writing, finally to discredit the Christian form of Theism. It is taken for granted by well-known authors *who themselves write in defence of religion*, that the God who is at the centre of the Christian faith is no longer intellectually respectable. Not merely is the immeasurable vastness of the universe as we now begin to know it and the seeming impersonality of its processes thought to rule out belief in a "personal" God: it is argued that such faith is now unnecessary, and may in fact even prove injurious by inhibiting moral and spiritual enterprise. It was no doubt a necessary stage in the development of the religious consciousness, but it is a stage that has now been outgrown. Day by day, by the use of our own brains, we are finding out more about the world, bringing its processes and forces more and more under our control. What need is there now for belief in God ? Religion is an inalienable element in human life at its best and highest, but belief in God is in no sense vital to it. We can see now that God is a myth, which religion will be the stronger for discarding. God must die that religion may live. So Mr. Middleton Murry, for example, a man almost fanatically religious, rejoices that he is now at last emancipated or (in his own language) dis-intoxicated.

Now this, I think, is something quite new. There are now and always have been people who believe in God on intellectual grounds, but are quite untouched by the spirit of religion. Such belief is no test of moral character, though it is perhaps a criterion of intelligence. But we are faced now with just the opposite—a sincerely and genuinely religious outlook which yet abandons belief in God. This is not meant as an attack on religion : it claims to be a defence of religion. It believes that the only effective way of preserving religion in the modern world is to abandon belief in a "personal" God. Thus Professor Julian Huxley testifies that "the sense of spiritual relief which comes from rejecting the idea of God as a supernatural Being is enormous".[1]

I have no desire to speak disrespectfully of the gifted authors just quoted ; the less so since Professor Huxley's volume is a brilliant and constructive contribution to certain vital elements in Christianity. Yet even he seems to assume that Christian theology is pledged to a ludicrously anthropomorphic deity manipulating the Universe *ab extra*. "If the rainbow is generated by the refraction of the sun's rays on the falling rain, it is not set in the sky as a sign by

[1] *Religion without Revelation*, p. 53.

God."[1] And once more: "It seems to me quite clear that the idea of personality in God or in any supernatural being or beings has been put there by man, put into and round a perfectly real conception which we might continue to call God if the word had not acquired through long association the implication of a personal being: and therefore I disbelieve in a personal God in any sense in which that phrase is ordinarily used."[2]

Now, of course, if faith in a personal God meant what these authors think it means, it would be intellectually indefensible. And it is, no doubt, a service to true religion to deliver it from such philosophical crudities. There is a great deal in Mr. Huxley's writing for which Christians owe him real gratitude; and I do not think I am likely to be unfair to the point of view which we are now examining. I am keenly sensitive to the appeal of it. It delivers us from the pettiness and stuffiness which so often stifle the religious atmosphere, and the trivial ideas of God which are too frequently entertained by Christians, utterly unworthy of His glory and of the richness and wonder of the world. It offers escape from the trying people who talk as though they were His private secretaries knowing His plans in every detail. It launches out on the great deeps. It bids us watch this stupendous universe in all its majesty and beauty, alive in all its manifold forms of living, with new facts, new powers and possibilities ceaselessly emerging from the matrix of its inexhaustible resources, and mark what it is which is thus disclosed to us. Out of the dark background of its terrors there come to us "gifts" of love and beauty; out of it come forth spiritual values; there is—it seems—within it a tendency leading it on to fuller and fuller life. Let us turn towards it in reverence and gratitude: life in itself is veritably sacred and to recognize this is the true religion. "I believe in the religion of life."[3]

[1] *Op. cit.*, p. 46. [2] *Op. cit.*, p. 30. [3] *Op. cit.*, p. 381.

A Christian might, and ought to, say most of this. "Great and sweeping thoughts of God and Man are the presupposition for the Gospel." But if God be not, what does it all amount to? So far from rescuing religion from a dangerous intellectual predicament, this is to cut the nerve of religion by depriving it of a real Object. For religion, after all, is about God: but here religion has changed its whole nature and become an attitude to our states of mind. And that is death to real religion. If we ask what is the source and guarantee of this cosmic emotion which is proposed to us in place of God, it is clearly generated by ourselves. It is a short step and unavoidable to the idolatry of self-worship. Mr. Murry does not shrink from this conclusion. "God" (he writes) "does not exist, but we shall never be able to do without Him unless we know in ourselves the reason why He was created. That knowledge is dynamic, for no one can know in himself the demands which God was created to satisfy without determining that for his part his life shall be devoted to the perpetuating of those values which God was created to secure."[1] It is this new religion rather than the old which has fashioned God in its own image.

After all, we may ask, on which side is the mythology? For if we scrutinize the proposal and ask what it is that we are to worship, the answer which is commonly given is: The sacredness of life. And that is quite as mythological as anything to be found in Genesis. For the talk about "Life" is pure mythology—the personification of an abstract idea. It is no more true to say that "life" is sacred by way of supporting the religious consciousness, than it is to say that the "life-force" is cruel by way of disproving the love of God. As well call a triangle ambitious! Why it is considered crude and obscurantist to conceive God in terms of personality (at worst, the least inadequate terms

[1] *God*, p. 233.

we have) but philosophical and scientific to personify a fiction called life-force, I have never found it easy to understand.

But religion cannot be had on these conditions. Religion demands a real and a living God—precisely a " supernatural Being "—as the real Object of religious knowledge and the Guarantor of the religious quest, who both reveals Himself to us and imparts to us His own goodness. It needs a God who is (in the true sense) " personal ". Unless there be such a God as this then indeed religion is vain—" our preaching is vain and your faith is vain ". " Modern thought " is deeply concerned to redeem the traditional faith of Christianity from the bondage of its intellectual past. But the time has come to return the compliment. We are fast reaching a position in which contemporary thinking will need the assistance of Christian theology to save it from intellectual liquidation. Some trends in scientific utterances seem to be definitely towards a scepticism which abandons all claim to rationality. Exulting in its recent emancipation from the tyranny of " mathematical " categories, science is only too keen to assure the world that its so-called truths are but " pointer-readings " and in no sense true accounts of things as they are. They are but ways of looking at things, and Religion is free to look at them in a different light. Thus there is ample room for both points of view. But neither is concerned—so it is suggested—with what is ultimately real. " The religious experience is no more and no less in touch with the real than scientific experience."[1] Thus religion and science are *both* " true " because neither is concerned with truth and neither is the knowledge of what is real.

If this way of thinking proceeds much further it is the

[1] Needham, *The Sceptical Biologist*, p. 258. In this section I have used material published in *The Guardian* eighteen months ago. But I am glad to find the same point made in a review of Mr. Needham's book in the *Hibbert Journal* for July 1931.

high road to intellectual suicide. It will not be long before Theology will have to rescue contemporary thought from a completely irrational scepticism. The world will need the ancient religion to set it free from the new superstition. It is now beginning to become clear not only that "evolutionary" thinking admits of a Theistic interpretation but that it makes nonsense without it.

If there is to-day any philosophy dead beyond all hope of resuscitation it is the Victorian scientific naturalism, till lately so secure and dogmatic. Scientists themselves have broken it to pieces. Everywhere it is now being recognized that a merely "scientific" interpretation of the universe of which we form part is no true account of the world we know. The rising philosophy of science insists that we cannot interpret our world truly unless we include as part of the subject-matter our moral and spiritual experiences. These are factors in human knowledge at least as verifiable as electrons—and many would wish to say, a good deal more so. Thought is moving along this line so rapidly that the Bishops at Lambeth were justified in saying that "There is much in the scientific and philosophical thinking of our time which provides a climate more favourable to faith in God than has existed for generations . . . views of the universal processes are being formed which point to a spiritual interpretation. We are now able by the help of the various departmental sciences to trace in outline a continuous process of creative development in which at every stage we can find the Divine presence and power".[1] This is true, but it might be put more strongly. The new movement needs Christianity to rescue it from the sceptical sentimentalism into which, as we argued, it may too easily fall. It is the Christian philosophy which does justice to these modern demands while yet supplying what they most need to save them from their inherent weakness. The evolutionary

[1] *Encyclical Letter* of Lambeth Conference, 1930, p. 19.

philosophy needs Theism in its Christian form to give it support and to make it rational.

I must not trespass on Dr. Matthews' field nor beyond the hedge of my own limitations.[1] But we cannot answer the question raised in this chapter without an attempt to vindicate this contention.

Evolution is a " blessed word " : and half the confusion of thought and language in current theological controversy comes from its use in a hundred different senses. Its proper usage is biological : at any rate it involves an adaptation of some part of the world to its environment. The universe as a whole cannot " evolve ". Nor can Truth or Goodness " evolve " : they are not within the evolving processes. Men can grow to the knowledge of more truth, and may come to appreciate new forms of excellence ; and popular language may describe these movements as " the evolution of ideas ", " the evolution of morals," and so forth. But it is important to realize from the start that such common language *is* inaccurate. It is the minds of men which evolve, not the goodness or truth which they realize. Valuations may evolve ; but values are the measure of evolution. If they evolve, there is no sense to be made of it. We may say of them what St. John says of the Logos : they are and always have been *in* the world—in a sense they come out of its processes : it is equally true that they come *into* the world. They are its meaning, not merely its resultant : transcendent to it, even though they are within it.

For what is commonly described as evolution is no mere unrolling or unpacking of factors which have been always present. The acorn develops into an oak, and the whole process is truly continuous. But we cannot say that the oak is *in* the acorn ; and there is no reversing the process. We

[1] The reader is referred for a brilliant and satisfying treatment of this whole question to Dr. Matthews' volume in this series : *God in Christian Thought and Experience.*

could never resolve an oak into an acorn as we can take down a clock or an engine and resolve it again into its component parts. We can take a machine to bits and reassemble it: we made it and can unmake or remake it. But this is what we cannot do with an organism, for an organism is something which *makes itself*. This is the characteristic thing about it. It is evolution, not manufacture. Something is there in the finished product which was not present in the initial stages.

It is not necessary for our present purpose to discuss the various theories of biologists as regards the place which can rightly be assigned to the working of mind in organic evolution. Indeed it would be impertinent to attempt it.[1]

All that concerns us is to notice that Biologists are almost all agreed in principle that at any stage in the evolution of life there is something "there" which was not there before. It is not so much that "life" is developing as that something new is constantly coming into it. There is continual irruption, or (as Lloyd Morgan called it) "emergence" of new qualities and factors which are products, indeed, of previous conditions but cannot be thought of merely as their resultant. Out of two added to two comes four, and four is resolvable into two *plus* two: there is nothing in the product or result which was not present in the constituent factors. In vital processes it is otherwise. Life may be the product of pre-existent elements, but it cannot be resolved back into them. The child is the product of its parents, but something has emerged into existence out of the conjunction of the parent cells which is more than merely the sum of the two factors. At each stage in the unending process something new, not merely in fact but also in individual quality and

[1] It is, however, worth while to remark how precarious is our foundation if we try to build a Theistic position on the "vitalist" or "animist" hypothesis which some writers have made widely popular. That is one psychological theory, but it will not necessarily hold the field. Any day —so far as I am able to judge—it may be torpedoed by bio-chemistry.

character, emerges into the field of reality. And as Mr. Joseph pertinently enquired in his Herbert Spencer lecture a few years ago, "If the properties are really new why not allow that they are created?"[1] (It is strange to notice the close affinity between this conception of emergence and the irruptive, catastrophic world-view native to the writers of the Bible and most probably to our Lord himself. "Evolution" and "catastrophe" are not necessarily so incompatible as liberal exegesis tends to insist.)

We have made free use of the word development and there is no way of dispensing with it. But in using it we are begging the question. Clearly, we can talk of development only if there is something which develops, permanent through the whole changing process and more fully expressed and realized in the final than in the initial stages. What is it that is developing in the universe? In the life history of any organism, it is certainly not the physical particles, which are either constant (and thus have not developed) or else have changed (and in that case are not constant). So that, as Mr. Joseph argued, the idea of development becomes intelligible only in the light of the finished product.[2] What develops is the form or idea which is progressively realized and expressed. This cannot mean anything but that what develops—in the organism or in the universe—is a Purpose striving to express itself. Development thus presupposes Purpose. But the popular phrases about an "impersonal purpose" immanent in the evolving process are only a substitute for thinking. On close examination they become meaningless. There cannot be a thought which nobody thinks, nor a feeling which is not felt by anybody. Similarly we can attach no meaning to the widespread modern notion of a purpose which is yet not purposed by any personal

[1] H. W. B. Joseph, *The Concept of Evolution*—1924, p. 11.

[2] *Op. cit.* 15, 22–end. "We shall not fully understand organic life without first attending to the life of mind."

will. If there is purpose there is a will which purposes. If we think there is purpose in the universe we are committed logically to Theism. No other hypothesis makes sense. What is " developing " is a divine Purpose.[1]

If we build upon this foundation, we shall say that the constant which is developing is the purpose or the will of God, and that it is this which gives meaning to the whole life and movement of the universe. For if we descry signs of purpose at any point, we must admit it over the whole field. It is absurd to suggest that the universe is purposive in parts, like the curate's egg ; for in that case it would not be a universe ; or began to be purposive when Man appeared in it ; for we still retain some sense of humour. We shall thus be led to interpret the whole story as the progressive realization or disclosure of a divine Purpose at various levels of response.

If this be so, we shall only achieve our true end, shall only become what is truly "natural" to us, by a partaking in that divine Purpose, But this will offer a constructive principle for the actual conduct of the good life only if we can have sufficient knowledge of the nature and character of the Purpose and the positive content of the will of God. And at this point the Christian faith claims to possess its decisive revelation.

3. The Content of the Will of God.

Christianity stands or falls in the world by its unique disclosure of God. He is God, the Father of Our Lord Jesus Christ. It is that precious intimacy of access, that incomparable wealth of religious reality, which He brings to the

[1] Cf. Aristotle's dictum, " The potential is only actualized by the agency of the already actual ". I should like to refer here to Prof. A. E. Taylor's paper on Dr. Whitehead's *Process and Reality* in *Theology*, August 1930.

hunger of human hearts. We have seen that while our Lord's own vocation lay specifically in the sphere of religion His thought of God was through and through ethical; and that a new richness of ethical content is inherent in His revelation. His life was a filial consecration to the holy will of the Father in heaven. His meat was to do the will of Him that sent Him. The nearest approach that the records attribute to Him towards defining the life into which He invited men was that it consists in doing God's will. That, He said, was the heraldry of membership in the new Family which He was to create. "Who is my mother? and who are my brethren? Whosoever will do the will of God, the same is my brother and sister and mother." This Family would be perfectly realized only in the Father's eternal Kingdom; for (as is at least probable) the Lord's Prayer is essentially Messianic in connotation. Yet the Father's will is to be done on earth. It is therefore the most important of questions for those who would walk in the way of discipleship to discover what the Father's will is. But we have allowed the idea of God's will to become threadbare, vague and conventional, with little positive and defined content. It does not speak of definite things to be done, of high adventures and heroic obediences. It has become a formula of the pious and its main suggestion is that of abstaining from sin. But this is a mortal danger to the Christian life. It makes it fatally easy for Christians to allow vaguely religious aspirations to take the place of a realistic endeavour to fashion the concrete materials of life into conformity with the Divine Purpose. Nothing can be more morally enervating or more destructive of religious sincerity.

It is thus wholly vital to our enquiry to ask what positive meaning should be attached to the Christian phrase: Doing the will of God. What kinds of conduct does it suggest or enjoin? What fields of activity does it cover? We have seen already that nothing short of holiness or consecration to the divine will satisfies the Christian moral ideal. But in what forms of act should this be expressed ? We have been too ready to say that it means " being good ", which is only a formal definition and cannot be said to give us moral guidance.

This is the point where one feels most acutely how inadequate in content and precision are the traditional statements of the Christian life. In the Book of Common Prayer, for example, the living heart of the Christian ethic is richly and magnificently stated ; it is to love the things which God commands and to desire that which He doth promise. But there is very little to suggest to us what kinds of thing God is supposed to command. The result has been to give too much cover to the suggestion that the life of a Christian means what is described as " being good ", not being good at anything in particular.

The effect of this in popular thought has been to leave the Christian life isolated as it were in a vacuum, a form empty of any content. It has thus come to seem a devout alternative to fulfilling the actual tasks which life sets us. Thus in the minds of most English Church-goers it is probable that " doing the will of God " is practically confined to and equated with the minimum obligations of Church membership. Amongst people of religious temperament it degenerates into " little Churchinesses ".[1]

If one were to ask the average Churchwarden what he understood by doing God's will, the answer would almost certainly be conceived in terms of Churchgoing, " saying your prayers ", punctual payment of the diocesan quota, and avoiding the less respectable vices. The more devout members of the congregation would answer in terms of devotional exercises, Communion, meditation and so forth. We must not be unfair to such answers. The Christian life

[1] Von Hügel, *Letters*, p. 288.

has a " religious " content: and it is at his peril that a would-be Christian neglects such duties and obligations. If the Christian life is not hallowed by worship and sustained and enriched by sharing in the common experience of the Christian society it will rarely, if ever, bring its fruit to perfection. Indeed to ignore the devotional and institutional moments in Christianity is to sink to a sub-Christian level. There is no popular maxim more dangerous to spiritual and moral well-being than the tag *laborare est orare.*

There is no doubt at all that it *is* the will of God that Christians should take their " religious duties " seriously. If we lose conscious contact with Him then the whole temperature of life drops, and our thinking and our willing become second rate. To insist on this is utterly necessary; but is there nothing more to be said? Can this be the entire content of God's will? Let us put the case in a thoroughly concrete instance. The clergy are apt to invite the laity to turn aside from the office or the golf course, the laboratory, garage or consulting-room, at the end of the day or maybe in the lunch hour, in order to " give part of your time to God ". But what do we think they have been doing all day? If God is not present in the enterprises, the scientific research, the " city " life, the school, the home, and even in the pleasures of this richly coloured and absorbing age, I cannot conceive where in the world He is. It is vital that we should acclaim the work of God, His power, His presence, His creative activity, even where men cannot consciously recognize Him. We must, of course, equally insist upon this, that these gifts fail of their full fruition—lack, indeed, just that redemptive touch which releases them into richest grace and energy—unless they are gathered in the focus of personal and public prayer and worship into conscious relation to our God and Father. The latter statement is of the utmost importance. But what for the moment most needs to be emphasized is what religion is most prone to forget—that the gifts of life, its tasks, its claims, and its pleasures, can never be brought within Christian ethics until we have trained ourselves to conceive them, not as alternatives to the Christian life, but as its material and its opportunity.

It may well be urged that this is so much of a truism that to write it down is superfluous. I can only reply that in my own experience this, which might be regarded as platitude, comes to many people as a surprising paradox. This may be salvation for the preacher: but for the teacher of Christian morals it is rather a disabling handicap. So it seems worth while to establish the point here.

Behind this circumscription of outlook is obviously an inadequate Theology. The question is really What do we mean by God? And here once more there are two truths to remember. He would not be what the word God implies throughout the whole range of religious history were He not the Object of religion—of personal faith, worship and communion. As such He meets us "in the face of Christ". He is the Father of our spirits. But unless He is more than that He is not God in the sense we profess in the creeds of Christendom—One God, Creator of heaven and earth and of all things visible and invisible. "God is not the private property of religion"[1]: He is at work throughout the vast universe. We must recapture that authentic note which Father Thornton has expressed so admirably. The astronomer at his telescope—we may add the man of business at his desk, the Resident Magistrate in his Indian district, the teacher in the school, the parent in the home—is every bit as much a concern to God as is the Churchman at his prayers.[2] God is the Source of all Value: and all Goodness, wherever found and in whatever forms it is manifested, is a present revelation of God.

[1] Valentine, *What do we mean by God?* p. 140.
[2] Cf L. Thornton, *The Incarnate Lord*, p. 455.

Now this implies, in the language of Theology, that God is fully revealed indeed in Christ, but that not all of God is thus revealed.

"The Unincarnate God," as Von Hügel said, "is wider in His range, but less intense in His working than the Incarnate God." There is that in the depths of Divine Being which cannot be revealed in human experience—which our finite reasons and imaginations can never either perceive or understand. There are also manifestations of His presence on levels lower than self-conscious spirit. Neither can these be revealed in Christ. Christ is the revelation of the Father —of God in His redemptive, manward activity: to know Him thus is the ultimate need of Man and in that knowledge is life eternal. But Christianity has never taught that Christ is the only revelation of God. Indeed the whole orthodox theology depends upon the contrary proposition: it claims that the thought or meaning of the world, ever informing the whole creative process, comes to full disclosure in Christ—that the true light which has always lighted every man, all that is good and true wherever found, is there "coming into the world" in undimmed and unrefracted radiance. The very presence of the Old Testament bound up in our Bibles with the Christian Scriptures is standing witness to this contention. It cannot be urged too often or too emphatically that to claim divinity for Jesus is not to claim honours for Him, but to make an affirmation concerning God—to say that the Ultimate Purpose of the world is best conceived in terms of the Spirit of Christ. The whole Christian faith is really meaningless unless we conceive God's work in Christ in relation to the whole sweep and range of God's work throughout the cosmic processes. It was thus presented, in the forms of their own thought, tradition and inheritance, by St. Paul and St. John in the New Testament, and the classical Christian writers ever since. It is this which demands rethinking and restatement in our own new intellectual climate. Christianity, if it is to claim the world, must now be presented in a wider context—as at once interpreting and sustained by the length and depth and height of God's work, creative and redemptive, in the whole universe, so far as it is open to human experience. Christ can hold the cosmic significance which orthodox Christian thought has always claimed for Him, only so far as we refuse to isolate Him. And there is this paradox about it, that while the richest personal religion can be nurtured and sustained only by Christ, yet if we think to know God in Him alone then we cannot know God at all.

The very breath of the Christian way of life is uncompromising insistence upon the Christ-like character of God. All false ways of thought and conduct plainly derive, in the last analysis, from false and inadequate ideas of God. Nothing is more important at this moment than to lead men to conceive the Divine Purpose in terms derived from the Gospels and not from Samuel and Judges. Hence the Bishops at the Lambeth Conference prefaced their attempt at interpreting what is implied in the Christian "way" in the changed conditions of the twentieth century, by an appeal to all Christian people "to banish from their minds every thought of God which is incompatible with the character of Jesus Christ". That can never be said too insistently. But the Bishops' language is admirably restrained. It is not the crude, unqualified equation of God with Jesus in the Synoptic Gospels which is the temptation of popular modern preaching. This is commonly expressed by saying "God is like Christ and like nothing else"; or, "If we want to know what God is like, we must look to Jesus Christ and nowhere else". The affirmative statement is splendidly true; the implied negative seems to demand criticism. For if we know nothing of God apart from Christ, how do we know God when we find Him? It may be urged that this "Christocentric" theology which we are rightly keen to emphasize is exposed to certain disabling restrictions. Its effect is really to minimize Christ's significance by cutting Him out of the fabric of history and isolating His revelation of God from what is revealed in science, art and philosophy and our experience of life as a whole.

Now this, as we have seen, has been recognized by nearly all the great Christian thinkers. But it needs now to be rethought and restated. For the form in which the tradition has been embodied serves too often only to conceal it from the average Christian, or the average critic, with no training in technical theology. It is, for example, preserved and emphasized in the constant references to the Old Testament, and the passion for finding Hebraic precedents, so characteristic of the English Prayer Book. But we cannot say that this is what strikes the eye. It appears to our thinking rather ludicrous to exhort Christians in the twentieth century to model their lives upon the Hebrew Patriarchs. We are all fully aware that Judaism is the mother and matrix of the Christian movement. We realize that had it not been for Judaism the vision of God in Christ could not have come to us. We know that in all His words and works of grace " the mother of Jesus "—the Jewish Church —" was there ". All this we recognize with reverent gratitude. We cannot, however, believe that for us moderns the faith and worship of the Christian Church is tied for ever to its Judaic origins.[1] For one thing, the scientific criticism of the Biblical writings, which we all take for granted, has inevitably modified our attitude to at least some parts of the Scriptural tradition. We cannot appeal to the writings of the Bible simply as authoritative, " given " texts. Further, the growth of the historical sense and the wider knowledge now available of other cultures and other religious systems, is bound to open ampler horizons in our whole conception of God's work in Man. We may still claim that the Gospel is the

[1] Cf. Resolution 4 of Lambert Conference, 1930.

Truth, but no longer that nothing else is true. History for St. Paul meant Jewish history together with recent events within the Empire. For us it has an infinitely wider range. Correspondingly the reach of our thought of God and man must be infinitely wider.

If we claim that Christ is the Logos, the Purpose of the world made articulate, then we must find ways of presenting Him which will be less unworthy of that Purpose in the width and range in which it is now discovered to us. We must learn to appreciate God's revelation in all the activities of the human spirit along all the avenues of history and in the whole life of this "emergent" universe, as the setting of the crucial disclosure which comes to us in the face of Christ. The entire work of the creative Spirit as seen in all outreach after value, in all insight into love and beauty, in all brave, pure and humble hearts, is the true *preparatio evangelica*.

The revelation of God in the face of Christ is the focus of this divine self-disclosure. In the previous section we sought to establish that the long story of cosmic evolution only becomes significant and intelligible if interpreted in terms of Divine Purpose. For us, that Purpose is, in its inmost quality, the will of God the Father of Jesus Christ. Our Lord is the key by which we unlock the secrets of the sealed book of the Universe. He opens the book and breaks the seals thereof. If we take the story in its broad outline, what we find gradually emerging is a series of levels or stages of development to which we attach a scale of increasing value. Life emerges within the inorganic, and begins to climb up the spiral; within life emerges rudimentary consciousness, which in turn gives birth to intelligence and the faculty of directive purpose. Within intelligence, at the end of the story (though perhaps it is still more like the beginning), emerges Man as self-conscious spirit. It has not, needless to say, been a straight line. We cannot shut our eyes to the facts of evil, terror, ignominy and failure. Nature, as St. Paul's insight realized in the one passage in the New Testament which shows any real appreciation of Man's organic relation to the universe, has "become subject to frustration" (Romans viii. 20). No one is likely in the twentieth century to blind himself to these and similar facts. Yet it remains true that the general tendency has been a process increasing in complexity, in richness of content and experience, from the first dim stirrings of life through various grades of structure and response, culminating in self-conscious spirit, which is the climax of the whole development as we men know it in our range of knowledge.

But what "emerge" as the process advances are essentially, if we think about it, new *attitudes*, at least new modes of response to environment. The artist's life realizes a richer content, is further advanced in the scale of progress, than the cow's effortless self-nourishment, just because he finds in his world more "meaning", which evokes from him a more sensitive response to it. "The stress is on the new attitude, for it is this that is, as I think, emergent."[1] Compare the human mind with the sub-human, the spiritual man with the carnal, any "higher" type with any "lower", and this, it would seem, is the standard of valuation. The higher type is that which exhibits capacity for recognizing and responding to deeper and richer aspects of Reality. The progressive disclosure of Divine Purpose in the processes of creative evolution consists, then, in evoking this response with increasing clarity of insight to the spiritual factor in environment—that is to say, in the end, to God Himself in whom we live and move and have our being.

At every grade of organic response we should see the disclosure of creative Spirit at that level, with that degree of adequacy. Everything as it fulfils the law of its being is, at least at that level, doing the will of God. The organism

[1] Lloyd Morgan, Gifford Lectures, Vol. II, Preface.

responding to environment is making response, in the last resort, to God. As it finds out by trial and experiment the way in which its life can be lived effectively, God may truly be said to be revealing to it and through it as much of His will as He has committed to it power to express. Man's life is a still unfinished adventure. It is clear, however, that personal spirit must be at least a more responsive medium for the realization of Divine Purpose than the sub-human forms of life and consciousness. That is, of course, the basis of religion and of Christianity in particular. It involves that man is made in the image of God, and that the end and meaning of human nature is communion with the Divine Spirit. In the fellowship of men with the Father the Divine Purpose comes to its fulfilment, so far at least as concerns our experience. Thus it is that in the life of Christ we find the clue to the story of evolution : in Him the Divine Purpose is incarnate. Sonship is the true end of our being. But if this is the Purpose informing the whole it is operative also at all the lower levels. There must be included within the will of God all that conduces to the full development—material, intellectual and spiritual—of persons made for communion with Himself. Thus all the complex technical issues involved in modern life and society are brought within the circumference of His will. We can thus begin to see that doing God's will involves much more in fact and idea than religious attitudes alone can account for.

God's will is conformity to those laws which express His Purpose at any given level of life and experience. For Man it is, at the highest level, the specifically religious response of love, communion, trust and adoration. But that is not the whole of God's will for man. By no means all our life is lived or can be lived on the altitudes which we call " spiritual ". Nobody can be always religious. We remain part of the natural order still : we must " trade with time ", with things and with other persons ; we live in a number of different spheres and kingdoms—economic, civic, technical, æsthetic—each ruled by its own proper laws, each of which expresses the Divine Purpose at that level and within that context. We cannot hope to be doing the will of God in face of a problem in science or politics by taking refuge in religious phraseology or by introducing transcendental inferences into technical discussions.

Pious people sometimes need a reminder that primarily God's will for them may consist not in more devotional exercises but in observing the laws of health, or paying their bills, or answering their letters, or some other " worldly " and prosaic duty. What is God's will at the level of religion cannot be in opposition to His will in the natural or the economic order. But its expression, as well as the kind of conduct which it demands, must differ in different circumstances. What may be the immediate will of God cannot possibly be stated in abstract. There are many situations in which we find ourselves when the specifically "religious" response is not that which God's will requires of us. God's will in engineering, for instance, is primarily (though of course not only) obedience to the laws of mechanics. The religious engineer says his prayers : but that will confer no absolution from fidelity to his professional technique. At the least he cannot hope to be doing God's will if he is insensitive to that obligation. The same cardinal principle holds over the whole area of men's enterprises. The will of God is that we should respond adequately to the " truth " of each given situation, that is, to the values inherent in it as the expression of Divine Purpose, when measured according to the mind of Christ. The " mind of Christ " is the decisive factor. For if God is indeed the Father of Jesus Christ, then the truth of a given situation will present itself to us in a different light—as richer in content and in possibility as well as more exacting in its demands—from that in which it appears to the worldly judgment. This is the standard of Christian ethical values.

But the whole question of what we mean by values is at present so confused and so ill thought out that it needs much more thorough examination. This we shall attempt in the following chapter.

CHAPTER VII

THE REDEMPTION OF VALUES

1. What are "Values"?

"A RELIGION which is perfectly at home in the world has no counsel for it which the world could not gain by an easier method."[1] Yet if it does not live in the actual world, to direct its enterprises and redeem its values, religion has equally no message for it. How can the Christian faith maintain itself in the midst of the many-coloured human drama and yet not surrender that otherworldliness without which the redemptive salt perishes?

We have argued that the content of God's will for us in this, that and the other situation, lies in the endeavour to realize the highest values which are inherent in it, when measured by the standard of Christ. But this sounds intolerably abstract. It demands far more intimate analysis if it is to be brought into such close touch with life as will make it workable as a moral principle. At least we must rescue the idea of value (which is becoming deplorably jargonized) from its esoteric associations and make it significant for common men. If value means anything for conduct, then it must be something which may be sought and recognized in quite humble and elementary grades of our response to the gifts and claims of life—in paying the grocer and watering the garden—not less than in the pursuit of pure knowledge or the thirst for the beatific vision. The traditional triad of "absolute values" is unsatisfactory and artificial. Imagine our telling a Christian

[1] Reinhold Niebuhr, *op. cit.*, p. 177.

group in Bermondsey that if they wish to be doing the will of God they must seek to realize Beauty, Truth and Goodness! If we are to work with this threefold classification, we are bound to try to explain it in such a way as to cover the whole field of our experience. And this in practice is quite unworkable.

We may try, for example, to stretch the idea of *Knowledge* till it covers all attempts at every level, whether theoretical or practical, to introduce order into our experience, reflecting the rationality of the universe. This may be manifested at all levels, from the farmer's study of the seasons to the metaphysician's treatise on the nature of things. Thus it will embrace not only research and scholarship, which must always be the luxury of the few, but all effort to form true opinions, to rid our souls of prejudice and ignorance, to think fairly and to judge justly. It will have to include also every degree of technical and professional skill and craftsmanship, in which the spirit of man co-operates with the law and order of the universe. It will mean, for instance, steering a motor-omnibus round the curves of a slippery London street—a triumph of ordered control over matter at which the sons of God shout for joy. We may try, again, to include under the head of *Beauty* all delight in the graces and joys of life and every kind of expression of what is good. Thus it will cover not merely " Art ". It will mean the desire of the dweller in a tenement for a pot of geranium on the window-sill, which is very surely a hallowing of God's name, and all attempts to clothe ourselves, our homes and our surroundings with grace and dignity, within the limits of means and opportunity.

We might attempt some such delimitation of the frontiers between Truth and Beauty, and try in such ways to appraise them in terms of life. This is, to be sure, a desperate expedient: for what beauty may be without order is impossible to conceive or imagine. But even if such an attempt were forced through, yet when we come to the category of *Goodness* there is scarcely anything left that can be covered by it—unless it be personal relationships; and that is certainly not what the word means. We shall find ourselves left alone with the famous paradox of a good will that wills nothing good in particular. And that can have no strictly ethical meaning; though Kant's position (as we shall see later) can be re-stated in such a way as to be almost the heart of ethics in its Christian interpretation.

In fact all such attempted analyses prove themselves arbitrary and unreal precisely because the scheme is too abstract for the persistent variety of life. The trinity of Beauty, Truth and Goodness seems to be simply assumed in book after book as an almost irreformable dogma. But it hardly survives close intellectual scrutiny. At best we can say that it is a convenient shorthand, employed by philosophers as a useful symbol but frankly and avowedly diagrammatic. Even as that it fails rather badly. And for practical guidance in the Christian life it is, in my belief, almost useless. It is fatally lacking in just that precision and concreteness which is most needed. We must either abandon the formula entirely or else re-examine it from the start. As it stands, it has little help to offer us.

It is difficult to maintain, on closer inspection, that the symbols genuinely correspond to three modes or aspects of reality. There are not three co-equal absolute goods, for they mutually involve one another. It is questionable, as Canon Quick suggested in his brilliant volume in this series,[1] whether knowledge is of absolute value. (Truth is a quality of propositions; what is meant, clearly, is true knowledge.) For while it is clearly good to know truth, yet the value of any particular knowledge seems obviously to be relative to the terms or relations which are known. Some of our know-

[1] *The Christian Sacraments*, pp. 24 *sq.*

ledge we might be better without. At least the value of knowledge seems to depend on some external criteria. Thus it might be easier to defend the theory of absolute values if it were "binitarian" rather than "trinitarian". But even if we agreed to ignore this criticism we should not evade the weakness of the formula, that the three supposedly absolute values mutually involve one another. Where one is present there is the whole trinity. For what constitutes any of them "values" is precisely the goodness which they share in common. Their goodness is their generic quality. There cannot be three ultimate goodnesses. There is goodness, variously manifested in all those partial and fragmentary values which express, at their level, the underived Perfection, which the theory of absolute values seeks to safeguard.

It has been proposed to salvage the formula by regarding the so-called absolute values as the objects of three spiritual attitudes—scientific, æsthetic and ethical—all of which are of unconditioned worth. This, too, breaks down under cross-examination. For these three spiritual attitudes are quite obviously interdependent. There is a logical element in beauty: in the highest forms of creative art this logical and intellectual factor counts for much—and perhaps for more and more as art comes nearer to perfection—in the excellence of artistic achievement. The rational quality of a great poem is at least as significant as the lyrical. In the composition of the plastic arts this seems to be still more obviously true, and of course most conspicuously in architecture. It was not for nothing that the great masters like Leonardo and Michael Angelo urged their pupils to study mathematics as the highest expression of rational necessity. The kinship of music and mathematics is too plain to demand elaboration.

There is undeniably an æsthetic element in the majesty of a fine act or character, and there is, as certainly, a moral factor in full æsthetic enjoyment or creation. I am not suggesting that art should teach " a lesson ", or that the artist's function is that of preacher. That would be destructive both of art and morals. But it is true that we cannot enjoy the complete sense of enjoyment and repose, and full and complete æsthetic satisfaction, unless there is that in a given work of art which satisfies moral intuition.[1] And yet once more—that we may complete our circle—there are æsthetic and moral elements implicit in all our intellectual processes.

We could only defend the formula on these lines by endorsing the old faculty-psychology, with which indeed it suggests some correspondence. But we know that it is not my " mind " that thinks, my " emotions " that feel and my " will " that acts, but rather the one manifold-in-unity, the one psycho-physical self or consciousness, which is active in these various responses. And if so, we can no longer posit one absolute value that corresponds to " thought ", another to our " æsthetic sense " and so on. There is just goodness, and we have glimpses of it, apprehend and express it in many different ways, but all as responses of our complex selves. Indeed the more coherent and unified our insight into and concept of goodness, the more truly " selves " shall we become.[2]

Now the ultimate " unity of the good " is of crucial importance to Christianity, both as a philosophy and as a way of life. On other terms, as Professor Taylor points out, the goal of the moral life is unattainable. For if, as some philosophers hold, there is an ultimate plurality of " goods " —economic, æsthetic, ethical and so forth—irreducible into any organic unity, then the more good we seek to realize the more distraught and unharmonized are we. But to insist

[1] Superficially, of course, some great art—e.g. tragedy—may appear to shock and to come into conflict with the maxims of Sunday-school morality. But " satisfies " means a great deal more than this.

[2] See below, pp. 186 *sq.*

on this vital truth is incompatible with the theory of three ultimate absolute values, co-eternal together and co-equal. At least it is thus deprived of any real significance as throwing light on the business of living. So, too, this essential mutuality and interdependence of the modes of goodness, all implicit in one another and all responsive to personality, is of immense philosophical import for the vindication of Christian Theism. But to recognize this must mean withdrawing support from the stock theory of absolute values; at least in its customary presentation.

Thus even as philosophers' shorthand the traditional scheme is hard enough to maintain. For practical guidance in Christian living it appears to have very little to offer. We must surely begin nearer to actual life. We cannot fruitfully discuss what may be meant by absolute values till we have formed some clearer idea of what values in themselves are, whether absolute or otherwise. And indeed the whole notion of values demands closer thought and definition than it always receives in theological writing—or, for that matter, even in philosophy. The current idiom talks so much about values as almost to make it into a "blessed word" which serves to conceal confusion in our thinking. But Christianity cannot direct our conduct by murmuring facile phrases about values. The word itself has become lamentably degraded as the mere *cliché* of æsthetic coteries. As a second-hand philosophical technicality it makes any discussion seem enlightened; but it means very little to the unsophisticated, and (if we may judge from their treatises) not always anything very clear to philosophers. Thus it easily confuses and obscures thought. We must therefore try to get behind phrases and nearer to the concrete realities. Temerarious though the attempt is, we must ask quite naïvely and bluntly what we imagine that "values" really are.

In one sense, no doubt, the idea of value is ultimate and

perhaps unanalysable. But that does not mean that it is unintelligible. We all know, more or less, what we mean by it, until we bemuse ourselves with argument. For that we recognize and respond to value is the most characteristic thing about us, and is almost the meaning of life itself. Let us for the moment drop the word "value", which suggests all manner of abstruse speculations, and substitute the homespun word goodness. Then, although we may never succeed in elaborating a perfect theory of it, at least we know what we are talking about. We cannot get behind the idea of goodness: it is no more definable than truth; but it conveys some meaning to all of us, and we all recognize goodness when we see it. Now whatever goodness is in itself, it is clear that goodness *as we experience it* is correlative to the idea of purpose. We approve some things or disapprove of others—we call some things "good" and others "bad". We desire some things and we shrink from others. We desire things because we think they are *good* and that therefore to have or achieve them will satisfy us.

Thus goodness is the correlative of our consciousness of our own finitude. Our spirits know themselves to be incomplete. All men are constantly reaching out towards something other than themselves in which they believe that their lives will find fulfilment. That which claims us, that to which we give ourselves, is what invests our lives with such measure of direction and purpose as they possess. And the things we live for, which we regard as good, in which we believe that we shall find satisfaction or escape from the prison-house of self-centredness, are exactly what we call our "values". All of us find some worth or value in this or that experience or activity, and these are, as we say, what life means to us. We all find value in life itself—i.e. we believe that it is worth while, despite all that may challenge this conviction. There is no other reason why we should go on living—often in face of desperate pain and tragedy—beyond the fact that for us life is " good ".[1] And what makes it good is the values we find in it, the interest, meaning or ideal with which we identify ourselves and expect therein to find self-fulfilment.

If this be true, the value is what we live for—that in which we hope to find the end or purpose of our experience as spirits. A man may live for whisky or for dividends, for his wife and children or for the New Jerusalem. Whatever he lives for, that is what life means for him. That is what he believes to have " value ". And normally we appraise the worth of a man by the scale of values which he appears to acknowledge.

There is scarcely need to elaborate further what is a primary fact of our experience. And if this reading of value is true, it will carry with it highly important consequences. Popular language tends to imply that there are concealed somewhere in the universe a number of things or essences called values, more or less as there are (or are assumed to be) a number of unseen forces called electrons. And we half-suggest that as physical analysis can reveal the existence of the latter, so trained moral and æsthetic insight can somehow detect the presence of the former. But, if our suggestions are true, we cannot claim that values exist as so many substances in their own right, and independently of any mind. The idea of value, in our interpretation of it, is always related to the idea of Purpose. And if this be so, we shall know how to turn the flank of a dangerous movement in modern philosophy which imperils the whole doctrine of value, and threatens to make nonsense of our experience.

The core of the philosophy of values, as conceived so

[1] Cf. Streeter, *Reality*, p. 111. "If life is real, value in some form or other must be real also; for implicit in the will to live is the unexpressed assumption that is worth while."

magnificently by Plato, is to take this fact of our interior history as the clue to our understanding of the universe. If we ask Why did A do this? the only answer which gives a real reason is "A thought it a good thing to do"—or, in other language, A found value in it. The idea of value is what explains the act. Even thus then, it is suggested, must it be with the universe itself. If we ask Why? we must answer in terms of value: it makes sense because it is good. A teleological interpretation presupposes the concept of value, which the implied purpose seeks to realize. In this sense values "explain" the universe: they are the reason why it exists. They are "in the world"—as St. John says of the Logos—yet it is by them that "the world is made". The kinship between this line of thought and the Christian doctrine of the Logos is obviously very intimate. And this Platonic theory of value has been used as the basis of Christian Theism in Dean Inge's *Confessio Fidei* and Archbishop Temple's *Christus Veritas*.

It is faced, however, with a pressing difficulty from the evolutionary standpoint. For Plato the values are ideas—i.e. unchanging archetypal Forms eternally subsistent in the "real" world, and investing this changing world of time with whatever reality we can rightly claim for it. For this system of thought the temporal order is wholly derivative and secondary. But for "evolutionary" philosophy the temporal order is alone real. Time is regarded as the form of reality. Thus, if we claim that values are real they too must be within the temporal order, evolving in its "emergent" processes. But to say that abandons the whole position. For if what life is supposed to *mean* is itself in process of evolution it is hard to contend that it has any real meaning. If values are a product of the process they are not principles which can explain it. If values are a result of evolution the world seems to be hopelessly irrational. It will mean something different every morning. Yet no philosophical system can maintain itself in the twentieth-century intellectual climate if it seems to be based on the Platonic theory that what is real is necessarily static.

Here, as in many other apparent dilemmas, the question turns partly on terminology. Behind it lies a confusion of language. For when it is said that values " emerge " what seems really to be intended is that *valuations* emerge—that is to say, minds or persons valuing. What the world " means " cannot change or evolve. But we who come out of its evolving process may advance to a less inadequate recognition of its worth, its meaning and its purpose. " The sources of religious belief," wrote Professor Whitehead, " are always growing," as experience grows in richness and complexity: the same is obviously true of the material for our valuations. The race may find value to-morrow where yesterday it was unaware of it. If so, it will be we who have changed, not the meaning or value which we find. To whatever extent there is progress in the world, what it seems to consist in essentially is the progressive adequacy and richness of the valuations by which we live—i.e. our increasing recognition of the things that are genuinely worth living for as true objects of a life-purpose. This indeed is the calculus of progress in any such sense as religion can endorse. The only situation which it can recognize as being ultimately " better " than any other with which it may be compared, is one which is measured in terms of persons valuing in a " higher " way rather than a " lower ". The worth resides in the qualities of spirit which express themselves in the new valuations, and inspire these new responses to life.

Yet here we seem to be arguing in a circle. We have denied that values evolve, and have argued that what is really happening is the emergence of new recognitions of values which have always been " there " to recognize. Yet we have also argued that values are not so many immaterial substances which are " there " independently of mind, but always stand in relation to purpose. The two contentions seem to be inconsistent. And there is, as we shall see in the next section, an apparently irreducible inconsistency, and even it may be illogicality, involved in the whole conception of value. But for Theism, at least, this is not ultimate. Value and Purpose still remain correlative. But our purposes are blind and fragmentary—our "values", as we say, are imperfect. They are only fulfilled, clarified and harmonized in co-operation with the perfect Purpose which is the meaning and value of the universe. The "absolute values" of metaphysics mean, in fact, the complete realization of that which God wills: "and behold it is very good". All recognition of and response to value is a partaking of the Divine Nature and a foretaste of the life eternal.

2. Values and Valuations

We have argued that what is really meant by phrases about the evolution of values should be stated rather in terms of valuations—that is to say, of minds or persons valuing. But we then proceed to appraise valuations by reference to some scale of real values. And this argument, as any freshman reading formal logic can point out to us, seems to be involved in a hopeless circularity. I have freely admitted that it appears illogical. But the more one ponders, the more is it forced upon him that this seeming illogicality is inherent in those facts of our experience, which the theory of values is an attempt to summarize. And, as was suggested in the last paragraph, Theism offers the one way of escape from it.

For there is, as was pointed out by Meinong[1] in his subtle if inconclusive analysis, no inherent quality in things them-

[1] Alexius Meinong, *Zur Grundlegung der allgemeinen Werttheorie* (Graz, 1923).

selves in virtue of which we attach value to them. There is nothing however bizarre or trivial to which someone may not attach value. Any attempt to equate worth or value with properties of things in themselves breaks down under cross-examination. We cannot say it resides in utility; for we value gold more highly than iron, although for most purposes it is far less useful. It is certainly not the same thing as price; for when we pay a price for a given object it is not as representing its value, but because we value it more highly than the money we are prepared to give for it; if, on the other hand, a man sells it, he values the money more highly than the object, otherwise he would not be willing to sell it to us. Nor can it be (as the "Labour theory" holds) a sort of *quantum* locked up in the object by the amount of work expended on it. For we do not always value most highly what has cost most labour to produce; on the other hand, men are only willing to "put work into" something that they value. Nor is it possible to escape by the suggestion that what we value is that which we desire: the whole point is Why do we desire it? We desire what we regard as desirable; we feel a *need* (*Bedurfnis*) for that which we value. Value is relative to persons valuing; the characteristic of what we call value is to be sought in the subject's attitude.[1] The essence of qualitative value resides in this specific experience (*Werterlebnis*, as Meinong calls it) which we have described as valuation.[2]

Now in this we may seem to be abandoning any recogni-

[1] "In dem es sonach eine Beziehung zum Subjeckt ist, vermoge deren ein Objekt . . . für wertvoll gilt, so ist bereits die Vermutung nahegclegt das für Wertthatbestände eigentlich Charackteristische werde nicht so sehr im Objekt als im Subjekt zu suchen sein. . . . . Die Werttheorie wird kaum fehlgehen wenn sie zum Zwecke der Characteristik der Wertthatbestände vor allem nach einen ausreichend characteristischen Erlebnis sucht" (*op. cit.*, p. 33).

"In Werterlebnissen das Wesentliche des Wertgedankens zu suchen" (p. 37).

[2] The word was first coined, I believe, by Prof Urban of Yale See his contribution in *Contemporary American Philosophy*, Vol. I.

tion of objective values and falling back on a statement which says nothing, equivalent to " I value what I value ". And in one sense there is no more to be said than that. We certainly cannot *define* what we mean by goodness: it cannot be brought under any higher principle, since goodness is in itself something ultimate. There is nothing behind it to which thought can reach. In like manner we cannot define truth. And in the relationship of mind to knowledge we seem to encounter just the same paradox which confronts us here in this matter of values. Truth is not true because thinking makes it so: and if the mind makes or constitutes truth, then what it makes is just not what we mean by truth. Truth is " there " for minds to discover. Yet there is no truth unless there is mind to know it. It exists in this specific relation between thinking mind and its object. And the same seems to hold in the sphere of value. It seems that values, too, can exist only so far as they are " possessed by mind ", as Dr. Alexander rightly insisted.[1] In Lloyd Morgan's phrase they are " projicient ".

This should certainly not be taken to mean—as it is taken in Alexander's philosophy—that the mind makes or confers the value as a kind of tertiary quality read into things which are in themselves neutral; any more than the thinker can be said to make truth. But as truth has meaning only for thought, so values exist only for mind. It is only in this specific relation between the subject and the object valued that values can be regarded as real. Apart from any relation to any subject nothing could be said to possess value. No valuations, no value. What we call beauty would not be beautiful if there were no subject to enjoy it. It exists in that specific experience. This does not mean that beauty is subjective, in the sense of being " merely a matter of taste ", or in the sense that the subject's enjoy-

[1] " Values belong to the object as it is possessed by mind and not outside that relation." (Alexander, *Space, Time and Deity*, Vol. II, p. 43).

ment invests the thing with the quality of beauty. It means simply that the idea of beauty presupposes both the " beautiful " object and the subject of that experience, and is significant only in that relation. Thus when we say that values " emerge ", or that new values come into the world, what we really mean appears to be this—that minds have now come for the first time into that specific relation to environment in virtue of which new objects are seen to have value. Value and valuations are correlative.

But it is at this point that the line becomes a circle. For we attach value to valuations. It is for example notoriously true that a man's valuations may be pathological ; or through lack of training or moral insight valuations may be so meagre that we call them definitely false or wrong. Can such objective judgments be justified ? " I value this " is a statement of fact which admits of no more discussion than such a statement as " I like cocktails ". But we often wish that the person concerned would not value what he says he does : we judge that his values are mistaken and in some cases morally depraved. In other words, we do not admit that every recognition of value is its own jury as well as its own evidence. For in that case moral judgments are illusory ; we cannot assess men's choices at all. Each of us would be like the Cyclops giving dooms to his wife and children, and our moral choices and valuations will be on a par with tastes in tobacco. It leads straight back to moral sensationism where " this is right " means " I feel like this ". Just in what sense then are valuations *true*, or the values which they recognize right or wrong ?

We seem here to be standing over a precipice of disastrous scepticism and relativity. For if we discard the absolute values, as hypostatic self-subsistent realities, there seems to be no ultimate standard of reference. And the suggestion is dangerously close that not only is there no standard but in the nature of things there cannot be one. Philosophy used to attempt to differentiate between primary and secondary qualities—those which are inherent in things themselves and those which are due to the work of our minds upon them. Things are not in themselves " red " or " sweet " : they have certain primary, mathematical qualities in virtue of which they affect our senses in ways which we describe as colour or taste. We call the rose red and the sunset golden : but the red and the gold are our contribution, and are not inherent in the " real facts ". The facts have in themselves no such qualities. In the last resort it is our minds that put them there. The current philosophy of our time makes precisely a similar attempt to differentiate between fact and value. We read our " values " into our " facts ", but the facts in themselves have no such properties. Values are but " tertiary qualities ", imposed by us on the " real " facts, which are morally and æsthetically neutral.

If this is a true account of the situation, it is a blow not only to Christian ethics but to all standards, whether in art or morality.

> " Any tradition of living would soon cease to be a living tradition if men could be persuaded that it consists of ' valuations ' manufactured by themselves and imposed on the ' real facts ' of life from outside. A tradition thus degraded would lose all its power of inspiring to fresh endeavour and better action. The ideals of good which in actual history move men to fresh efforts only move so powerfully because they are not taken to be an addition imposed on the facts of life but to be the very bones and marrow of life itself."[1]

This suggested divorce between fact and value is the philosophical justification of that moral scepticism and

[1] A. E. Taylor, *The Faith of a Moralist*, I, 61.

disillusionment which describes itself as the "modern temper".[1] But it is the result of a false way of thinking. It hopes to achieve scientific objectivity by applying laboratory methods to the varied and concrete material of experience. Thus it comes to think of the facts as one thing, and the valuations placed on them as another. But, if so, the latter are wholly subjective: they have no foothold in the realities of life and are, at the last, but cherished illusions. "The hungry generations tread them down."

But we do not and cannot attain to "objectivity"—in the sense of knowing life as it really is, without prejudice and without illusion—by this needless and dangerous surgery. For "what confronts us in actual life is neither facts without value nor values attached to no facts, but fact revealing value and dependent for the wealth of its content on its character as thus revelatory, and values which are realities and not arbitrary fancies, precisely because they are embedded in fact and give it its meaning. To divorce the two would be like trying to separate the sound of a great symphony from its musical quality".[2]

There is no such thing as a fact apart from its meaning. But its meaning will never be revealed to the attitude of the impartial onlooker contemplating it from outside. The impartial critic of religious experience is, as we know, often the man least qualified to pronounce any true judgment upon it. And the same holds good for all our experience. For we know life, in fact, "from inside": and only from within the experience can we draw materials for our interpretation of it.

After all, living experience is unitary. It cannot be chopped into artificial segments. And all our experience, at every level, is an awareness of, and a response to, facts which are given by our environment. All growth, whether

[1] *Supra*, Chap. V, pp. 112–113.
[2] Taylor, *op. cit.*, 62.

physical or mental, is by way of assimilation. We do not put the vitamins into our diet: we discover and assimilate what is there. So we do not put the glory into the sunrise or "impose our values" on a heroic character: as we grow in grace we discover them. In other words, what we are here concerned with is a response, more or less adequate, richer or poorer, better or worse, to the moral and spiritual realities which are integral factors in our environment—that is, in the end, to the Divine Mind "from whom all good things do come". All goodness is derived and communicated—to be sure of this is the life-blood of religion and the very essence of adoration. In every recognition of value, on however humble a level, mortal men are admitted to communion with the creative goodness of God. For the source and standard of goodness ("absolute value") is in God's holy will and purpose, eternally and completely satisfied within the experience of the divine life, yet still to be realized in the time-process—"on earth as it is in heaven". Ultimately, the meaning of value is that in which God is well pleased.

Thus the subject-matter of Christian moral judgment is really those qualities of spirit which express themselves in what we call our "values" and in the acts in which we embody them. Hence the goal of the Christian moral life lies, as it were, on the other side of the frontier, in Christian worship and adoration. For the Christian, the absolute moral standard is the vision of God in the face of Christ. The demands of the Christian life are never fulfilled on the level of "mere morality". Duty passes over into worship, and thereby transcends itself and is transfigured. Not that moral distinctions are obliterated in an Absolute "beyond good and evil"—that would be the negation of Christian Theism. But that the worship of a holy God, unconditioned in absolute perfection, opens to us such new depths of insight into the meaning and worth of life itself, and the richness, range and searching demands of goodness, that thereby our values are transvalued and we are reborn in a new moral order. It is only as we are thus born again that we can enter into the realm of God.

3. God's Holiness and Christian Values

This somewhat technical discussion may have seemed to the reader a little wearisome. It was, however, a necessary stage in the journey which we are travelling ; and we have thus, I hope, brought our argument to the threshold of what primarily concerns us. Precisely what difference is imported into our moral judgments and attitudes if we accept the Christian form of Theism ? There are many "good" men who do not believe in God : there are many noble and admirable lives which acknowledge no conscious Christian inspiration. Yet we have contended that what is truly implied in the demands and claims of the moral consciousness is only fulfilled in the Christian religion ; and that, within the Christian experience, goodness itself is so clothed upon with new richness and delicacy of colour as to be invested with a changed significance and to evoke new ways of response of life. What is it that works this subtle alchemy on the stuff and substance of our judgments ? How does it effect the transvaluing of our values ? This is the question of crucial importance and the real centre of our investigation.

Goodness is what all men seek after, as that which will satisfy some purpose. The purpose may be limited or temporary, the expression of some minor, local element in our whole psycho-physical constitution—as for example the quenching of thirst. Or it may be what we call our life-purpose. Every such satisfaction of purpose is, within its own limited context, good. Yet with reference to a more embracing claim, in the pattern of a wider and fuller purpose, it may contain so small an amount of goodness as to be a trivial or unworthy object for a man's allegiances and self-consecrations.[1] It is good that a thirsty man should drink. But a "chronic thirst" and a chronic satisfaction of it are commonly held to be incompatible with making the best that can be made of life. That does not mean that the quenching of thirst is evil. Drinking is good, in the context of our instincts. But because this is the context that defines it, it must rank as an elementary grade of goodness. It may have to give way to richer and higher expressions of it, in the light of a more embracing life-purpose and a fuller conception of Man's end and destiny. The positive value of any good that appeals to us seems thus to be relative to its power of satisfying the true possibilities of spirit and enriching our life with its full capacities. The higher the goodness a man achieves, the richer and more unified his character. He may live for the satisfaction of instinct. That is good, so far as it goes: but it satisfies only one element in his nature. Nobody can realise all goodness. A man may be perfectly "good" in the moral sense—i.e. he may be completely virtuous,—by giving himself to the realization of quite rudimentary forms of goodness relatively to his gifts and opportunities. But he may yet remain an incomplete man—less than the man that God wills him to be. The more he understands of God's will, the more of a man (as we say) will he become. And as spirit wakens in responsiveness to the influence of its divine environment, new modes of goodness are disclosed to it, fuller expressions of that will of holiness which is the creative life of the universe and the true Light which ever lighteth every man. "As we rise in the moral scale, under

[1] The position which I am trying to establish here is deeply indebted to Prof. Paton's volume *The Good Will* and to the Master of Balliol for advising me to read it.

the drawing of conceptions of good more and more adequate to sustain intelligent aspiration, living itself steadily takes on more and more a 'form of eternity'. For, in proportion to the level we have attained, each of our achievements becomes more and more the reaction of a personality at once richer and more unified to the solicitation of a good, itself presented as richer and more unified."[1]

That is not to say that goodness changes, in the sense that what is good to-day may become evil to-morrow. Goodness is never anything but good, and never can be, in time or eternity. But as the experience of the race grows, as the life of the individual is trained in depth, range and delicacy of insight, new forms of goodness are disclosed and their claim on us becomes more and more exacting.

As we grow in wisdom and stature so we discover new forms of goodness, into which the lower and more elementary forms have to be taken up and incorporated, or to which (if need be) they must be sacrificed. If we believe that men are sons of God, to glorify God and enjoy Him for ever, that will impart a new depth and tension into our appreciations of goodness. It will imply a transvaluing of our values. It will not deprive the subordinate forms of goodness of that genuine value which belongs to them, as true but rudimentary expressions of God's perfection on their own level. That is the fallacy of religious fanaticism. On the other hand, from the Christian standpoint, to seek goodness only within the context limited by our biological needs, or indeed within any horizons defined only by the time-process, is not only to fail in goodness conceived in any morally worthy way. It is to fall short of the glory of God. So far as any such limitation issues from failure in spiritual insight, from moral inertia or cowardice or from deliberate choice of the easier path, what we choose may not be in itself evil, but we who choose it are guilty of mortal sin.

[1] Taylor, *op. cit.*, p. 100.

It is thus that in the presence of Christ all men know themselves to be sinners. They may fairly claim to be "doing their best", and may even be conscious of no actual wrong-doing. But He comes as a sword-thrust into the heart of life, shattering our contentment and complacency; not merely to make us contrite for our failures but to make us ashamed of our best. When He confronts us, the poverty of our insight and the cheapness of even our highest aspirations is so shamefully and relentlessly exposed as to awaken in us the sense of sin. Our commonplace discernments of goodness are here challenged by the divine holiness. We are in the presence of Goodness itself. And we know that nothing which falls short of that holiness can hold or deserve our ultimate veneration. "Without holiness no man can see God."

Hence, too, the paradox which we meet so often—that the people who seem to be most keenly alive to the need of penitence and divine forgiveness seem, to our superficial standards, to be those who have least to be penitent about. No doubt there are plenty of pathologicals who torment themselves and exhaust their advisers by worrying over imaginary sins. But real saints, whose lives seem to most of us unattainable patterns of holy living, are normally or at least very often spirits clothed in a habit of repentance. To the commonplace judgment this appears irrational. To an awakened spirit it is obvious. The further a man has advanced, by the grace of God, in the recognition of goodness, the clearer his insight into its real demand and the keener his sense of his own unworthiness. The Greek psychology of temptation, as outlined in the *Republic* for example, was surely very wide of the mark here. There is no state that corresponds to *Sophrosyne*. There is no stage in an awakened moral life at which a man ceases to be vulnerable by the seductions of the lower choice. There is nothing which so glaringly exposes the self-centredness of the Greek moral ideal as this bland and rather smug suggestion. The truth is that only the finest souls can realize what temptation really means. It is they alone who are fully sensitive to what is involved in the real claims of goodness and alive to the guilt of the less exacting choice. The classical instance is in the Synoptic Gospels. Jesus alone could have been tempted as He was.

Now this implies, from the Christian standpoint, that a sense of sin is a rather advanced stage in our moral and spiritual experience. There are those who keep on deploring that the modern age suffers from a defective sense of sin. But that is putting the cart before the horse. Its essential need is a living sense of God. You cannot have any genuine sense of sin (in its full religious connotation) until you have seen some vision of God's glory. You may feel remorse or shame or desperation ; you may feel you have forfeited your self-respect, failed your friends or let down a cause ; but you cannot experience a sense of sinfulness without some vital experience of God.

Thus conduct passes into worship, and only thereby is the good life fulfilled. The contemplation of God Himself is the source of moral progress and fruitfulness. It is just not true that the " moral imperative " is self-sufficient and self-explanatory. The tradition which has built up its system on devotion to a sheer moral law has not, in point of fact, been conspicuous either for delicacy of moral insight or for any such genuine humility as must be the condition of growth in goodness. It tends to a rather unlovely moral priggishness. Thus it somehow seems to inhibit the moral integrity which it would claim to safeguard.

It is clear, moreover, that " obeying the dictates of conscience " cannot be a valid formula for the good life. It has justified half the worst crimes of history. Certainly it is in no sense equivalent to the Christian phrase, " doing the will of God ". For there is implied in that will the duty of submitting ourselves to such supernatural influences, and training ourselves in such spiritual aptitudes, as will open to us true, authentic insight into what any situation holds within it when seen from the standpoint of the " mind of Christ ". It is thus that the worship of God Himself is at once the condition and the " great reward " of that consecration to the will of God, in which Christianity finds the meaning of life and the absolute standard of value.

Worship is the fulfilment of the good life. But it is also the creative source of it. " The worship of a holy God saves the soul from premature satisfaction with its partial achievement."[1] There is nothing absolutely and without qualification good save the holy will of our God and Father. All other values are relative : all other goodness is derived. Only in a sharing of that eternal will can finite spirits fulfil their destiny. Thus the implications of the good life can only be brought to complete fruition in consecration to the supernatural. To suppress this otherworldly note would debase all Christian moral standards. Holiness, as we have seen already, and not merely virtue or conscientiousness, is the Christian ideal of character. The good we seek is none other than God Himself.

But this does not mean that we depreciate the genuine though subordinate forms of value which we find on the " natural " levels of experience. Nobody can be always religious ; to attempt it would almost certainly drive us to madness. Few people are able, and probably few should attempt to be always consciously aware of God. Christianity will, I think, be eager to emphasize that, as the created order has been endowed with a certain measure of independence even as against its Creator, so the natural good things in life possess a relative and imparted goodness independently and in their own right. *All* values have their source in God : however humble and elementary, they reflect some radiance

[1] R. Niebuhr, *op. cit.*, p. 51.

from His glory. But we need not be always seeking anxiously for a " religious " justification of the natural and subordinate values. It would, to my mind, be quite inconsistent with the spirit that breathes in the parables to live in this strained and self-conscious attitude. The dreadful advice which a preacher is fabled to have given boys in a public school chapel—" take God with you into the scrum "—seems to me to be really incompatible with the spontaneity of the Christian life.[1] If we demand an ulterior motive for enjoying games or keeping ourselves in health we are making life pietistic and unnatural—and that is surely profoundly un-Christian. To enjoy a game is a good thing to do and it needs no further justification. Yet a man who has reached middle life and is still too much preoccupied with games seems to be rather a pitiable person. He has established psychological harmony by ignoring things of far greater worth. And the Christian ethic will always bid us cultivate a measure of inward detachment even while we frankly enjoy the lesser good things. It is, for example, a sound rule of life that a man ought to cultivate some hobby which he finds so absorbing and enjoyable that he is always tempted to give to it more time and money than he can spare—and always to resist this temptation. And a tension of this kind between two levels of loyalty would appear to be a fruitful analogy of what is involved in the Christian life as at once natural and supernatural.

Once more, traditional morality—even if frankly utilitarian—growing out of social experience and men's actual commerce with life, has its place, not lightly to be repudiated. Honesty *is* the best policy : racial experience has discovered that and, so far as it goes, that truth is valuable. Human life would become a poorer thing if that maxim were set aside.

[1] Cf. the story of a well-known bishop who is said to have exclaimed, on seeing a goal scored, " Surely that shot was richly blessed ". Or was it an ecclesiastical idiom for the more familiar " a d——d good shot " ?

But that needs no Christian justification ; and the attempt which is made too frequently to justify Christian moral standards because they will lead to success in this world—even if this be true, which is highly questionable—is to degrade both religion and ethics. The real point to be urged by Christian ethics is that the accepted values of common-sense often prove to be fatal hindrances to moral and spiritual progress. The standards of reference which they presuppose are but the obvious and immediate standards of their own particular and limited context. But we cannot, in fact, realize the values inherent in any given situation—as parents, citizens or whatever it may be—unless we include the eternal horizons and are seeking to measure by absolute standards. It is the paradox of the moral life that so many obviously good things may prove themselves to be " hardly " reconcilable with what goodness in itself demands. This note sounds clearly enough in Christ's teaching. " How *hardly* shall they that have riches enter into the Kingdom of God." Yet riches are themselves good, not evil.

This recognition supplied the true motive of the mediæval Christian asceticism. Men were then more keenly alive than we are to the moral and spiritual dangers which are lurking in the most innocent and most obviously good relationships. The only safeguard they could devise was to abolish the relationships, and to propose chastity and poverty as the evangelical counsels of perfection. Their problem still remains unsolved. It is easy enough to refute the Manichee. But that rather annoying pose of masculinity, with its affectations about public-houses, which some modern clergy are prone to adopt, is itself witness to some maladjustment, some sense of unfreedom and uneasiness in their whole relation to physical satisfactions. We can only be perfectly free and perfectly " natural " in our acceptance of bodily enjoyment if our spirits are truly at home in the supernatural.

But apart from this, the best things about us, family devotion or loyalty to our country, are themselves fraught with grave moral weaknesses. The more intensely a man cares for his family, the more blind is he prone to be to its imperfections, and the less sensitive to the wider claims of national welfare and public service. And still more obviously on this latter level. The more passionately a man loves his country, the more ardently he desires to advance its welfare, the less alive is he to its limitations, and the less capable of thinking of it as part of a world-wide human community. The ethical attitude of the individual to the group which is the context of the good life for him serves to frustrate its moral fulfilment. It is only loyalty to the absolute standard, a hunger and thirst after God's holiness, which can rescue us from this moral impasse.[1] We cannot be " good " in our family relationships, our citizenship or our daily duties, unless we are endeavouring to be more than " good "—to be conformed to the holy will of God. " Our affections must be set on things above, not on things on the earth," or we shall spoil, frustrate and degrade the most precious things that we know on earth. This bi-polarity of allegiance is of the essence of Christian living.

The distinctiveness of the Christian moral standards depends largely upon this wider context, these eternal and divine horizons which define for us the meaning and worth of Man's life. Goodness is seen in the light of that holy Will which shines on us in the face of Jesus Christ. Within life so interpreted and so appraised new forms of goodness disclose themselves, to compel the re-valuing of our scales of value. There emerge new visions of what goodness may be, out of which are fashioned new qualities of character, and new estimates of worth, bringing with them sterner obligations.

It may serve here to suggest one illustration. If we take the cardinal virtue of Justice—the Greek summary of all

[1] Cf. Niebuhr, *op. cit.*, pp. 88 *sq.*

moral excellence—as an element in the Christian moral ideal, we can see that it is not so much superseded as filled with immeasurably new content, because of the meaning that we find in man's life, as interpreted by the mind of Christ, in the framework of the divine society. "Love" is "Justice" in a transfigured setting. The development of the moral ideal depends largely, as T. H. Green[1] taught, on the widening of the "area of common good"—i.e. of the context within which mutual obligations are recognized. The moral ideal of a savage tribe is outgrown in a civilized community; chiefly because in that wider life there are more human claims to be recognized. What is good for man is seen to be something richer than was understood by the primitive society. Thus the extension of our moral area involves *pari passu* an enrichment in the implications of our moral values. So too, conversely, a clearer insight into the meaning of man's life carries with it a repudiation of all that, whether by design or accident, restricts the area of co-operation. When a man has seen deeply into goodness then the idea of privilege becomes intolerable, and barriers of class, race or government seem to him an affront to human dignity. So it is that St. Paul and all Christian teachers who have seen life through the windows of the mind of Christ can assert that in Him all barriers are down. In Christ there can be neither Jew nor Greek, male nor female, bond nor free.

But this recognition must transfigure our whole conception of what "right" conduct implies. "Who is my neighbour?" is the crucial question which controls all estimates of our duty. The idea of justice plainly illustrates this. If justice means to render to all their dues, then if we ask what is due to others, the answer depends partly on our estimate of the needs and capacities of human nature, and partly also on the range of neighbourhood within which we admit mutual obligation. Christianity revises both these

[1] *Prolegomena to Ethics*, Book III, Chap. III.

estimates; and the process of re-valuation brings to light such new facts and standards that Justice itself is filled with a new content. In a society resting on privilege men may regard the slaves and manual workers or some oppressed racial minority, as little more than "living tools" or animals. They do not come within the area of neighbourhood and no human claims are accorded to them. By this standard the most that can be "due" to them from the dominant class is a subsistence wage. When they come to be recognized as neighbours, their rights—that is, their claims on others—are seen to include the means for developing the fullest life of which they are capable. What before would have been thought generous will now be understood to be barely just. When men are seen in the light of eternity, there appear yet new standards of measurement. For if a man is a member of Christ's family, if he is an inheritor of the Kingdom of Heaven, a potential citizen of the divine society, and capable of communion with God, and if this is his claim to be reckoned as my neighbour; then what is due to him can be nothing less than all that can help to equip him for that vocation.

Thus Christianity clothes the term Justice with an immeasurably enriched significance. It will not be content with the overthrow of privilege and a real respect for the rights of backward peoples; though both of these are ahead of current standards. It will rather insist that if God so loved the world; if a man is worth that in the sight of God; if the Spirit can evoke such qualities out of very average human nature as are the commonplaces of human history; then a man's due has never been rendered him till Society has helped him to realize all the goodness for which God designed him. On that level Justice is so transmuted as to be more truly described as redemptive love.

This is but one obvious example of the ways in which, within the Christian context, new forms of excellence manifest themselves, bringing new claims and obligations. It is in this way that Christianity evokes, and raises high in its scale of honour, attitudes and qualities of character which are little esteemed in the context of the world. These are the characteristic "fruits of the Spirit".

This illustration may serve to suggest how the Christian interpretation of life, in its true context and with its eternal background, elicits new insight into goodness, enriching our conception of God's will with ever fuller and more concrete meaning, and thereby transvalues all values. How this can be worked out in practice, how Christian values can be vindicated in some actual moral situations, we shall have to suggest in the following chapters.

But meanwhile we have reached a position from which we can at least see our way towards the solution of our earlier problem. Is religion co-extensive with the whole of life? In what way may it be claimed that Christianity can offer the world such moral guidance as will unify, redeem and direct the whole complex life of the twentieth century? It is clear by this time how we shall answer that. Christianity is a religion: and religion, though it is mutually involved in all the other activities of spirit, penetrating, transforming and sanctifying, must not itself be confused with any of them. Their autonomy must be respected. Thus, for example, Christianity must not attempt to impose any limits on freedom of intellectual enquiry or to ask for any particular conclusions. It must not suggest that a Christian education is committed to any other hypothesis in Biology, Physics, or even History, than those which these sciences themselves demand. It must not say that a vitalist hypothesis is "more Christian" than a biochemical. There is no such thing as a Christian Biology. There is just Biology. And in so far as a Biologist pursues it honestly, seeking truth without fear or favour, he is doing God's will in his own particular province.

Von Hügel used to insist upon this with an almost monotonous reiteration, as in the following characteristic sentences. "The creature is not the Creator either in quantity or quality; it is not a little god; and yet though it is indefinitely lesser, the Creator respects the inferior and different nature. Even so science and all the departments of life are not religion, or to be absorbed in it, or to be anything but as scrupulously reverenced by religion as would be a bevy of young women by some strong mature man." To recognize this, said the Baron in the same letter, was Eucken's most fruitful contribution. "If you ask Has not religion to do with everything? Eucken would answer: Most certainly. Does it not embrace everything? He would say: Yes and no. Yes, if by religion you mean here a motive so all-embracing as to make you respect the various laws immanent in all the various departments of life. No, if you mean a set of laws or motives which can be taken as the simple regulators and commanders of these other laws. Hence religion will have to come to see that it cannot attain to its own depth, it cannot become the *chief thing*, if it does not continually renounce aspiring after being *everything*."[1]

Thus Christianity vindicates its claim to be coterminous with life in all its range of interest and activity, not by attempting to dictate to the other, non-religious activities—æsthetic, scientific or technical—but by inspiring a new attitude to all of them. It does this both as a coherent world-view (based upon its own experience of God) and as a redemption of men's appreciations.

1. On the one hand it offers a synoptic view. It will not seek religious or moral lessons in the findings of the departmental sciences; but it will remind them that it is often easier to understand what a tree means if you see it in the whole pattern of the wood. It means more seen in that context than if you consider it in isolation. It then becomes

[1] *Letters*, pp. 93–94.

part of a larger scheme of things; and you cannot truly interpret anything except in the light of the whole of which it is part. And this may involve reconsideration of the "laws" which are thought to apply to the part—just as the laws of chemical reaction have to be revised or stated differently when they are studied on the biological level. The same will apply to the technical factors which enter into most of our moral judgments. Thus the phrase Christian Economics, so much beloved in Copec circles, immediately provokes the rejoinder: "There are no Christian economics any more than there is a Christian geometry." In one sense that is a perfectly true statement. No amount of Christian aspiration can make two straight lines enclose a space; nor if consumption exceeds production will Christianity save us from bankruptcy. Economic laws must be respected; but that does not mean that they are the only laws which are operative even in economic life. Christianity will insist that Man's life is part of a divine-human pattern, in which economics have a rightful place: but it cannot allow that they are independent of the social, moral and æsthetic concerns which are equally integral to human nature. And this may involve a different reading of what is implied in economic law when subsumed under laws of wider application. The same consideration will hold of judicial, medical or any other laws, regarded as elements in moral judgments. On the technical factors involved Christians, as such, have no competence to decide; yet the technical factors are themselves gifts of God and disclosures of His will as operative in the created order. They are therefore to be welcomed with reverence as held within the will of God for His world—not as so many obstacles to be overcome, but rather as opportunity and material for the working out of Christian solutions. There is surely a very hopeful field for mutual counsel and co-operation between the technical experts on the one hand and the representatives and custodians of Christian moral values on the other. This might be done on a quite small scale in almost any parish in England with reference to some particular moral issue. Nothing would give more sense of confidence in Christianity as no mere Utopian sentimentality. Few things would help more to deliver Christians from a spineless and amateurish pietism.

2. But even more important than this, because it is applicable to all Christians, however ignorant and however humble, is the contribution of Christianity in the clarification of our insight. In approaching the question : What is our duty ? or (to put the same thing in different words) : What is the best we can do with this situation ? the Christian will bring his own scales of measurement. If a man's heart is indeed right with God he will find *more* in a given situation —richer possibilities of goodness and therefore more searching claims and obligations—than are revealed to the worldly mind. To make the most that you can of life is excellent advice for a young man, even if not startlingly original. But it moves on an entirely different level from the injunction : "Ye shall be perfect even as your Father in heaven is perfect." To the life that is hid with Christ in God, the surrendered heart and dedicated mind, there are disclosed such deeper and richer insights into what is contained within the will of God as are not apparent to the children of this world. Hence, first and last, the Christian ethic is dependent upon the Christian religion as the source and safeguard of its specific values. " Be not conformed to this world but transformed by the renewing of your minds *that you may prove what is the will of God*, that good, acceptable and perfect thing."

PART II

CHAPTER VIII

THE FAMILY

1. The Christian Values at Stake

THE Englishman's home used to be his castle. In modern life it is coming to be regarded as somewhere to sleep next door to the garage. How can it be made into a home again ? This is the most searching moral issue that Christianity to-day has to face. If we wish to try out in practical application the theory which we have attempted to establish, here is the obvious field of investigation. For here pre-eminently is the situation in which the natural good is fully realized only by partaking in the supernatural. Moreover, the moral and social bewilderment of the modern world centres on the family. Here is the ganglion of all those new reactions, economic, psychological and moral, which the Christian ethic is forced to encounter. The weakening of the Christian belief and the disintegration of the family seem to be mutually involved together. Here the Christian faith is on trial at the very heart and nerve centre of the world's ethical and religious problem. For it is probably true on the whole that the religious and moral scepticism which is paralysing our contemporaries is due less to intellectual solvents than to the seeming failure of home life. The modern man thinks he has been betrayed in the citadel of his inmost personal intimacies. Bertrand Russell no doubt exaggerates when he asserts that in nine cases out of ten the relations between children and parents are a source of unhappiness to both parties. He must have moved and formed his social judgments in a sombrely monochrome environment. But he is, I believe, profoundly right in saying that " the failure of the family to provide the fundamental satisfactions which in principle it is capable of yielding is one of the most deep-seated causes of the discontent prevalent in our age ".[1] If the world is to recover moral mastery it is here that Christianity must help it.

We cannot escape from the twentieth century, or think to heal its hurts by " deploring " them, like undergraduates' debating societies. We have to deal with facts as they are. The primary moral issue of our time is the rehabilitation of family life as the home of free, rich, spontaneous living as against the intimidation of the State, the pressure of depersonalizing forces and the anæmia of mediocrity. This, as the Bishops at Lambeth truly said, is " a supreme interest of the Christian Church ". But we find ourselves now in a totally new position. Such phrases as " the sanctity of home life " are irritating more than informative. They do not ring with the tones of authority, since there is so much in the modern temper which repudiates the idea presupposed in them. The sanctity is what has to be rediscovered. And much more than that, the Christian Church is itself adrift in uncharted waters. It must now steer its way through perilous seas without the guidance of familiar landmarks. Here is, indeed, the crucial case in which the Church is compelled to face the question how far it possesses an ethic of its own. Can it meet the challenge in the open ? For the Christian standards here are hard pressed. It is taken for granted by our modern prophets that the Christian ideal is hopelessly discredited. The domestic virtues of the Victorians seem to the young false as well as funny. Contemporary drama and fiction assume that conjugal fidelity

[1] *The Conquest of Happiness*, p. 186.

involves a dismal, repressed existence of joyless suburban domesticity. All our standards are tumbling round us.

The present situation is intolerable. Everybody who thinks at all seriously is alive to the need for some valid standards. "Love has its own proper ideals and its own intrinsic moral standards. These are obscured both in Christian teaching and in the indiscriminate revolt against all sexual morality which has sprung up amongst considerable sections of the younger generation."[1] The misunderstanding and misinterpretation of the whole Christian outlook on the question which is so flagrant in Earl Russell seems to be common to all the "advanced" writers. They seem to agree only in these points, an invincible ignorance of Christianity and a conviction that the Christian ethic seeks to preserve irrational taboos from which free men demand emancipation. The Christian rejoinder must not be shocked or shrill. The Church must set forth its own philosophy as its own constructive contribution : and then the world must make up its mind. We have thus to ask how far is it possible in the changed conditions of the twentieth century for the Christian ethic to offer convincing guidance for the rebuilding of the family.

I prefer to put the question in that way. We shall do well to avoid the familiar *cliché* about "Christianity and sex". Not only because it is an exhausted *cliché* but because it makes a thoroughly false suggestion, that this one aspect of the whole relationship is a peculiar challenge to Christianity, which is chiefly concerned with holding it in check. That this suggestion is false, needs no emphasis. It has been the *damnosa hereditas* of far too much Christian moral teaching, which has always been prone to identify sin with concupiscence, in the sense of sexual desire.[2] But this is a relic of

[1] B. Russell, *Marriage and Morals*, p. 103.

[2] "The King Charles head which has obsessed so many speculators on the problem of evil in man." N. P. Williams, *The Ideas of the Fall and Original Sin*, p. 66 : cf. also pp. 34, 155, 304 *sq.*

primitive taboo, which dies hard even in modern Christianity. Perhaps it is kept alive artificially by what seems to me to be the disastrous practice of giving such prominence to "straight talks" in preparing adolescents for confirmation. It is clear in any case that our moral teaching has failed in the past through being so largely negative. It has stressed too much the avoidance of sexual sin, reinforced by appeals to self-interest based on the supposed results of wrong-doing. Apart from the question of sub-Christian motives, such arguments are no longer possible *because they are known to be true no longer*. It is just not true that your sin will find you out, at least in any crude and obvious sense. You can purchase immunity at a small cost. That line of attack must now be abandoned, and that is all to the good from the Christian standpoint. The question must now be discussed on its merits as a moral and spiritual issue, unclouded either by fear or favour. It is not how to avoid doing wrong that is the chief interest of Christianity, but how to attain the best life and make the most of it.

We need a philosophy of the whole question seen in its widest and richest context. Most of the professed solutions fail because they isolate one or another of the delicate and far-reaching relationships which are involved in the life of the family. For the family is the achievement in little of all that human society seeks to be. No thinking about it will be true which ignores any factor in this complex. We must see it as woven into the whole pattern of man's life and his eternal destiny. One may study it from the standpoint of biology, or of economics or of sociology. But none of these views will be realistic unless it also includes all the others; and unless it be remembered that man is not merely a civilized animal nor a moralized social being, but that he is also an immortal spirit with a soul to save and a destiny to realize. Christianity must always be suspicious of any too simple solutions. It must set itself against such proposals as offer harmony at too low a level. It will thus regard from its own detached standpoint most of the current philosophies of the family and most of the current popular proposals which are offered by the new morality; not because they offend the prejudices of clergymen, but because they are in fact untrue to the delicacy and richness of the subject-matter.

It is fatally easy for matter-of-fact ethics to offer solutions which are superficial because they thus over-simplify the data. And these Christianity cannot but reject. Thus (1) we shall fail to discuss the question adequately if we think solely in terms of the family as a self-contained and self-sufficient group, torn out of its wider social context. For it only comes to its own true fulfilment as a creative and redemptive force in the social order of which it forms part. It is clear that intense devotion to his family may hold a man back from the wider claims of his citizenship. It may be that some sense of tension between the immediate and the remoter loyalty is essential to the ripening of both of them. In any case the tension is felt; and it is an impoverished attitude to the family which is blind to this wider social reference. There are no short-term solutions and no short cuts. So far as the family fails to pass over into the fuller relations of society, its potential values remain partly unrealized.

(2) On the other hand it is equally fallacious so to insist on the wider reference as to make light of the immediate intimacies. Communists have always been sensitive to the clash between family devotion, as the nurse of personal individuality, and the needs of the collectivist state. They have sought to adjust an imperfect relationship by abolishing one of the terms to be related. It has not, however, proved true in practice that to weaken family allegiance has strengthened the ties of civic obligation. The family is the school of civic virtues. And this should warn us against

a like tendency which can be traced in contemporary discussions, to consider family life and what is implied in it from a purely sociological point of view. It is not hard to be so preoccupied with the social necessity of eugenic breeding, or again with the family group as the unit of consumption or production, as to ignore the specific worth and preciousness of the inner life of the family itself. But if these rich values evaporate, then in effect we shall have destroyed the family, together with all its possible social significance.

(3) Once more, thinking may be so much concentrated on the rights and privileges of the two partners and what is best for their health and happiness as to ignore the claims of their children. This is a flagrantly one-sided attitude and we are in full reaction against it. But it is possible to be so concerned with the rights and claims of the children as to overbalance on the opposite side. We rightly assume as a fundamental axiom that it is wrong for children to be born to parents who (for whatever reason) are unable to give them a fair chance in life. "Bad" parents, we say, ought not to have children. Yet we must not allow ourselves to forget the redemptive influence of children on parents who seem to be otherwise beyond redemption.

(4) The pattern is thus much more subtle and intricate than is realized by common-sense ethics. But to these general considerations Christianity adds its own sovereign principles. No thought about the family can be true which thinks merely in terms of this world. Man is made for life eternal; and all social groupings and relationships must therefore fall short of their real significance if they are not so constituted and ordered as to school men for that eternal destiny. The family, in its Christian conception, is an incarnation of life eternal. Hence even into its best and dearest intimacies Christian thinking will introduce a certain note of detachment and distance. 'I could not love thee, dear, so much, loved I not honour more." True Christian

thought will go beyond this. It will see that love is only made perfect if the lovers love God even more than one another. Christ Himself is lovely and adorable in His genial appreciation of the values and sanctities of the family. Yet that other note cannot be muted if we are to be true to His mind: there are times when a man must "hate" his family, not because it is not good in itself, but to sanctify it in the perfect Good.

Thus, if we would think creatively and usefully, we must eschew short-term propositions. I do not know any better summary of the way Christianity regards the matter than this admirable sentence: "In what special ways can the family help us to prepare for life in the world and for everlasting life, for a realization of that in ourselves which is the key to our relation to a present that grows out of the past and leads to the future?"[1]

In this matter the younger men and women are left lamentably without guidance. Yet here are the most momentous decisions which any of them are called upon to face. Other big issues can be left, however foolishly and irresponsibly, to professional politicians and economists. This cannot: it presses on them personally: it is for them all the imperative moral issue. Most of the talk and all the denunciation comes at present from people over sixty. The doing, and most of the suffering for mistakes, fall on people under thirty. The weight of Christian responsibility rests, therefore, chiefly on their shoulders; for they alone can discover the way out. Not every utterance of bachelor clerics, safe in harbour beyond the age of passion, is necessarily to be accepted as oracular.

We must ask, therefore, what considerations the Christian ethic will rightly invite the younger men and women to bear in mind in embarking upon this urgent moral enterprise.

[1] Mrs. A. D. Lindsay in *Christianity and the Present Moral Unrest*, p. 176.

There is no ready or cut-and-dried solution. They can find their answer only by experiment. For the old conventions no longer hold now, and to try to revive them would be futile. They have lost their compulsive social force and (in the minds of the rising generation) most of their claim to inward allegiance. They were secured partly by subterfuges, partly by keeping women "in their place"—i.e. economically dependent and intellectually undeveloped. That age is past. Economic causes, such as the break-up of domestic industries and the entry of women into the wage market, have no doubt been largely responsible; though Christianity is surely entitled to claim at least a contributory influence. Inevitably this transitional period in the rightful emancipation of women is bound to be difficult and experimental. At its worst, it involves a new claim by women to imitate the vices of men. Even at its best it calls imperatively for creative insight and readjustment. Unless we can help them to find a constructive attitude our younger contemporaries will soon find themselves drowned in that flood of fierce, crude hedonism which is washing over from across the Atlantic. If Christian standards are to be re-created it can be only by commending themselves freely to the reason as well as the feelings of the rising generation.

Changes of habit and fashion do not matter much. Christianity is not necessarily committed to any particular social convention. We are not concerned with mere respectability, which has lately been described with some justice as one of the seven deadly virtues. What we are concerned with is the Christian ideal: the particular legislation or conventions by which that is expressed or supported are, after all, of secondary importance. There is thus no need for Christian people to oppose the demand for changes in the marriage law. It would seem too obvious to need much argument that the existing laws do need changing; and it is not a concern of Christianity to make people unhappier than they need be. In the political and social circumstances in which modern Christianity finds itself, Christian opinion is certainly not justified in attempting to force upon the Statute Book laws which Christians themselves regard as binding. It is doubtful, indeed, whether the Christian principles are well served by legislative sanctions even within the Christian society. This may read like a plea for moral anarchy: but it is, I think, much more consistent with the real genius of the Christian spirit to throw moral choices and decisions quite relentlessly back on individuals. The Christian way of life is an Honour School—not merely guaranteeing a minimum standard, which is what all sound legislation aims at, but ambitious for the achievement of an optimum. The question thus turns upon the nature of that optimum. What ideal should Christians try to realize, at the cost if need be even of heavy sacrifice to their personal desires?

For without willingness to face such sacrifice no fruitful solution is conceivable. All the current talk about instinct and the supposed dangers of repressing it, would be bound to result, if acted out consistently, in making any civilized life impossible. It is the voice of an atavistic barbarism. Society is unthinkable at any level without the constructive, voluntary repression of at least the more violent anti-social instincts. The Cross, after all, stands at the centre of any living attempt at community life. "The beginning of culture," as Malinowski says, "implies the repression of instincts, and all the essentials of the Œdipus complex or any other complex are necessary by-products in the gradual formation of culture."[1] That refreshing cold bath of sanity is tonic in our Freudianized climate. It keeps the problem at its proper temperature. For Christianity, like all sane thinking, at least has sense enough to insist that the special problems bound up with sex are insoluble in a strained and feverish atmosphere. Sex finds its level naturally and

[1] Quoted by Dawson, *Christianity and Sex*, p. 19.

quietly in a general scheme of disciplined, ordered living: it bursts through the dams and rages uncontrollably where the general attitude to life is one of emotional, unrestricted effusiveness. That, unfortunately, is the atmosphere which tends now to invest the whole discussion People are thus more likely to take it seriously if they refuse to exaggerate its importance. Nothing is more fatal to right thinking than the tense, violent, furtive way of approach which Bertrand Russell has called " bootlegged sex ". On the other hand, it is only cool thinking which can avail to deliver the younger people from their present day obsession with this problem, as though it were the supreme fact in life. It is worth showing how wide is the range of activity and interest in a sane life in which sex plays no recognizable part. To be obsessed with this fragment of experience is bound to make life hectic and unbalanced—thin and joyless if marriage comes, sterile and embittered if it does not.

The frank, open and natural companionship which now prevails between the two sexes seems to offer this generation such a chance as the world has never yet had of finding its way to a genuine solution.

The worst enemy of sane relationships between men and women in our day is the romantic attitude to love. Intense as may be the moth's desire for the star, it throws little light on our problem. It is rather lacking in exact analogy. It is this unreal sentimentalism, this thought of a love that can never be satisfied, an exalted bliss for ever unattainable, yet to be sought for in momentary raptures, which fatally vitiates the whole discussion. It is a survival of chivalric notions. But the preacher's appeal to the " knightly ideals of chivalry " points the young to a highly dubious precedent. The fair lady to whom the knight owed fealty was in fact always somebody else's wife! As Huizinga's brilliant chapters remind us, " marriage had little to do with love ".[1]

[1] *Op. cit.*, p. 113. See especially Chapters VIII and IX.

Marriage, in mediæval society, was a matter-of-fact business arrangement: " love " was a fiction of courtly society. The romantic appeal consisted in just the fact that it was illicit and unattainable. Dante spiritualized such love: but not Petrarch nor any other. Christianity tried to Christianize eroticism by throwing the cloak of religious consecration over the knightly orders and courts of love: but the smile remained on the face of the tiger. It was one of the worst mistakes the Church made.

" Erotic thought," as Huizinga remarks, " never acquires literary value save by some process of transfiguration of complex and painful reality into illusionary forms."[1] The world of the mediæval romances was imaginatively compacted out of such illusions. But a passion fed by romantic siren-songs is hardly the bond of such a realistic and enduring human relationship as the twentieth century needs to establish. Yet it is this literary convention, gathering all that love holds or promises into one burning point of rapture, which (in a cruder and less refined form) is the great illusion of our contemporaries. It goes without saying that to make an ideal of what is in fact a phantasy of day dreams is the surest way of making life unsatisfactory. It is strange that an age which takes Freud as its prophet should so blind itself to the " principle of reality ". For it is assumed in most current literature that this phantasy of illicit love is something in itself more pure and holy, more sublime and more genuinely " spiritual " than a mere suburban compatibility. The former has all the romantic values; the latter is held to be something grey and dingy.

Love, in most of our contemporary literature, means quite avowedly sexual desire. This is part and parcel of that enormous fallacy which tends so to interpret our inner life as to make it a " collection of separate impulses, each of which can attain its private satisfaction ".[2] Thus the gratification

[1] *Op. cit.*, p. 99

[2] Lippmann, *op. cit.*, p. 306.

of one instinct is isolated from the whole rich complex of bodily, mental and spiritual experience within which it plays its rightful part. That is what Christianity repudiates. This is not a matter of arbitrary conventions imposed upon the young by the middle-aged. It depends upon our conception of human nature. Christianity takes account of all the facts. It certainly does justice to the life of instinct, which is (says the Prayer Book) implanted in us by God. It is good to satisfy sexual desire: to suggest that it is unholy is not Christian. But this goodness is but one element in the goodness realizable by man: if it is so attained as to exclude other and higher elements in goodness, then its realization is positively evil. A man attains to his full stature only so far as biological impulses are woven as one strand into the pattern of his whole psycho-physical constitution, and his own individual life is woven into the fabric of society. Love is a self-giving of the *whole* man; and therefore it must involve some inhibitions upon the crude impulses of some parts of him. Nor can it ever be fully realized either by himself or by anyone else, save by willingness to submit himself to such restrictions, standards and loyalties as make any form of social life possible. This is what a "good man" will wish to do; and this is the moral basis of monogamy. Christianity, of course, goes further. If Man is indeed made in the image of God, if in communion with his God and Father he attains the real fulfilment of his being, then love, as a self-giving of the whole man, is lifted into the eternal order and becomes shared communion in the Spirit. This is the Christian ideal of marriage. Thus, as is well known, the New Testament banished *Eros* from its vocabulary and coined (or perhaps re-minted) the word *Agape* to describe the Christian interpretation of love. Our age is busily re-enthroning *Eros,* and not only in Piccadilly Circus.

This is a disastrous psychological fallacy: how widespread it is and how fallacious, the whole apparatus of modern life bears witness. The whole atmosphere of our society is drenched and saturated with sexuality. The Stage, the Film, the Novel and the daily Press are preoccupied with crude sex-appeal. All the massed suggestions that play upon them are such as to lead boys and girls to imagine that this is the main interest of adult life. And yet, to judge by the tone of the stage and fiction, zest and enjoyment in this preoccupation are fast giving way to cynical satiety. " The contemporary love story opens cheaply and ends in dispute or dull resignation."[1] The very titles of Aldous Huxley's novels, those brilliant mirrors of this aspect of life, supply in themselves speaking commentaries. *Barren Leaves*, *Brief Candles* : the titles are quite admirably adapted to that mood of disgusted, wistful disillusionment, to which their author gives such masterly expression. People who despise and distrust love are becoming sceptical about life. This hardly suggests a creative attitude.

But in fact this whole line of approach is false. It is wrong, not because it is not " respectable ", but because it deals in illusions, not in facts. Love, in the sense of romantic literature, is a rapturous moment of exaltation succeeded by either remorse or boredom. Love as Christianity understands it is a thing that grows through mutual companionship, shared interests and common sacrifices, into a union of personalities.

" The emotion of love is not self-sustaining ; it endures only when the lovers love many things together and not merely one another. It is this understanding that love cannot successfully be isolated from the business of living which is the enduring wisdom of the institution of marriage."[2] It is largely failure to appreciate this which underlies the contemporary attitudes. There is, I suppose, no serious

[1] H. G. Wells, quoted by Streeter, *Adventure*, p. 85.

[2] Lippmann, *op. cit.*, pp. 308–309. Far and away the best part of the book.

thinker who would advocate the removal of all restraints. No one who considers the welfare of society can acquiesce in complete sexual anarchy. The advanced writers like Earl and Lady Russell, and Judge Lindsey in the United States, are trying to make a serious contribution from the standpoint of real human happiness. They admit the responsibility of parenthood, which, indeed, they desire to rescue from the moral chaos of promiscuity. They emphasize that where children are born there the parents must continue to live together until the children no longer need them. What they are seeking is some effective compromise which will reconcile the rearing of families, with its social and civic responsibilities, with the wayward desires of the average sensual man. Thus the attempt is made to differentiate between " love " in its romantic sense and parenthood, as the sharing of a home. The so-called companionate marriage rests on this psychological foundation. For this very reason it is built on sand. But we cannot dismiss the idea by scornful phrases. Christianity, I feel sure, must reckon with the growing doubt in the mind of this generation whether the procreation of children really is the primary aim of marriage. People do not think that this is as axiomatic as the Bishops and the marriage service say it is. I shall have to return to this point a little later. But meanwhile, when parenthood is in question, how can it be seriously supposed that people can share in that common enterprise on a basis of mutual infidelity ? Whether Christian marriage should always involve parenthood is a question needing a great deal of discussion. But parenthood without love and joy and delight in mutual acceptance is precisely the ideal of a stud farm. It is even biologically dysgenic. For what hope is there of successful issue where children are born out of a sense of duty ? Christianity knows more about human nature.

It is sometimes thought that the Christian attitude is expressed by saying that marriages are "made in heaven". Christianity is not so sentimental. Its feet stand in the world of life: it does not lose its head in nebulous sentiments. Face to face with the romantic attitude the Christian ethic is far more realistic. Its claim on human nature is more exacting, but it knows more clearly what it is dealing with. Thus, for example, it is fully aware that while marriage ought to be made by love yet it often happens that love is made by marriage. It therefore admits the "avoidance of fornication" as a ground for matrimony which it can acknowledge, though of course it will always hope for more than this. For it knows, being fairly old and wise and much concerned with average men and women, that the romantic standpoint is false. It is sure from its own experience of life, both in its splendours and its humiliations, that the so-called realism of modern writers moves in a world which is only half real because it includes only half the facts. It knows at least that experience is cumulative, that Man is compact of instinct and of spirit, and that love is not a momentary excitement but a plant that grows in a life-long companionship. Thus the indissolubility of marriage is a vital element in the Christian conception of love.

There is no need to be obscurantist here or more rigorous than Christ Himself would be. Obviously there must be machinery for dealing sensibly with breakdowns.[1] We must not give grounds for the suggestion that the Church is barking up the wrong tree. The first interest of Christian ethics is not to prevent people from getting unmarried: it is rather to help them to get married rightly. The current proposals about trial marriage which are really, I suppose, recrudescences of the old folk custom of legal betrothal, have at least this much justification, that they are designed to serve an end which is of the greatest importance to morality. But it is not likely that they would work out that way. For

[1] See pp. 230–236.

if a marriage can be dissolved at the first disappointment or disagreement, how can its success be estimated at all? Its chance of surviving the incidental strains largely depends on the fact that the two partners both know that they have made their contract " for better for worse, till death us do part ", and that therefore they must weather the storms together. The psychology of marriage is thus quite different from that of any experimental union. It matters profoundly to the Christian ethic that people should not fall into marriage casually. Far more thought has to be exercised on the best ways of helping men and women to choose their partners wisely and hopefully. But that method we cannot recommend, because the so-called " trial run " is in fact the trial of an entirely different engine.

But we cannot dismiss the suggestion in this airy way. The Christian society itself should feel a vivid sense of responsibility towards those of its members who are facing the most momentous of Christian enterprises. No more than the State does the Church discharge its function if it is content merely to hold the ring, to applaud the victors and punish the defeated. It must at the best be a true partner in an undertaking which concerns vitally the health and wealth of the whole body. And at the worst, where there is defeat and failure, the Church is there to redeem and restore, not merely to regulate the damages. The ideal towards which we should be working is one which it is singularly hard to keep free from the taint of priggishness and patronage. Moreover, when the affairs of a family are controlled by well-meaning people outside then it is something else, not a family. Nevertheless, just as in a decent family all " care " for what concerns each, yet without interference or inquisition, so it should be in each Christian group. It is really committed to every betrothal as much as the State is committed to every contract. And the parties should be able to feel that its prayers and sympathies are with them, enriching their joys and sustaining their difficulties, helping them steer round the dangerous curves. Yet modern writers lose all sense of proportion about this question of unhappy marriages. Anyone who took current literature as a true reflection of Western life would conclude that since about 1927 no married life in England has been happy, and that the normal family is a storm-centre of hatreds, discords and inhibitions. One would like to know how many of these writers have ever been guests in a Christian home, such as they would find in thousands all over England ? If they were, it would mitigate their headlines.

Failures there must be, and they must be rightly dealt with. But the question put by the world to Christianity is rather How can we hope for real success ? Indeed the whole climate of this age is, as Thornton Wilder has grasped, strangely like that of the late provincial Hellenism.

" It seemed [to Pamphilus] that the whole world did not consist of rocks and trees and water, nor were human beings garments and flesh, but all burned like the hillside of olive trees with the perpetual flames of love, a sad love that was half hope, often rebuked and waiting to be reassured of its truth. But why, then, a love so defeated, as though it were waiting for a voice to come from the skies declaring that there lay the secret of the world ? . . . His heart suddenly declared to him that a sun would rise, and before that sun the timidity and the hesitation would disappear."[1]

That is the great liberation of Christianity. It draws the individual life within the pattern of a divine scheme, at the heart of which is victorious love, creative, redemptive and undefeated. There is the rhythm to which life must conform and in conforming find its fulfilment. We cannot be atomists in our thinking, either about ourselves or about our relationships : otherwise what is the meaning of " Our Father " ? The pattern of life is the Great Society, at once

[1] *The Woman of Andros*, p. 46.

temporal and eternal, instinctive and spiritual, divine and human. Men and women partake in eternity so far as they form part of that Community, penetrated, enriched and transformed by sharing in spiritual reality, the physical sustaining the life of Spirit, the life of Spirit redeeming the physical, within the mutual responsibility of the whole family of God. Thus the Christian home is not a mere synonym for a commonplace, virtuous domesticity. It is, as the Christian Church claims, a sacrament of human relationships in their ideal—at once the symbol and instrument of redemption through the Love Divine.

2. New Data for a Christian Ethic

But if this ideal is to be accepted, there are various concrete considerations, due to the present condition of society, to which the exponents of Christian ethics must give some searching and courageous attention. If this chapter is not to become a volume we must be content to mention a few of these and to indicate some line of approach to them.

1. The circumstances of industrialized society introduce into family relationships some new and disturbing economic factors. These are bound to affect in various ways both our moral judgments and our social standards. Thus, first, the age of economic maturity does not synchronize with the biological. It must be faced that early marriage is becoming increasingly difficult, and, as things are, probably undesirable. This at once gives rise to those situations from which it is proposed to find a way out by the so-called companionate marriage. The suggestion has been much misrepresented and many of the attacks which are made on it proceed either from ignorance or unfairness. Judge Lindsey repeats again and again that he is not advocating "trial" marriages. He is merely trying to find a sane remedy, within the circumference of established custom, for a wrong which threatens to become

scandalous, and is making havoc of countless lives. There are various different forms of the proposal, but they are in essentials the same. Judge Lindsey, Earl and Countess Russell, Mrs. Sanger and many others would all agree on the central idea. It is that young people whose means do not permit of setting up home together should yet be rescued both from promiscuity and from social and psychological disaster, by being united in lawful wedlock on a " companionate " basis. That is to say, they are to be instructed in reliable contraceptive methods and to live together as man and wife ; so long as no child is born or expected either party may obtain divorce, without stigma and without alimony. Meanwhile they will each earn their own living ; the wife will not be dependent on her husband. Thus their love will attain its satisfaction unfrustrated by economic pressure and without danger to society.

This proposal is seriously intended : it should not be answered by mere abuse. There is little doubt that many young couples will try the experiment along some such lines. And that they should do so may be far better than the merely promiscuous sex life which existing conditions too often foster. It is also a strength in this suggestion that it does emphasize very strongly the civic responsibilities of parenthood. Once there are children born of the union then the two parties must make a home and live together so long as the children need them. The " companionate " union has then become " procreative " and must submit to those disciplines involved in the changed situation.

The notorious confusion of marriage laws among the different States in the Union has at least one considerable advantage. It allows various social experiments to be tried out in an " isolated " medium, without exposing the whole national life to their dangers and unsettlements. It is arguable that it might be a good thing for human welfare if the " companionate " were given a trial by the legislature of

Denver, Colorado. It is, significantly enough, in Russia that a fully developed form of the system is already actually in operation. "Under the Russian system, with birth control and free divorce, all marriages are trial marriages, all matings are companionate matings".[1] And it must be remembered that the avowed object of this gigantic adventure in Communism is the supersession of the family. It is almost as certain as anything that this is how the proposal would work out. Grant the sincerity of those who advocate it; grant also that some such regulation is to be preferred, socially and morally, to the chaos which it aims at superseding; it remains that the system could hardly fail to destroy the life of the family altogether. It cannot be a lasting solution. It seems to offer a kind of social harmony; but it is at too dangerously low a level. It is hopelessly vitiated, from our standpoint, by its perilous over-simplification. It isolates "love", as sexual desire, from the responsibilities and sacrifices involved in the sharing of a permanent home. And this, though it may do something to accommodate the appetites of the average sensual man to what is demanded by social well-being, can never do justice to love itself. We have seen that to isolate love from the whole context of social experience is a certain way to making it insecure.

But perhaps the most permanently important element in the companionate proposal is this attempt to disengage love from its traditional economic network. We are here in touch with a new system of forces which are bound to make an exceedingly heavy impact on established moral judgments and institutions. "The entire world is moving," says Mr. Hindus, "not away from but in the direction of the goal which Russia has achieved."[2] There are many tendencies

[1] M. Hindus, *Humanity Uprooted* (New York, Jonathan Cape and Harrison Smith, 1929), p. 131. I have drawn again on this brilliant book in the subsequent chapters.

[2] *Op. cit.*, p. 138. This paragraph owes much to this stimulating chapter on the subject.

in the modern West, working for the most part unnoticed towards those ends and those valuations which the Communists consciously desire. The Russians wish to emancipate love from all irrelevant associations and the bonds of all outward extraneous sanctions. Love, they claim, will be richer and more spontaneous when it lives simply in its own strength. Thus, as private property is abolished, economic motives and necessities will cease to coerce or complicate affections. All matings will be love matches. So, again, the communalization of the material functions of home life, community kitchens, *crèches* and so forth, will liberate love as vital expression from all ulterior motives and obligations. "No nation can be free," said Lenin, "when half the population is enslaved in the kitchen": and some moderns would add: "or in the nursery." Man and woman will each have their job, with complete legal and economic parity, with perfect freedom to separate if they will or to live together if and as long as they like. There are no social stigmas or restrictions, no obligations to hold together because of economic necessities, none of the ties or drudgeries of home-building. If they decide to live together permanently it will be because they genuinely wish to do so, and for no secondary reasons. That will be the triumph of love.

So this queer flirtation with romanticism decorates the Marxian philosophy. Whether love can indeed survive in so rarified an atmosphere, whether it can sustain the life of the family in face of the mighty forces pitted against it, can be discovered only experimentally. If our previous contentions are true, its chances seem to be infinitesimal. But it has to be realized, all the same, that some of the forces we have been describing are already operating in our societies.

The changed economic status of women, even more than their legal and social freedom, is penetrating and influencing profoundly the whole idea and ideal of family life. A man will no longer " keep " his wife. Less and less as the new order develops will the wife be dependent on her husband, either intellectually or economically. Both will have their own professional competence and both, in more and more cases, their own income. The woman's mental and emotional stimulus will no more be drawn *only* from her home life. Moreover, changes of domestic arrangements due to the urbanization of life—flats, restaurants, " Hoovers ", etc.—will make the wife less markedly than she used to be the mistress (or the slave) of her home. But all this means that the ideal of love and indeed the whole conception of family life is bound to pass through far-reaching changes. There are still found conservatives to deplore the effect of women's colleges and hockey clubs and literary and professional interests in killing love, as they understand it. What is really happening is not this. It is rather that love is finally emerging from its old chivalric associations towards something different but in fact far better. Inevitably the next generation will honour love in quite different terms. In other words a " companionate " ideal, rather than one which is primarily " domestic ", is likely to hold the allegiance of the Western world. And this, in its turn, must profoundly modify our whole attitude to the family, and not least to its sexual relationships. The Christian conscience is faced with something new here, which calls for keen and courageous thinking.

2. For rightly or wrongly the thought of this generation does not endorse the traditional idea that parenthood is the primary aim of marriage. There are many to-day who regard it as secondary—not in the sense that it is to be avoided on lower grounds of mere self-indulgence, but for the much more Christian reason that it is a declension from the best ideal of the partnership of man and wife to regard it as *chiefly* a means for producing children. There are many

who are genuinely convinced that on this point the traditional Christian ethic moves on a level lower than theirs.

Such a book as *The Retreat from Parenthood* indicates clearly which way the wind is blowing. There are plenty of serious and sincere people, with a high and spiritual ideal of marriage, who are not prepared to give their moral assent to what has hitherto been axiomatic. The report of the Lambeth Conference, for example, shocked some people not because of its liberalism, but because of what seemed to them the obscurantism of its fundamental assumptions on this point. Whether or no this attitude can be justified, at least it is plain that the Christian ethic is faced, here too, with fresh moral data.

The Victorians may be judged to have sat loosely to some of the demands of Christian social duty. But at least they obeyed with staggering fidelity the primal command: Be fruitful and multiply. Their children have broken with this tradition. Partly on obvious economic grounds, of which some are both right and necessary, some such as Christians cannot endorse. Christian ethics will censure the motive so far as it is bound up with social snobbery—as expressed in needlessly costly education—and needlessly high standards of luxury. From the Christian standpoint a human baby is of more value than a Baby Austin. It is also true, on the whole, that a one-child family involves impoverishment for the child in ways that cannot be measured in terms of money.

No serious thinker, least of all the Christian, can blind himself to the grave moral symptoms involved in *undue* restriction of the family. But families cannot be reared on a sense of duty. It is no good saying that people *ought* to have them. Shall we fill the world with unwanted babies? The procreation of children is bearable only as the crown of delight and joy. And the so-called retreat from parenthood which is said to be traceable amongst younger women cannot be rightly dismissed as mere unwillingness to face the pains and perils of childbirth. It has behind it a better motive—the idea that a woman in the modern world ought not to be asked to submerge herself entirely in the duties and demands of maternity. The Christian conscience surely endorses that. The vast Victorian families appal us not least because nowadays we are more sensitive to the terrible burden laid by them on the mother. And this marks an advance in Christian ways of thinking. On all grounds, sociological and Christian, the smaller family of the modern fashion is preferable to that of our predecessors.

But the modern family means, amongst other things, that only five to ten years of a woman's life will be claimed entirely by motherhood. It seems, therefore, to be undesirable that a woman who has a profession of her own should necessarily abandon it on marriage.[1] There are many cases in which it would bring great moral enrichment into life if both parents had professional interests. Moreover, when the wife is left widowed—and in the ordinary course of nature most married women will become widowed because of the shorter average male life—she will have resources, mental as well as financial. Motherhood framed in that general context would, I believe, lose most of its terror. It *must* be wrong for men to ask women to surrender everything to the claims of motherhood, to be left in the end forgotten and impoverished, or dependent upon the charity of their relatives.

3. But so soon as we mention smaller families we find ourselves in the heart of the moral problem. The presupposition of any modern ethic is its attitude on the question of *Population*. How it is right for people to act partly depends on how many people there are and how

[1] The attitude of education authorities which dismiss a woman teacher on marriage is on all points to be strongly condemned. It is a survival of Stone Age mentality.

many people we think there ought to be. This pertains, presumably, to the moral judgment. It is not wholly an economic question, since men are more than producers and consumers. Yet the material for a moral decision must be supplied very largely by Economics.

I do not know on what grounds it is assumed that an absolute increase in population is necessarily a Christian ideal. A declining birth-rate may be a symptom of moral attitudes which Christianity must condemn. But an indefinite multiplication of the human race is surely no Christian concern. There are no Christian values involved in a quantitative increase of *Homo Sapiens*. The obligation is relative, not absolute. It depends on what population is needed to produce the best way of life under the conditions of a given area. In the sparsely inhabited spaces of the Dominions, or, again, where a small European colony is trying to maintain its own standards in the midst of a people of lower culture, there a definite increase seems desirable. On the other hand, our own country is by common consent overpopulated. A large increase here would be a disaster. But there is no reason to anticipate that. The unparalleled growth of our population since the time of the Industrial Revolution was due to temporary and local causes, and was by no means a typical development. "If we regard history as a whole a stable rather than an increasing population seems to be the rule."[1] The normal checks are already in operation. The rising standard of life restricts the birth-rate and is likely to do this with an increasing stringency. (The great fallacy of Malthus's thesis was his failure to appreciate this principle.) On the other hand, the death-rate falls steeply and the curve is likely to drop further downwards. Thus it is calculated by statisticians that for a hundred years from 1931 the population of the United Kingdom will probably remain fairly constant.[2]

[1] Carr Saunders, *Population*, p. 21. [2] *Ibid.*, p. 49 ff.

It may prove to be true that even this population will prove to be more than the nation can carry properly. That is a matter for economic experts. It may be true that it should be reduced still further. " But it is certainly not always the case that the fewer there are the more there is to go round. On the contrary, it is sometimes true that the more there are, the more (in virtue of the law of increasing returns) there is to be distributed."[1] There are also moral factors to be considered. An ethic that ignores economics is bound to result in futile sentimentalism. But an increased material prosperity may be bought at too high a price, in such an increase of the urbanization and mechanization of life as destroys the soul. So too with biological efficiency. Christianity ought to set itself decisively against the multiplication of the unfit, and to work for a far more sensitive public conscience in all that concerns hygiene and eugenics. The Church would do better to concentrate on this rather than on inventing imaginary sins such as marrying a deceased wife's sister. But the Christian values are not fully realized in the production of pedigree stock. We might breed a race of perfect physical specimens who would yet be, in Bishop Berkeley's phrase, " sorry citizens and sorry patriots ". Christianity could never be so stupid as to speak of Eugenics as a " new religion ". It will take full account of all these factors. Yet it must itself preserve a certain detachment, regarding them all from its own particular standpoint.

Nevertheless, all that has been said assumes the rightness as well as the necessity of deliberate restriction of births. Christian ethics *must* emphazise that. It cannot teach the sanctity of marriage and the responsibility of parenthood unless it teaches with equal emphasis the obligation of reverence and self-discipline in the sexual intimacy of married persons, and of restraint, foresight and deliberation

[1] E. Barker, *National Character*, p. 107.

in the bringing of children into the world. That being admitted, the question becomes simply the choice of the right method for securing this. It is easy to say : By abstention from intercourse. But such advice demands searching scrutiny. One cannot but question whether those who give it have always a very close acquaintance with the conditions of working-class homes. In the circumstances of middle-class life it is often possible for married partners to agree on this course and carry it through victoriously. In the homes of the poor the question is very different. Both the absence of space and privacy and the far more restricted range of interests which are available for working people make such abstinence harder for the husband. Refusal on the part of the wife is likely to lead to desertion or infidelity. The working mother has frequently to live in contemplation of this dilemma—another pregnancy or " the other woman ". Abortion or self-induced miscarriage is often the only solution she can devise.[1]

It goes without saying that Christianity cannot acquiesce in the use of contraceptives merely because abstinence is difficult. The Christian life presupposes discipline ; and the only enduring Christian contribution is the building up of Christian character. Nor can it sanction the evil subterfuge of teaching " the poor " to use contraceptives by way of shirking the nation-wide challenge to deal faithfully with slum properties and provide improved working-class dwellings. It will be insistent upon the provision of all such educational facilities as will help to enrich and extend mental interests and to brace and fortify character. In particular it will desire to use its influence to secure the effective raising of the school age ; not only to keep juveniles out of industry or (from what is worse) years of enforced idleness, but also to help break the vicious circle by diminishing the numbers

[1] See the paper by Mrs. J. L. Stocks in the Conference number of *Modern Churchman*, September 1930.

of unskilled workers. There is also, I think, another way of approach which Christian opinion may do well to explore. When the French tried recently to increase their birth-rate by the provision of family endowment, it was found (for reasons easily understandable) to work in precisely the opposite direction.[1] Should not the State provide free education, medical attendance and so forth up to a limit only of four or five children ? These and other subsidiary proposals will help to ease the incidence of the problem. But if we look at the whole question broadly, from a wide moral and national point of view, I cannot see how Christian opinion (or for that matter the British House of Commons) is justified in resisting the instruction—under trustworthy medical supervision—of working-class parents[2] in contraceptive methods. This at least we may say with some confidence—that it cannot be a sound Christian line for a number of elderly well-to-do people to seek to withhold legally from the poor the knowledge of methods freely employed without censure in the middle classes.

This, however, is not the end of the matter. For we might justifiably take that line on broad social and humanitarian grounds, and yet hold that for professing Christians such conception-control is illegitimate. We cannot pretend that the nation is the Church. In other words, we have still to face the issue from the standpoint of strictly Christian morals. And the true point here is essentially one of values. Can we rightly allow Christian value to the pleasure and delight of connubial intercourse which is not intended to issue in parenthood ? Here, I think, modern Christian thought is moving away from older assumptions. As is well known, the report of the Lambeth Conference definitely gave

[1] Carr Saunders, *op. cit.*, p. 65.

[2] Why should it be always only " mothers " ? Must women always bear the whole weight of the burden ?

Christian sanction to this " secondary aim " of intimacy as the physical seal and sacrament of love. Abstinence, if it is to be effective, is bound to involve almost complete abstinence ; it is not the same as that " moderation " which must be recommended by any serious ethics. And it must be doubtful, at least in normal cases, whether married people ought to live together in a state nearly equivalent to celibacy. (Even St. Paul, that common-sense misogynist, warns people against " platonic " marriage.) If that be conceded, the consequence follows.

Many Christians feel an instinctive repugnance—with which I am bound to say I can fully sympathize—against the whole notion of contraceptives. It seems like the final invasion by the mechanism of the modern world into the citadel of private intimacy. But in my opinion most of the counter-arguments are rationalizations of this repugnance rather than reasons which can be taken seriously. To say that it is " unnatural " says nothing. Everything in civilized life depends on conscious control of natural processes. " Nature " left to itself will solve the problem by devastating infantile mortality. But Christian ethics will hardly wait for that. Nor can one see how the use of contraceptives is in itself any more " unnatural " than is the recourse to the so-called safe period (obviously a defiance of nature) which has always been sanctioned by the Christian Church. If a more scientific method can now be employed to achieve the same end it is hard to see how Christian moral principles can consistently bring it under their censure. That is not to say that they will recommend it, save for " morally sufficient " reasons. But even if we must choose between two evils, the lesser evil is the right choice. And the Christian conscience must interpret strictly the restraints and limitations implied.[1]

[1] One of the weightiest vindications of the Lambeth Resolution is the brilliant paper by the Master of Corpus, Cambridge, in *Theology*, December 1930. It was far too good for small print in a magazine.

It is not possible for the Christian Church to legislate for its members on this matter. It seems to be one of those moral choices which must be thrown on individual consciences, seeking such guidance, insight and strength as are offered by Christian life and discipline. But, I think, it must say in the last resort, what is in effect the conclusion of the Bishops: "If, after conscientious thought, assisted by medical and moral counsel, you believe yourself justified in doing this, then, having regard to all the circumstances, you cannot be judged to be committing sin. Only remember that such solutions are not to be enterprised nor taken in hand inadvisedly, lightly or wantonly, to satisfy men's carnal lusts and appetites . . . but reverently, discreetly, advisedly, soberly and in the fear of God."

4. Divorce

The battle tactics of the Church militant, as it sets itself to hold or reconquer the ideal of marriage for the Christian standards, do not suggest very brilliant generalship. It has always been prone to defend the wrong line. Thus we wasted our strength and energy in resisting the Deceased Wife's Sister's Bill, which involved no vital Christian principle, and spoke as if Westminster would disappear like Sodom and Gomorrah in mythology for sanctioning the revision of the marriage laws. And meantime we marry first cousins, and gaily confer the blessing of the Church on countless marriages which are really wrong and should not be permitted by any legislation. We are now in danger of making the same mistake in our attitude to the question of divorce. We are never going to Christianize marriage by opposing demands for a change in the divorce laws. The laws as they stand are impossible to justify.

Surely it cannot serve the cause of Christian morality that the State, while recognizing divorce as a way of ending unsuccessful marriages, should confront those who wish to have recourse to it with a choice between perjury and adultery. Moreover, the law as now administered is an actual incentive to immorality. In the hope of putting a check on " hotel cases " judges are tending to refuse divorce on grounds of merely a single lapse from rectitude. The courts thus say, in effect, *Pecca fortiter.* Thus divorce is refused, on the one hand, if collusion is proved between the two parties ; that is to say, they are still tied by the marriage bond as a *punishment* for reprehensible conduct, or for the sinful desire to be separated. On the other hand they can earn their release only by a sufficient amount of adultery.

On no grounds can it be held that this situation is morally healthy in any society. It makes for subterfuges and insincerity, and brings the law deservedly into contempt. It is hard to conceive how Christian opinion can suppose that the maintenance of the existing laws can serve the Christian ideal of marriage. For the Canon Law marriage is indissoluble. In 1857 the British Parliament took the law into its own hands and insisted that marriage can be dissolved. The legislation was drafted " on Christian lines ", i.e. in accordance with St. Matthew's Gospel. The resulting chaos warns us against the danger of trying to impose Christian laws on the social legislation of modern States.

That marriage should be lifelong and indissoluble follows from the Christian conception of it. But you do not necessarily serve that ideal by compelling people to remain married legally when the marriage has ceased to have any real meaning. Rather you drag the ideal through the mud. It is not possible, in my opinion, to take the debated text in St. Matthew as the basis of any legislation. Its authenticity is extremely doubtful : for nothing is less in accordance with Christ's method than such qualifying exceptional clauses. He flung out uncompromising principles, leaving the world to work out their implications. It is probable that the Marcan and Lukan versions give the original form of this saying. But that, too, is a statement of principle, not a piece of Christian legislation. It appears to me to be slightly disingenuous to claim this as positive legislation to be put into force by the laws of Christian states, when we gaily explain away " Resist not evil " and similar paradoxes in Christ's teaching, as challenging presentations of an ideal rather than laws to be obeyed literally. How can we justify this discrimination ? All these sayings must stand on the same footing. Jesus stood for the " Christian " ideal of marriage. It is the task of the Christian Society to work out such regulations and arrangements as will best help this ideal to come true in the changing circumstances of social life. (The existence of the " exceptional clause " at all shows that the early Church claimed that liberty.)

It is clear that such promiscuous divorce as the laws of some American states permit is not only destructive of family life but also makes marriage itself a mockery. No sane thinker will wish to proceed to that length. But no healthy moral opinion can be formed in the general mind of society by holding compulsorily together two people who belong to one another in nothing except a tie imposed by the Law. That also breaks up the family and certainly does not enhance respect for marriage. We must recognize that there are bound to be cases where a marriage proves to be morally unworkable. It is arguable, at least, that the best way of making " real " marriage unions possible is to provide opportunity for a fresh start. Legal separation is no solution. It recognizes the failure of a marriage but provides no chance of one that may be successful ; it results only in an increase of illegitimacy. It preserves the shadow of the Christian ideal, but only by emptying it of all substance. Christians cannot seriously argue that this comes nearer to the mind of Christ than a realistic acceptance of facts. By trying to secure that in such cases non-Christians may not start again, Christians really defeat their own object. The

Church has no right to try to prevent the State from sanctioning divorce on such grounds of moral integrity and social well-being as public opinion is willing to recognize. It is in influencing such opinion towards the highest ideals of marriage that Christianity will discharge its function. It cannot do this by insincere pretences, or by imposing its own views by law on people who do not share its moral axioms. But of course it will best exert its leavening influence by a stricter expression of its own ideal inside the Christian society.

For Christianity marriage is indissoluble—*but only on Christian presuppositions.* Those whom God has truly joined together it is not in Man's power to put asunder. But it does not follow that every couple who happen to be married in Church or Chapel are therefore joined together by God. Often this is quite obviously untrue. Every clergyman must have used that formula when the words almost choked him as he uttered them. Here, I suggest, is the radical insincerity.

There is one way out of the present chaos and that is to recognize the distinction between the State and the Christian society. The suggestion has much to be said in its favour that the custom of Continental countries (and of British Dominions overseas) should be introduced into our own country. The religious ceremony should be religious, and not confused with the legal contract. The latter should be a civic and legal ceremony. Civil marriage should become universal ; and this, if performed in a decent stately fashion (not in a dismal Registrary Office) would help to emphasize—as is greatly needed—the civic responsibilities of marriage. It would also rescue the Church from the hypocrisy of blessing marriages which it ought not to recognize. This legal contract would be dissolvable only on such grounds as the State might determine. It would then be open for those who desired it—that is, who wished to identify themselves with the Christian ideal of marriage—to proceed to Church for the religious ceremony. By that action they would then mean something: they would be solemnly taking upon themselves the full obligations of Christian matrimony. The Christian Church would, of course, withhold its blessing from any such marriage as it could not approve. It would make its own regulations, and among these the informed Christian conscience would give their due place to medical requirements. I feel strongly the force of this proposal as a means of evading administrative difficulties.

Against it is the strong probability that only a very small number of Christians would be willing to ask for the religious ceremony; and the net result of the whole arrangement might be a gradual de-Christianization of the marriage ideal in the popular mind. It would be destructive of our whole purpose if the Church came to suggest that civil marriage was something of which to be ashamed. On these grounds, therefore, I am not at all sure that we should endorse this attractive suggestion. There is much to be said for a touch by the Church even where the parties have not yet reached the level of fully developed Christian thinking. But in any case the Church must have its own rules, or its whole moral position is stultified. It need not mean that its standards are lowered if it makes its rules more realistic, and more adaptable to changing conditions.

Christian marriage *should* be regarded as indissoluble. The Church should lay down the rule that only in quite exceptional circumstances, would it again perform the ceremony for either party in the other's lifetime. (If we take the highest Christian standpoint, this qualification would be hard to justify. If marriage is really and truly a union of two immortal spirits it is hard to maintain that the death of either partner sets the other free to re-marry. Though there are many obvious cases where the sheer demands of human need seem to be more binding than any theory.) Christian people who marry as Christians, with these warnings, safeguards and assistances, desiring to live true to the mind of Christ, would thus deliberately commit themselves to the solemn intention of making a Christian thing of it. They would in this way voluntarily accept more searching standards of obligation: and if the marriage proved to be disappointing the Christian Ethic could rightly ask of them to be ready to pay the price of discipleship, and to try to abstain from the easier way out. All the resources of love and forgiveness should be expended before they acknowledge failure. And to help Christians battling with this horror should be one of the first claims on Christian charity. Nevertheless if, as must sometimes happen, the marriage yet proves morally unendurable or even destructive of spiritual health (as if one of the partners becomes imbecile), or if it has ceased to have any moral content (as through *unrepentant* infidelity), then I cannot believe that the Christian Church will really be serving the cause of Christian marriage by a rigorous and impossibilist attitude. In such cases, it may be fairly argued, the marriage has ceased to be indissoluble just because it has ceased to be marriage in the sense presupposed by Christianity. The legal tie corresponds no longer to any moral or spiritual realities. If the civil contract is then dissolved, the "innocent partner" should not be regarded as a deserter from Christian principles if he or she desires to re-marry. (The innocent party in the civil courts may as things are be the more guilty morally.) Such persons should not be excommunicated. It is really untrue to the mind of Christ to maintain that they are "living in sin". If the Church recognizes the marriage by readmitting the parties to Communion, there seems to be no logical justification for refusing its blessing to the wedding ceremony. (There is plainly an inconsistency in the "Lambeth" recommendations at this point; though it may not be impossible to defend it.) An aloof, half-disapproving attitude is scarcely calculated to help such people to perfect their union in the spirit of Christ.

History does not encourage us to believe that Christian standards are made more effective by the exercise of ecclesiastical discipline.[1] The Christian Church is a body of people who are trying to help one another, in the strength of the Divine assistance, to live true to the spirit of their Master. We are to have the salt " in ourselves "—not to sprinkle it on one another's tails. The weight falls on the individual conscience, strengthened and guided by the life of the Fellowship.

5. Women's Vocations

It was argued above (pages 204 *sq.*) that we cannot discuss the family in isolation from its social context. Much that is shaping the new ideals of marriage, and much that accounts for the peculiar difficulties inherent in the marriage relationship, draws from causes outside the family. No discussion can be realistic which ignores these collateral influences. We can hope for no adequate Christian ethic till we have given more thorough consideration to the whole standing of women in the modern world and the poise and rhythm of feminine life. There is no avoiding the unpleasant truism that most women are very heavily handicapped, not only by physiological constitution but also by the lack of sufficient opportunity for their mental and emotional satisfaction. My belief is that such considerations cut far more deeply into family life than most current discussion is willing to realize. In other words, an ethic of Christian marriage must involve more searching enquiry into the nature of women's education and their professional or vocational future.

There are those who declare that the breakdown of home

[1] " The lesson of history as we have tried to read it repeats the lesson of the Gospel. Penal discipline has always defeated its own ends " Kirk, *op. cit.*, 469).

life is due to the higher education of women. How much more blessed were the Victorian misses, content to make the walls of the home their world, and to find their whole life in " household duties " !

Now obviously the beginning of any movement must involve some risks and demand some readjustments. Whatever may be justifiably criticized in the person described as the " modern young woman " is largely due to the fact that male domination has been so firmly established for so many centuries, that the change can hardly be made within one generation without some crude and exaggerated reactions. But to urge that a merely " housewifely " education will most fit women for marriage and parenthood is surely much worse than a delusion : it imperils the whole Christian ideal. We need not stress the educational maxim that an awakened and disciplined mind trained by a specialized course of study can apply itself fruitfully to new circumstances, whether cooking a meal or administering a province. Oxford and Cambridge are built on this assumption. We are here concerned with the moral implications of this educational axiom on the success or failure of married life.

For the problems both of marriage and parenthood are intimately inter-related with this question of woman's education. If a woman's mental and emotional life is wholly dependent on her home, two dangerous consequences are threatened : (*a*) Just in proportion as the care of her children has been her entire interest and concern, the less will a mother be willing to let them grow up. To do so means the emptying of her own life. The over-mothered child, as everyone knows, offers a moral and psychological problem hardly less acute than the neglected one. Much of the tension between parents and children is probably due to the lack of mental stimulus derived from other than purely domestic sources. It seems to be therefore of the highest importance that the mother should have been put in-possession of such intellectual and artistic interests as will give her inner life a secure content. It is well if she has been trained for some profession with which, as circumstances permit (for example, after the birth of her last child), she can retain some effectual contact.

(*b*) It is only in very few professions that a woman can share in any effective way in the public work of her husband. Behind a great many of the failures and tragedies lies this elementary fact. The more completely a wife depends on her husband for her mental and emotional satisfaction, the more likely she is to regard his professional work as competing with her for his affections. The stronger, again, will be the consequent pressure to seek elsewhere for satisfactory companionship. This situation, which is apt to arise in proportion to her genuine devotion to him, is the base of half the triangles of modern life. And the cruel dilemma "my wife or my work" shatters the nerves of too many husbands, and introduces a subconscious anxiety into the heart of perfectly happy marriages. The more one observes the more it is forced upon him how many a disaster might have been avoided had both partners had a "professional" interest. (It does not follow of course that the wife will always or even often "practise" professionally.)

Still more relevant is this question to the problem of the unmarried woman who constitutes, as everyone realizes, so grave a religious and moral difficulty in nearly all Christian congregations. This problem must be kept in its right proportions. It is obviously untrue to assume that all unmarried women are miserable! Nor is the scope of the problem very widespread. Roughly speaking, it seems to arise only, or mainly, in the "professional" classes where, for not very obscure reasons, more men choose to remain bachelors. Some such women are employed happily in satisfying work of their own, and some of them prefer not to marry. There remain, however, a fairly large number who are desirous of marriage but are denied it ; and the Christian conscience cannot merely ignore the moral and spiritual malaises of which they are too often the victims. About this there is much that needs saying ; not least as regards the vindictive cruelty which some married women mete out to the unmarried, and the average male contempt for the "spinster". But we must confine ourselves to our main question. The suggestion that a girl's education should aim only or chiefly at housewifery breaks down completely in face of this problem. She may be trained as a perfect *Hausfrau :* but if after all she remains unmarried, then she is left at the mercy of fate with no chance of an independent career. (For it surely cannot be right to expect that grown-up unmarried daughters ought in all cases to stay in their parents' homes. There are perhaps some kinds of sacrifice which the Christian conscience ought not to sanction.) If she falls back on Bridge and talking scandal or dominating some religious coterie, is it altogether her fault ? A great deal of the envy, hatred, and malice which disgraces some Christian congregations, and poisons other people's home life, is really due to defective education, and to the failure of our society to provide women with worth-while vocations.

For all this leads to a highly important corollary. It is easy enough for the text-books to say that women can "sublimate" unrequited instincts in careers of creative service. But how much creative work is in fact open to them ? The chronic problem of College-trained women is to find employment adequate to their training and satisfying to their capacities when they go down from the University. All their professions are hopelessly overcrowded, and the present economic depression will make the outlook even less hopeful for them. During this transitional period this is as urgent a question as any for an ethic that seeks to be realistic. It is foolish merely to claim on women's behalf the right to crowd men out of employment.

Yet we cannot dismiss with a note of interrogation a problem on the right solution of which depend such far-reaching Christian concerns. Christians are surely bound to take seriously this vast new question of women's vocations. It is urgently necessary for the Christian ethic that we should attempt to lay open fresh avenues of useful and worthwhile service which will offer women a richer and wider scope for their contribution to community life. This is a fruitful field for research which might well be undertaken by Christian groups. The question about the ordination of women should be re-examined in this context, not merely as one of ecclesiastical order but as part of a large problem of Christian morals.

CHAPTER IX

CITIZENSHIP

1. The Two Cities

THERE is a deep-rooted English prejudice against "bringing religion into politics". This idea may be explained partly by our subconscious national memories of old, unhappy far-off things. Englishmen cannot forget the Armada. Moreover, the ferocious civil conflicts of the two most formative centuries in our history were due to the desire of religionists to enforce their faith and polity on all citizens; countered by the demand of dissident groups for the right of free religious association within the unity of the national state. Religion served to envenom political controversy; and this no doubt helps to explain the prejudice. But the English feeling becomes remarkable when we reflect that the principles or assumptions most characteristic of our constitution are themselves primarily a religious legacy. The genius of our democratic convictions is in fact a political application of what had been learned by Puritan leaders and the members of non-conforming Churches from experience of the working and government of small, local Christian congregations.[1] British democracy has a religious ancestry. It is clear, too, that the logical conclusion of this stubborn English preconception involves an almost complete denial of all that the Christian tradition stands for. It amounts to the claim that the concerns of politics—the relationships of men in society—should be conducted apart from any reference to the relationship of Man's life to God. That

[1] Cf. A. D. Lindsay, *The Essentials of Democracy*, Lecture I.

means, in the end, to discuss the business of citizenship without any regard for the prior question of the end which the State exists to serve. And that is either the fundamental atheism which conceives the State as an end in itself; or else it regards the function of Government as merely that of a piece of technical mechanism for the advancement of non-political aims, whether cultural or economic. That would be to evacuate the life of citizenship of all moral and spiritual content.

The platonic and Christian position is the diametrical opposite of this. It is that we cannot think rightly about politics unless we think rightly about theology. Citizenship is a concern of religion, and religion a vital concern of citizenship. For the social order—in the final analysis—has its roots in the nature of God. Thus society will most nearly approximate to preserving the good life for its citizens, when its leadership and constructive principles conform most truly to God's will. Hence failures in political thought and practice are the reflexion of false ideas about God. Yet history is laden with warnings that civic life is impoverished and frustrated by attempts at theocratic administration. Where men have attempted to take religious principles and apply them in their naked immediacy to the complex issues of law and government, they have only too often succeeded either in repressing spiritual freedom or in secularizing religion. Such short cuts make the worst of both worlds. To forget that man must live in the body—in the world of necessity and determination and of political and legal mechanisms—is as silly as to deny that he has a soul and therefore cannot be bounded by that world. "Natural law" has its own goodness and its own measure of relative independence as much in politics as in physical science. Political life is never merely a means: even though, from the Christian standpoint, it cannot be recognized as an end in its own right. Citizenship, like the life of the family, is the intersection of temporal and eternal. It belongs both to nature and to supernature.

Hence Christian ethics invests the State with at least a relative and derived authority as an instrument of the divine purpose. ("The powers that be are ordained of God.") Against all absolutist pretensions it will urge that it is an inherent impossibility for the State to satisfy or respond to all the needs of spiritual personality. It can never, therefore, claim us entire. That would be to worship before the devil (Luke iv. 7) in the guise of the Great Leviathan. But against those who decry the State as a "merely secular" organization with no claim on spiritual allegiance, Christianity is the champion of its prerogatives, as the precondition of the good life. There is always this tension and duality in Christian thinking on all political issues, and from this it derives its richness and vitality. The Christian belongs to *both* of the "Two Cities": and so long as he remains an embodied spirit he cannot live wholly in either.[1] The Christian goal is the perfection and development of spiritual personality for life eternal in communion with God. But personality is a social fact. Every advance in the integration of the will and desires of any individual is always relative to his social context. In an ill-organized social system no man can become what he is meant to be. He cannot become a completely harmonious self. On the other hand, in no social system set within merely political horizons can he realize his spiritual capacities.

The integration of the individual and the organization of the social order are thus inextricably interdependent. For our various interests and desires, and the "constellation" of our various sentiments, are centred in and attached to a variety of social groupings. Every man lives in a number of

[1] Cf. Osborne, *Christian Ideas in Political History*, pp. 97–105, and Troeltsch, *op. cit.*, p. 255 *sq.* For the equivocal position of the secular state in St. Augustine, cf. Figgis, *Political Aspects of St. Augustine's "City of God,"* pp. 56–67.

different societies each with its own claims and each ministering to some element in his personal life. We are members of our family, our College, our club, our professional guild, our Church, our city; each provides us with certain interests, and demands from us in its turn certain duties. The richest life will be that which embraces the widest circle of these varied interests in a unified and harmonious life-purpose. But for most men there is bound to be some conflict; some men live in a state of constant tension between what is due, for example, to their families and the claims of various hobbies and side interests or the obligations of professional loyalty. (Think, for instance, of the moral conflict which every trade unionist must face when his union is called out on strike. Shall he be a blackleg and earn big money, or be loyal and let his children starve?) So far as these claims remain unreconciled a man's inner life cannot be unified; he cannot become in the full sense a person.[1] Thus the organization of our lives reflects the organization of society.

So far as we are at war with ourselves, we manifest as individuals the "dissociations" of the social order. So far as men are denied any element which human nature needs for its realization—æsthetic enjoyment, or education, or adequate economic endowment—the social order is found wanting. Thus men and women depend for the attainment of their full spiritual stature on the harmonious organization of those groups and subsidiary societies which minister to the various forms of goodness, material, spiritual and intellectual.

This must be achieved by the Great Society. Ideally, and to a large extent in fact, the various subordinate societies which give us the means of realizing goodness are brought into harmony by the community which, for the modern West, is the nation. Whatever forms of goodness are open to us, whatever (as we say) life can offer us, are secured and

[1] Cf. Paton, *op. cit.*, pp. 255–280.

safeguarded by the community. Hence derives the moral right of the community—and of the State as its executive organ—to demand from the citizen the sacrifice of health and wealth and, if need be, even of life. The State is the presupposition of the good life. Thus it may claim to be of divine authority, within the conditions of temporal life, as the means of realizing God's will. Its authority is relative and derivatory. As Christian ethics has never sanctioned any absolute right to private property, so it has never been able to recognize any absolute duty to obey the State. Both the right and the duty are relative to the needs of spiritual personality. The State, said St. Paul, is God's minister; he does not say that Nero is God. The divine-right theory of the Stuarts was no more than a fantastic parody of the true Christian position. The Christian claim was in truth the precise opposite. Establish the State on a purely secular basis and you have no check on its absolutist pretensions. Erect it on supernatural sanctions and you have a bulwark against its tyranny. "The only effective way to limit the authority of the State is to regard that authority as bestowed by God for certain purposes."[1] That was the Christian concern—to submit the State to an absolute standard of reference, and to demand that its claims should be justified before the very judgment of God. The State had a lawful demand on men's loyalties so long as it discharged its legitimate functions in accordance with the divine law of Justice and the Christian interpretation of Man's destiny. If it did not, it forfeited its authority and its subjects were released from their obligation. This is the persistent Christian position throughout the mediæval period, both in the papalist school and the imperialist.[2] The papacy as conceived by Hildebrand was at least in part an experiment

[1] Temple, *Essays in Christian Politics*, p. 32.

[2] For the way in which the "Lex Naturae" was taken over and elaborated in the Canon Law see Bryce, *Studies in History and Jurisprudence*, Vol. II, pp. 142 *sq*.

in safeguarding this magnificent bulwark of freedom in the rough and tumble of actual politics. The collapse of that splendid failure and the birth of the secular nation-state it is unnecessary to describe here. "The Reformation substituted a papal Cæsar for a Cæsarian Pope."[1]

Our citizenship is in heaven. Yet the claim of the early Apologists—"We are the best citizens of the Empire"—is one which we ought to be able to make. Secular civilization is disfigured by much that seems to repudiate Christian standards. Its follies, cruelties and false values are so glaring and so disastrous that Christian thought is sometimes in danger of rendering it less than justice. Yet we certainly fail in recognition of God's activity in the "natural" order if we blind ourselves to those signal qualities of honour, courage, kindness, goodwill, mutual sharing and responsibility, exhibited in our Western civilization. It is only when the system breaks down in time of war or industrial dislocation that we realize all that is involved of fidelity, enterprise and co-operation in the rationing of a great city. It is literally and demonstrably true that we do not and cannot live by bread alone. It is easy, again, to be scornful and contemptuous of democratic institutions, which are often as stupid as they are inefficient. Yet the presuppositions of life in any democratic society are genuine manifestations of the Spirit. So, too, in all the new movements of educational reform and of international understanding, the Spirit of God is at work in the secular state. It is of the very highest importance that we should appreciate how great goodness, how large a measure of the divine Spirit, is manifest in our social order, despite its sins, negligences and ignorances. Devoted and eager participation in the interests and duties of citizenship must indubitably be doing the will of God.

Yet no State exists in the world which can command our unqualified allegiance. The State is, in its essence and nature,

[1] E. Barker, in *Social and Political Ideas of the Middle Ages*, p. 15.

a legal and political institution. It is not, and should not be, a Church. This involves that the highest form of goodness is necessarily excluded from it. The State itself cannot satisfy the ultimate needs of spiritual persons—their capacity for communion with God. Thus we cannot be "saved" by the State, because it is not able to make us whole. And indeed to the writers of the New Testament this fragmentariness and limitation seems to invest "the world"—which means in effect what we now call secular civilization, the whole complex of social organization without any conscious reference to God—with a taint of actual and positive evil, "The 'world' lies in the power of the evil one." Moreover, all existing States fail in providing for many of their citizens some essential elements in the good life—whether economic or psychological—and keep them stunted and starved in body or mind. To this extent all political States involve some frustration of personality. And this, as we shall see, is inherent in that very national organization which is the condition of the political State in its present phase of development.

But further than this, those moral qualities which inspire the fullest and most devoted citizenship have in them an element of self-contradiction. For the more intense is a man's patriotism, the more wholehearted his loyalty to his group—and this is through and through an ethical attitude—the less is he able to appreciate either the limitations of his own group or its place in a richer and more embracing system. But the imperfections of modern States and their failures in justice and freedom are bound up with those very limitations. Hence it is only a pledged allegiance to an absolute and supra-political standard which can bring citizenship to its perfection. The State can only fulfil its true ends if it is seeking an end more than its own. Its subjects can serve it as good citizens only if they try to be something more than this—to fashion their lives by the will of God.

There are recurrent crises in history where this detachment and discrimination is presented in violent perspective. One was the fall of Jerusalem—the end of the world as it must have seemed to the Jews and Jewish Christians who witnessed it. The shock of that terrific experience is reflected inside the gospels in the fierce, blind recrudescence of the Parousia expectation. This was the sign of the impending Judgment. The world's sin had now found it out. The hour for the Son of Man had sounded. He would now come, as Judge and Deliverer—to pass sentence on a guilty society and to raise the righteous to life eternal. The fall of Rome was another such revelation. To that shattering, overwhelming tragedy St. Augustine replied in his book on the City of God, with its famous doctrine of the Two Cities—the two planes and standards of loyalty. (*Civitates duas fecerunt amores duo.*) It would be a fascinating study to trace the different presuppositions concerning God's action in history involved in St. Augustine's reaction and that reflected in the Synoptic Gospels. The sack of Rome in 1537, the French Revolution, the World War, all confronted men with the same challenge. As I write, the Press is resounding with " crisis ", and our nation stands indeed at a critical moment. But the true meaning of crisis is judgment —a discrimination and sifting of values. The call to such a judgment and scrutiny is knocking at the doors of the civilized world. This lays upon Christians imperious obligations. " If the modern Church is really to become an instrument of social redemption, it must learn how to divorce itself from the moral temper of its age, even while it tries to accommodate itself to the intellectual needs of the generation."[1]

Thus a certain detachment and " distance " is the condition of full Christian citizenship. Yet the Christian must throw in his lot with his earthly city. As we cannot

[1] Niebuhr, *op. cit.*, p. 73.

" spiritualize " marriage by shrinking from its physical implications, so we shall never Christianize politics by disdainful or inert aloofness. Failure to vote, for example, is sinful.[1] A vivid interest and informed sharing in common civic responsibility is a primary duty for Christian people. Ideals remain ineffective and futile unless embodied in concrete policies. We must " condescend to particulars ". It would seem, for instance, to be a false virtue which claims to stand above party politics. There are times, no doubt——we are living in one of them—when " the Country must come before party ". At such times to exploit a national danger in the interests of party manœuvring is rightly held to be morally contemptible. It is also true that the present party alignment corresponds to nothing real in politics. But that only means that electoral machinery and the methods of parliamentary representation must be brought more into touch with political realities. For the British parliamentary system presupposes political parties and its working demands an effective Opposition. Normally, therefore, we are not free to choose between " parties " and some other method of advocating the policies we approve. The choice is between " getting things done " through the machinery of the party system, and not getting anything done at all.

This is not to say that " all Christians " ought to vote for this or that party. There is scarcely ever a public question where opinion will not be legitimately divided as regards the best means to be adopted to the attainment of an agreed end. All Christians ought to agree that the welfare of every citizen is the responsibility of all citizens. But whether this will be best secured by the economic methods of Socialism is a matter on which opinions must differ. On the technical

[1] Deliberate withholding of a vote obviously involves moral choice as much as deciding how to give it. What I mean is saying, " I can't be bothered with it."

issues involved Christians, as Christians, have no expert knowledge. We can only say that it is a Christian's duty to inform himself to the best of his power on the questions which he must help to decide. A " Christian vote " would probably be disastrous in the normal field of political controversy. So, again, a Christian falls short of what Christian citizenship requires of him if he allows any sectional interest—that of his own social class for example—to dictate his political decisions. He must think in terms of the whole Community and of the true end which it is to serve. And this means that he must not give his support to that party which seems most favourable merely to his own Church or ecclesiastical " colour ", as one element in the whole Community. He must not, for example, support a Government whose policy he regards as detrimental to the widest interests of the Community merely because it opposes Disestablishment, against an Opposition which favours it.

It is best both for the Church and the State that Christians should be found on both sides in most current political debate. Yet there are certain great moral issues on which Christian opinion ought to be unanimous—the demand for Disarmament for example—and able to act as an organized Christian force. There cannot be any doubt in a Christian's judgment that world-peace is the will of God. If he doubts it, his judgment is less than Christian. And it is of paramount importance that in this and other like primary issues Christian opinion should make itself felt as avowedly and explicitly Christian. The moment may come when it will be required of Christians as the condition of fully Christian citizenship to withhold their allegiance not from the Government only but also even from the State. They may have to save the State from itself by a firmer loyalty to its true end than the State is able or free to profess. They would then, in fact, represent the Community against the betrayal of the political State.

2. Freedom and Community

Here, indeed, is the central issue in contemporary political evolution—What is the State trying to be or do? For the vital problem in all existing States is the seemingly irreconcilable tension between the claim of personal development and the stability of the social structure. We cannot reverse the rhythms of history. "When the War came," writes Dr. Wilenski, "Picasso's attitude to art was seen to be the only possible attitude to life itself in the new conditions. The first shell blew nineteenth-century romantic individualism to blazes. The cult of individual sensibility and individual freedom was clearly an obsolete ideal in this new phase of life. Order, centralized control, co-operation and discipline became the new ideal and cubism was seen to be the symbol of twentieth-century life."[1] The whole pattern of twentieth-century life is collectivist rather than individual. Steel and concrete are its natural medium and the skyscraper its most significant symbol. This is seen, too, in the Bolshevist posters, which express so startlingly and unforgettably the avowed ideal of that experiment—the organization of man-in-the-mass, the New Man, regimented and mechanized, which is to supplant the Christian tradition of men and women as individuals, with souls to save and a destiny to realize.

We vehemently repudiate the social philosophy of the Soviet Unions. But the tendency of all modern States is inevitably in the same direction. Everywhere the individual citizen finds himself increasingly at the mercy of tyrannous impersonal processes which threaten to crush out free personality. Whatever the form of political government, life is becoming more and more mechanized. This is partly due to the fact that all the issues of public policy have become so infinitely complex that they altogether outrange

[1] *Miniature History*, pp. 72–73.

the mental capacity of the private citizen. Decisions have to be relegated to specialists. And, as so much intractable material, so many varied and conflicting interests, have somehow to be brought under control and worked into a functioning system such as will secure life for all, a vast deal of personal initiative has to be sacrificed to efficiency. The whole trend, whether we are communists or fascists or parliamentarians, is towards the Omnicompetent State. The individual citizen, in all States, counts less and less every day. But this individual self-submergence is, as the world is now organized, the condition of individual survival. In a world so complicated as ours any Government that is not efficient fails to discharge its essential function. It exposes its subjects to those capricious and often destructive, uncontrolled forces against which its duty is to protect them. Yet it is possible to be governed too well. The brilliantly successful bureaucracy of the Roman Empire under the Antonines administered the Empire to ruin. And to-day there are grounds for apprehension lest we be exposed to the same danger. " Disgusted reader ", " Civis Britannicus " and the other intriguing anonymities—the village Hampdens of our age—who appear in *The Times* with indignant protests against the violation by Government of the (real or supposed) rights of citizens are spokesmen of a much-needed vigilance.

The centralization of responsibility and the relative helplessness of the individual has within it grave moral perils. Its tendency is to reduce all citizens to a common level of mediocrity. Life and thought are everywhere standardized. In modern industrialized democracies all tend to be cut to one pattern. Spontaneity and enterprise wither, and the fact that everybody does it becomes a sufficient motive for action. Indeed we sometimes seem to be moving towards the ghastly ideal of the termitary, as described in Maeterlinck's *Life of the White Ant*. The tragedy is that we seem to have no alternative. This depersonalizing of life appears to be the condition of living. We seem to be compelled *propter vitam vivendi perdere causas.*

There seems to be thus some inherent conflict between Freedom and Community. The Community is morally valueless save as the common life of free persons. And Freedom, in its turn, has no meaning save as realized in Community. Is there any way out of this impasse ? There is one vital if elementary truth which politicians too willingly forget—the strict and narrow delimitation of the State's moral and legal competence. The State is the executive of the Community in its legal and judicial aspect. It is concerned to enforce on everybody that which everybody must do if Community is to survive at all in its varied, manifold interests and activities. It must not prescribe the behaviour of citizens in their non-political functions and capacities[1]—as members, e.g., of the Royal Society, the Free Foresters or the Guards' Club or the Order of Ancient Virgins.[2] Here it has merely a general right of veto as the custodian of the whole body. These non-political forms of association—whether social, religious or educational—are the training-grounds of personal enterprise and the safeguards of individual freedom. The more they flourish in genuine independence, the more clearly the State is led to recognize their constituent place in that common life of which it is the political organ, the stronger the dykes that resist State-encroachment. It may fairly be claimed that the Church of England in setting up the Church Assembly and the Ecclesiastical Committee has established a new political principle immensely important to the cause of freedom. The machinery set up by the Enabling Act secures citizens in their capacity as members of a religious association direct

[1] Cf. Figgis, *Churches in the Modern State*, pp. 54–98, and MacIver, *The Modern State*, pp. 149–182, 467–486.

[2] Incredibly, this Friendly Society does really exist and has members.

access to the Crown-in-Parliament and guarantees the legislative autonomy of that association within its own sphere, subject only to the State's veto if its legislation infringes the legal rights of other citizens. This is an exceedingly fruitful precedent, probably destined to much wider extension.

But it is superficial to think that the problem before us can be resolved by merely administrative devices. The causes and remedies lie on a deeper level, and are bound up with the question: What is freedom? If it means the chance to live one's own life, then it must involve, quite inevitably, at least such control and regulation of the life of all in the common interest as will protect individual citizens from the incidence of excessive inequality. For no man is free to make the most of his life if he is victimized or restricted by social, legal or economic privilege. But this may defeat its own object: it may so tightly control individuals as to leave little place for individuality. On the other hand it is only too possible—as contemporary history shows—to abolish all legal privilege and secure to all citizens a legal equality, but yet to have failed to guarantee freedom. Acute social and economic cleavages, wide differences in education, or the toleration by public conscience of a virtually disfranchized minority (whatever its theoretical legal rights) may disastrously impede freedom. For then, however equal the law may be, it does not secure any effective freedom to the unprivileged section of its subjects. Such unofficial discrimination may be operative in several ways. It may be by a rigid "class" barrier, by some racial or sectarian ostracism, or by such economic organization as in effect subjects the consumer to the dictation of financial privilege.

Where there are such inequalities, then the equality guaranteed by law may in effect frustrate real freedom. For in such cases the life of the Society standardizes an outward uniformity but reflects no inward and spiritual unity. This truth is clearly exhibited in much that is happening at the present moment. "To-day, when men give at least lip-service to democratic equality, the unity which is necessary in a society which has not a democratic social structure is given by an irrational nationalism—as in Italy, Russia or China. Mere politics (that means the organization with force behind it) has got to do the work which in a real democratic society is done by voluntary cultural associations. The State has to become a Church, with bad results both for State and Church. For nationalism, one of the most powerful religions in the world to-day, is 'a very degraded form of polytheism'. . . . So long as our industrial system remains—what it is largely now—a sphere of unresolved conflict, so long will each of the parties of that conflict try to use the State's force for its own purposes, and the Marxian doctrine of the class war be partially true."[1]

It may thus turn out that a faulty social system frustrates political democracy. And, conversely, political devices which seek to correct inequality and privilege may have the result of aggravating them. In any event, political imperfections—such standardization, for instance, as makes private citizens insignificant—and failures in the democratization of the non-political elements in Community are disastrously involved together. We can watch this in Italy or the United States and survey the position from a safe distance. But no English conscience should feel comfortable when it turns its glass upon our own country. For here, despite our political democracy, yet socially and economically we continue to tolerate "inequality on the scale of a national institution".[2]

Few will be found now to argue seriously that we best secure individual freedom by the mere absence of "state-interference". There is no going back to Whiggish individualism. "The choice is not (as has been well said)

[1] A. D. Lindsay, *op. cit.*, p. 80. [2] Tawney, *Equality*, p. 24.

between an individualistic humanism and some form of collectivism, but between a collectivism which is purely mechanistic and one that is spiritual."[1] The State is not merely to " keep the ring " : it is responsible for the common good so far as political action can safeguard it. The proper range of state-interference is almost wholly a question of expediency—that is to say it is one for technical experts. It has no theoretical or ideal limits and involves no fundamental principle on which Christianity can pronounce judgment. It is merely a question whether the end aimed at can best be secured, in a given group of circumstances, by political or by some other methods. And this involves specialized knowledge of financial, economic and other " laws ". But the growing power of the modern State seems to reflect an increasing recognition of a principle which is essentially Christian and inherent in democratic convictions —that all are responsible for each. " To the Greeks, Democracy meant not the overthrow of privilege but merely the extension of its area. To them it seemed that Democracy was as much rooted in privilege as Oligarchy itself."[2] The modern conscience repudiates that assumption. It appears to us the denial of freedom. But we have yet to apply this conviction, to which we instinctively assent, to the organization of English society. We still acquiesce far too readily in the theory of two standards of life, whether in educational opportunity or in economic endowment and independence, as between the privileged and unprivileged classes. " Is [a man] free as a worker if he is liable to have his piece-rates cut at the discretion of his employer, and, on expressing his annoyance, to be dismissed as an agitator, and to be thrown on the scrap-heap without warning because his employer has decided to shut down a plant, and to be told when he points out that the industry on which his livelihood depends is

[1] Christopher Dawson, *Christianity and the New Age*, p. 100.
[2] E. M. Walker in *Cambridge Ancient History*, V, p. 102.

being injured by mismanagement, that his job is to work and that the management in question will do his thinking for him ? "[1]

It is scarcely possible for the Christian conscience to assent to the existing organization. Whether or not it endorses " Socialism " as an economic proposal, I fail to see how it can support an arrangement which entrusts so vast a share of the national wealth to the keeping of so minute a section, and thus puts the destiny of many so effectively at the mercy of few. And indeed it is everywhere recognized, quite regardless of political differences, that at least *some* measure of socialization of industrial enterprise has become inevitable. There is scarcely a modern municipality—however true-blue its members' political faith—which does not engage in some municipal trading on grounds of higher economic efficiency. And it certainly looks as though this process is destined to wider application. It is hardly doubtful that in due course of time the key industries and the means of transport must be brought under national control. At this moment it is being argued that the debacle of the late Labour Government is a refutation of Socialist theory in the sphere of economic practicability. But the text may be construed quite differently. It may afford further demonstration that the nation cannot effectively " manage its household " on the existing capitalistic basis.

This is a matter for technical discussion, on which Christian opinions will probably differ. But on the broadest and plainest moral grounds it seems clear that the Christian Conscience must demand some control by the Community of its industrial and financial enterprises. " The question is not whether there are economic movements which elude human control, for obviously there are. It is whether the public possesses adequate guarantees that those which are controllable are controlled in the general interest, not in

[1] Tawney, *Equality*, p. 252.

that of a minority."[1] And that is an ethical question, pure and simple. It implies the assertion by the Community of its equal concern for all its members. Without such effective assertion freedom becomes a merely rhetorical myth, as may easily be observed in the United States. Moreover, the so-called social services are but an elementary expression of that mutual responsibility and partnership both in sickness and health which is of the essence of Community life and the pre-condition of freedom. They are "Charity"—in its Christian sense—embodied in concrete legislation. That the American people should judge that it is consonant with real freedom to refuse all systems of state-insurance and hand over the care of the Unemployed to "Charity"—in its most shameless meaning—is, from our point of view, scarcely credible.[2] It would seem to us that the road to freedom lies rather by way of extension and improvement of the social services. For short of a complete revolution in our whole economic organization—which may or may not be desirable or practicable—these are the only methods available to redress inequality of opportunity and identify Freedom with Community.

But the Christian conscience ought to be keenly sensitive to the moral dangers inherent in this programme. To love our neighbour as ourselves means that everybody is to count for one and nobody for more than one. That is an irreformable Christian principle. Yet in practice it proves scarcely possible to avoid applying this principle in such a way as to involve a general levelling down of all standards, qualities and capacities. Mediocrity becomes a positive ideal. Whether we regard it biologically, or from the standpoint of education, or from almost any other conceivable angle, the same cruel dilemma seems to confront us. Can we

[1] Tawney, *op. cit.*, p. 250.

[2] Since this was written the State of New York has before it a proposa for a large increase in income tax to finance public works and relief-measures (*The Times*, August 29, 1931).

preserve a high general standard of physique, character or intelligence without supporting a privileged minority even if need be at the cost of the many ? The problem is as old as civilization, and we cannot pretend to have solved it. It may have been true, in an earlier chapter of history, that the old Noblesse did keep alive certain standards of conduct and devotion to public service, of æsthetic refinement and appreciation, which have in fact been the formative forces of what is implied in a " civilized " life. But if those values were conserved only on a basis of serfdom, are we to say that the price was too high ? It may be replied that all modern life is degenerating and becoming coarsened simply for lack of those magisterial standards. But is there not a cheat in this argument ? For the basis of privilege in the modern world is not birth or worth or public service : it is, quite frankly and brutally, money. And it cannot be argued that a bank balance is a test of integrity or of sensibility.

The pleas put forward for *such* an " aristocracy " must appear grotesque to the Christian judgment. And the argument may be reversed. It might be said that in actual fact the power of æsthetic appreciation and standards of personal refinement are continually rising, and that this is the direct result of restricting the area of privilege and widening educational opportunity. It might also be urged (and in my opinion with truth) that so far as contemporary life is vulgar and superficial, its values cheap and its pleasures inane, this is to be directly attributed to the domination of modern society by the tawdry dictatorship of the cash-box. If this be so, the reliable prophylactic against that coarsening of standards—which, as many critics aver, is endemic in democratic life—is a further extension and enrichment of opportunities for emancipation. This in effect means the development of cultural and religious associations as the schools of moral and spiritual training. And this in turn involves the diversion of wealth that is lost by wasteful methods of organization and socially sterile forms of expenditure into channels more rewarding to the commonweal. Nor must Christians allow themselves to forget that it is their essential contribution to the health and wealth of their earthly cities to be living by higher and more exacting standards than those endorsed by average public opinion. Only thus can the latter be raised.

Nevertheless, the difficulty is constant, and admits of solution only experimentally. But there is a more formidable criticism to which this position is open from the standpoint of Christian ethics—the destructive effects on moral character which may result from the communization of life. The objection has been well stated thus: "We should all be willing to be our brother's keeper: but none should consent to be kept by his brother." It is undeniable that in the last few years a demoralizing and dangerous attitude has begun to appear in our public life. It has come to be assumed that there are, somewhere, inexhaustible financial resources which can be drawn upon without limit to subsidize groups or individuals and preserve an artificial standard of life. And this, apart from its economic consequences, is beginning to prove debilitating to the moral fibre of our people. It is tending to paralyse initiative and the virile virtues of self-reliance. True, no doubt, that a feeling of helplessness and victimization by a social system "takes away half a man's manhood" and kills his readiness for enterprise. It is only by giving him a chance that we reawaken his power to help himself. But we need to beware lest, by eliminating all stimulus to self-betterment, we destroy his sense of responsibility to the common life of which he is part and do injury to his own character—which matters far more than anything else. Men are helped to become free not only by communal provision but by the tonic discipline of difficulty. It is, however, pleasanter to prescribe this for other sections of the community than to accept it as our own regimen.

There is, nevertheless, one proposal which should commend itself to the Christian's judgment as a way of counteracting these evils to which his own reforms may be liable. It is that of a universal income tax. On the smallest incomes it should be infinitesimal, and would thus inflict no real hardship. But its existence would serve to remind all citizens that the "tax-payers' money" means their own, and that the rights which a man claims for himself exact from him reciprocal obligations. "No representation without taxation" is an essentially Christian proposition.

But all this only serves to remind us that the good life which Community is to secure cannot be either measured or realized in terms of economics and politics. The ultimate good which is the citizen's due is the perfecting of his spiritual character. We are not loving our neighbour as ourselves unless we love God with all our hearts—i.e. unless the good which we will for him is the realization of his eternal destiny. It is not the final or even the chief concern of the Christian social ethic merely to make everybody comfortable. Some ascetic, otherworldly element must enter into the life of earthly citizenship. So far as the State is achieving its end, it has passed already into the supernatural. Till it does so, it remains imperfect. Love is of God: and only in God can the "royal law of liberty" be fulfilled.

3. The Community of Nations

The apparent clash between Freedom and Community is presented even more arrestingly on the wider stage of international life. The sovereign nation-state frustrates freedom. Without it no freedom seems possible: yet it seems that in exact proportion to its perfection as a national State it serves to inhibit and curtail freedom. This paradox is tragically apparent in the present world situation. There is an intimate mutual connexion between the frustration and inward disharmony of individual lives in our social system and the still imperfect relationship of nation-states to one another.

In his Fourteen Points addressed to the belligerents President Wilson was completely justified in assuming that democratic government goes hand in hand with respect for nationality. We can no longer nurse the delusion that democracies are necessarily pacific. We may be disillusioned about democracy. But the fact remains that for good and evil it rests on the foundation of the nation-state. We have no other experience of its working. "It is most interesting to observe how Turkey and China in their effort to become states on the Western model have had deliberately to begin by creating a sense of nationality. They begin indeed by trying to make the spirit of unity so strong that it does not admit of differences. They cannot become democratic states until differences are recognized and maintained alongside of the unity: but the feeling of unity which nationalism strives to create is the indispensable beginning."[1] Now the Christian ethic is not committed to any one particular form of government, whether democratic or any other. Indeed, it should be anxious to recognize that to transfer representative institutions to Indian or African society at its present stage of development may be an outrage to genuine freedom. But it *is* committed to Community—to that respect for mutual rights and keen sensitiveness to freedom of which European democracy is the rough-and-ready political expression. And this sense has chiefly been fostered by the development of the nation-state. Our generation is nervously awake to the dangers inherent in nationalism. But the nation-state has played its great part in the training of the Community-conscience. It has evoked and successfully maintained a richer unity-in-variety, a closer sense of belonging together expressed through more manifold groups

[1] Lindsay, *op. cit.*, p. 50.

and interests, than any previous political experiment. Despite its failures and limitations it has come nearer than any known polity to achieving freedom in Community. It was not merely an historical phase. It has made and makes its effective contribution to that realization of fellowship which Christianity values most highly. It is thus a hasty and impoverished judgment which thinks to call into being a world Community by the mere abolition of the nation-state. To substitute a watery cosmopolitanism for the rich fellowship of national loyalties, with their common memories and their common purposes, would be retrogression not progress.

Nevertheless, we are moving into the era when the inner logic of the nation-state can be seen to demand its transcendence. For the State is the executive of Community. And in the changing conditions of the new age Community is no longer coterminous with the confines of nationality. All the materials of community life, whether economic, cultural or religious, are trans-national rather than merely national. There is no such thing as national science ; a national Church is a contradiction in terms ; and every month demonstrates more conclusively that the economic life of all nations is inextricably interwoven. Thus the State is no longer representative of the realities of Community if it stands still on a purely national basis. Loyalty to its own constituent principle demands, not indeed its destruction but its organic incorporation into a larger international polity.[1] This development is in actual process. For the very existence of the League of Nations—hesitant and tentative as it may be—is tantamount to a deliberate abjuration of the doctrine of absolute State sovereignty by the States-members of the League.

But the politicians of nearly all countries are still living in

[1] Cf. Temple, *Christianity and the State*, Lecture IV—the best philosophical defence of the League of Nations which has been published.

an unreal world. And at present, till we have implemented what is implied by membership in the League, the nation-state frustrates Community by confining it within artificial frontiers. It impoverishes the lives of its citizens and deprives them of vital elements in full personal development by maintaining obsolete barriers in the path of trans-national intercourse. All attempts to solve national problems that work to a merely national scale of reference are as futile as they are dangerous. But here we must note a certain distinction. It is right for individual Christians to put the welfare of others before their own. But what is right for an individual citizen may be immoral for a responsible statesman. And it is certainly not Christian teaching that a Government ought to prefer the welfare of other people to that of its own nationals. Such an attitude would be treachery; for a Government is the trustee of its subjects. But the world has now reached a point where such distinctions have almost ceased to exist. The last ten years have shown unmistakably how complete is the interdependence of all nations on one another. If one member suffers all the members suffer with it. The day is past when in any department of life one nation can gain by another's loss. As the world now is, a purely national policy is a betrayal of national welfare.

But till that is more freely recognized national life remains unfulfilled. The existing economic depression thwarts and maims personal development. And it is an international problem admitting no merely national remedies. Politicians still make forlorn attempts to make economic frontiers march with those of political nation-states. But there are no economic frontiers. And policies which aim at erecting them, by way of helping a national group to recover economic prosperity, are out of tune with the whole trend of history and impede that international co-operation on which all nations are now dependent. Thus the policy of protective tariffs cannot be sanctioned by the Christian conscience. On the technical factors in that proposal regarded as a financial expedient Christianity cannot give a leading—though it will observe that in the United States, where the policy of economic nationalism secured by insurmountable tariff-walls has been tried out in the widest dimensions, it has proved itself a ruinous failure. But there is a perfectly clear moral issue. The Christian ethic cannot consent to purchase a small immediate gain in material comfort at the cost of a set-back in the more vital matter of international trust and co-operation, on which depends not only lasting prosperity but the whole cause of spiritual freedom. A protectionist Government in Great Britain would be more than a national calamity. On the other hand, a series of trade agreements—" We will admit your imports freely only if you will do the same to ours "—using the tariff as a bargaining asset, would not be exposed to the same moral criticism. For this might result in removing restrictive tariffs and increasing the area of co-operation.

Deeper than all temporary expedients for assisting economic recovery is the emancipation of nation-states from the ruinous wastage of competing armaments. Education, housing, public health and all the most vital concerns of Christian citizenship are sacrificed to the blood-lust of Moloch. This drain on industry and national wealth is the prime cause of the economic depression which is crushing Western civilization and falls most heavily on the most defenceless. Even worse than the economic results are the poisoning of the international atmosphere and the frustration of freedom in Community by the fears and suspicions which armaments breed. So urgent and so imperious is this burning question of Disarmament that it ought now in the mind of Christian citizens to take priority over all other issues. Every Christian ought to regard himself as a commissioned evangelist of this cause. Few things have more injured Christianity than the hesitancy and inertia of Christians where the cross of the Crusader is called for.

The States signatory to the Kellogg Pact have renounced War as an instrument of policy. The States-members of the League are pledged to rational methods of arbitration as a means of securing international justice. Armaments belong to a world order which is *legally* as well as morally obsolete. Those who give lip service to the League with the reservation of keeping their powder dry are as fishes who should decide to live terrestrially and yet to continue to breathe through their gills. But the solemn abjuration of war does not yet deliver us from the danger of it. Nothing so imperils the peace of the world as the maintenance of vast national armaments. The will to peace has yet to be made effective, and the inarticulate longings of the peoples to be embodied in real Community. The average voter is too ill-instructed or too supine to take resolute action for the securing of the world's peace. Unless this inertia is shattered and the will to peace made vocal and operative, the danger draws nearer with each passing year. It is hardly disputable that the Christian citizen should regard this as his primary contribution to the well-being of his earthly city as well as the mark of his Christian allegiance.

Republicans were invented, said Lamennais, in order to make republics impossible. And the cause of peace like most other causes has often been ill-served by its advocates. There is too often something ignoble about pacificist propaganda. An ideal of safety, comfort and prosperity is not one that appeals to the finest characters. The militarist ideal is finer: its demands on discipline, courage and adventure speak to what is noblest in Englishmen and win from them heroic response. No demonstration that war does not "pay" is in itself a convincing moral argument. We do injury to the cause of peace if we appear to base our appeal on the lower grounds of self-interest. The Christian case against war is not primarily that it is dangerous and painful and destructive of life and property; not even that it involves an appalling holocaust of the finest lives in a generation. Physical death and bodily suffering are not for the Christian the worst of all evils. Far more ruinous than these are the spiritual evils entailed. It involves the debasement of all moral currencies, the abandonment of standards and values, an assault on life's fundamental decencies. All belligerent Governments lie shamelessly; all seek to poison the minds of their citizens with irrational hatreds and blind animosities; all seek to unchain the ape and tiger, and to turn the sporting instincts of boys into the madness of wolfish fury. Thank God, they do not wholly succeed. But let any who still cherish delusions about chivalry in modern warfare re-read the instructions for Bayonet training issued in 1917. All Governments have to do these things; they are necessary war-measures. But it is no more easy to overtake them when the emergency is over than it is to repeal war-time legislation. The moral arguments on behalf of war are as rotten as the biological. It is true that a nation engaged in warfare achieves a strong unity of will and a common power of sacrifice and endurance: yet that is largely a matter of mass-suggestion and resembles rather the unity of the wolf-pack than a human sharing in a creative purpose. The net moral results of the world war have been preponderantly evil. An evil tree cannot bring forth good fruit.

This is the unyielding Christian position. It is not on a calculation of consequences that the Christian ethic stands in this question. It cannot give its moral consent to war because it is contrary to the will of God. The Lambeth Conference rightly "affirms that War as a method of settling international disputes is incompatible with the teaching and example of our Lord Jesus Christ".[1]

[1] Lambeth Conference, 1930—Resolution 25.

It is not true to pretend that Pacificism seeks to abjure the right of self-defence. The whole point of the Covenant of the League and of all movements towards disarmament is to substitute international security for the capricious arbitrament of warfare. It is to substitute law for mere violence. For war " as a method of settling disputes " is the exact antithesis of justice. It does not guarantee the triumph of the just cause: the right may rest with the defeated nation. War is not in the very least impartial; it may massacre just and unjust "impartially", but victory is with the biggest battalions, not with the nation whose cause is most righteous. The League is the instrument of security. The friends of peace are the friends of justice. They desire a rational decision by civilized legal procedure—enforced where necessary by armed sanctions—of disputes which are recognized as inevitable. They do not propose to abolish armed force any more than they would demobilize the police. They propose that it should be—like the police force—the instrument of a corporate will to justice.

Nor, again, is it honest to argue that Pacificism is the same thing as craven and inglorious surrender. If the State has any moral justification then, when its existence is threatened, it is morally obligatory to defend it. No ethic, Christian or other, would judge that it is a morally finer action to open the gates to an invading enemy than to die desperately in front of them. There is at this point a good deal of confusion in pacificist thought and in that of those who oppose it. What is right for a private individual may be wrong for him in his capacity as a citizen. A Christian should turn the other cheek—but not the cheek of his wife or his employés. And a Government, as the trustee of its subjects, would be profoundly immoral and treacherous if it yielded up the life of its country rather than resist the aggressor. Nor can the Christian ethic demand this. A State would be justified in this course only if its action embodied an expressed and genuine will of its people, inspired by avowedly Christian motives, to accept a sacrificial martyrdom. But while such a national crucifixion would be, as no Christian can doubt, the richest conceivable contribution to the moral welfare of mankind, such an attitude is still too remote to be a matter of practical politics. All war, in all circumstances, is evil. But it may be less evil than the alternative. And where two evil courses are the only possible alternatives it is morally right to choose the lesser evil.

Thus there may conceivably be "just" wars; though Governments are notoriously successful in making even their most shameless brigandage appear to their citizens as a just cause. There may be genuinely defensive wars. But no war has been waged in history which was not believed by the peoples on both sides to be a righteous struggle for self-defence. But in the changed world-situation the "justice" which would justify warfare is no longer appraised by the belligerent peoples, blinded by passions and "doped" by their rulers. It admits of exact legal definition. Amongst nations signatory to the Pact, the aggressor State is the State which refuses to submit the cause in dispute to arbitration. War "as an instrument of national policy" entered upon with such piratical motives is incapable of *any* justification. In such case it is wholly impossible for the Christian conscience to sanction it, or for the Christian citizen to take part in it. "The Christian Church in every nation should refuse to countenance any war in regard to which the Government of its own country has not declared its willingness to submit the matter in dispute to arbitration or conciliation."[1]

The Christian Church has not yet recovered from its humiliating surrender in blessing the arms of all the late belligerents. An open door now stands before it—the

[1] Lambeth Resolution 27.

greatest opportunity yet vouchsafed to it—to recover its hold on the world's moral allegiance and to lead the nations into the way of peace. Christianity ought to be the enrichment and the redemption of national life. But the Church is a supra-national society. It cannot, without moral abdication, identify itself without qualification with the cause or welfare of any one people. For this reason one cannot but feel misgivings about the development of "national" Churches. It is right that Christianity should express itself not in imitative Western forms but freely, spontaneously and naturally in accordance with the genius and traditions of the various peoples who accept its leadership. Only thus is it genuinely catholic; and the vision of the Lambeth Conference was as great a vision as Christians have yet seen. But there is a real and frightful danger lest Christianity should become the ally of crude, nascent Asiatic nationalism. For the same reason we cannot approve the popular "broad-minded" proposal of "closing up the religious ranks" in a united Church in each nation. A Church of Germany, France or Great Britain would be the worst conceivable kind of reunion. We have had sufficient historical experience to be forewarned of such a simplification, as an added danger to the peace of the world. If Christendom must remain divided, let the lines be denominational rather than national.

The time may come when Christian citizens must choose between their Christianity and their political allegiance. In any future war of aggression it will become the duty of Christians to refuse to support or co-operate with their Government. The provisions of the Pact and the Covenant clarify the whole issue. What may have been right for Christians in 1914 will no longer be right for them in the new age. In the pre-war world "conscientious objection" was not altogether easy to justify. In the new world it becomes morally binding. Where the war is aggressive (as now defined) Christians should refuse to take part or to help the State, directly or indirectly. The State would, of course, be entirely within its rights in executing conscientious objectors; though in practice it would not be easy to shoot millions of its own citizens, including numbers of women and children. So that in fact if Christian opinion in all nations made it clear now that it stands and would stand by this decision, that in itself would be almost equivalent to making war an impracticable expedient. No Government could carry a war through if faced with non-violent civil war at home.

But, when the emergency is upon us, nobody can trust his own judgment. The manipulation of mass-propaganda, the terrors, emotions and passions of imminent war, overwhelm moral independence. It is too late then : all go mad together. The essential mission of Christianity is thus to forestall these drastic decisions by helping to create such an atmosphere as will reinforce the chances of peace. War is a matter of moral disposition rather than of deliberate Governmental policy. Where certain spiritual attitudes are dominant in the mass of a population peace or war result automatically, uncontrolled by our conscious choices. Peace can be caused only by *Metanoia*—a disarming of men's minds and wills by the removal of those inequalities, those suspicions, hatreds and jealousies which frustrate the fulfilment of fellowship, within the nations and between them. Peace demands arduous adventure. " War in heaven " is the pre-condition of any abiding " peace on earth ". Christians ought to be found as protagonists in all causes that make for peace—not as avoidance of suffering and danger but as a creative moral ambition. It is *such* peace-makers who are the children of God.

This is not an ignobly passive ideal ; it involves sacrificial dedication. It is urgently necessary to insist on this. We have about us a new generation, brought up to revere heroic examples and eager to prove that they too could show themselves as ready for hardship and gallant enterprise as their fathers and brothers who fell in the last war. This is a very perilous moment ; unless these ardours and endurances are evoked and claimed by equivalent ventures in the constructive service of Peace. It is for Christian men and women to be leaders in all such redemptive works, all such experiments and hazards as serve to foster and strengthen Community. No man of my age and generation who has taken some part in active service and seen undergraduates mown down like grass (" second lieutenants unless otherwise stated ") is likely to be lacking in reverence for the Christ-like character of the Happy Warrior. " They died like men and fell like one of the princes." Yet none of these superb moral qualities but could be called forth and used as signally by the heroic demands of pacific enterprises. To fight disease, to drain tropical swamps, to stand out against conventional prejudice in the matter of " colour " or other social cleavages, makes every bit as high a claim on courage as the perils of service in the Forces.

The moral value of military training is, indeed, grossly exaggerated by the champions of a dying world order. It is much to be wished that the Churches would not avail themselves of semi-military organizations to inculcate discipline and public spirit and the other (rightly prized) manly virtues. " Rovering " and similar methods attain these results as well and better. To see the Scouts' Hostel at Kandersteg and watch boys of every nation and language working together to conquer a mountain peak, is to realize that the new generation is moulding a new moral ideal. There is something there infinitely more fruitful than presenting arms to a General on a cricket-ground or firing blank on chalk downs in Wiltshire. For in truth the feudal and chivalric ideal is becoming morally anachronistic. Dead warriors and weeping women belong to the old world of Homeric saga, not to the new age which we are to fashion.

The new age calls for a new kind of courage—no less exacting, no less sacrificial—in the evolution and fostering of life.

At present we are so steeped in the old tradition that all our symbolism is still bound up with associations of war-time heroism. We can only invest any enterprise with glamour so that men's blood tingles and their pulses quicken, by military trappings and metaphors. The causes of peace still seem tame and humdrum : they lack the note of " the trumpets that sound in the morning ". Even the Christian Church has succumbed to this. It loves to describe itself as a mighty army. But there is nothing in the whole world that the Church of God should less resemble : it is an adventure of creative fellowship. The task of our Christian generation is to devise new glamorous symbols—to invest the cause of peace in Community with the same splendour and the same appeal to all in men that is heroic and generous as the obsolete heroisms of war.

Peace is not the absence of strife—which is, indeed, an ideal of death. It is an energy of co-operation, through pain, strife, difficulty and danger, with God's ultimate purpose in history—to bring the race " unto perfect man ", in which the fulfilment of each individual is guaranteed in a perfect Community. But to say this is again to cross over the frontier from the natural to the supernatural.

4. Community and the Supernatural

We have seen that an eager participation in the citizen's life and responsibilities is implied in doing God's will. Yet no one individual and no one existing society can realize the whole will of God. Goodness in its perfection and fullness, in which all human wills co-operate, in which all mutually share, can be achieved in no earthly society centred round a local group loyalty. No community that is in the world can fully express the divine will. That can be only in the supreme Community, the *Societas Societatum*, of which the centre is the Absolute Good and its ruling purpose the Divine Spirit. The inner law of life in Community is fulfilled only in the supernatural—in the fellowship of the Holy Spirit. In it every element of goodness, every expression and aspect of excellence, finds its place in such mutuality that therein each individual may realize his own full development in the sharing of the Divine Life. Thus the true life of the earthly commonwealth comes to its full fruition in the heavenly. There Community finds its real meaning, in " a perfectly ordered and mutual fellowship enjoying God and one another in God ".[1]

Now to the English mind such language is apt to sound strained and unnatural, dangerously suggestive of " mysticism ". Yet it is clear that all human groups presuppose the presence of the supernatural. We are familiar with the attempts to trace the origin of society to one or another form of " social contract ". " Every schoolboy " can criticise the fallacy which vitiates all the historic theories. It is vain to seek for the origin of society, for society is itself the primary fact. It is the pattern of human life. We have no trace of *Homo Sapiens* save in some kind of social grouping. It is the expression of the nature of Man. But what is it which holds groups together ? What is it which makes a collection of men and women into a " group " (in the psychological sense), living together, acting together, conscious that they belong to one another ? On any level, primitive or developed, it is the sharing of a common purpose—the touch (if we will) of a common spirit. And this implies that the bond of society is something which is more than natural.

It is no mere product of biology ; it is not the resultant of economic pressure or the circumstances of geography or

[1] " Pax civitatis, ordinata imperandi atque obediendi concordia civium. Pax coelestis Civitatis, ordinatissima et concordissima societas fruendi Deo et invicem in Deo." Augustine, *De Civitate Dei*, XIX, xiii *ad init.*

history. It is something belonging to the order of spirit. Every human group, at its level, is the organization of a common life by something which is at least supra-natural. Christianity says that this is Man responding, in his measure, to the Divine. It is nothing less than the Spirit of God beginning, at least, to take control of Man's psychophysical constitution. This gives us as it were the matrix of the Christian interpretation. The meaning of history, in the Christian world view—the eternal purpose for which the world was made—is the gathering of the whole human race into one Community of the Holy Spirit, in which human life shall be fulfilled in all its range, its length and depth and height, in a common sharing of the divine Life. That would be God fulfilled in His creation, and the life of Man perfected in God.

At present that purpose is frustrated. It is still but imperfectly expressed in local manifestations of Community which cannot, as yet, transcend their own limitations. Thus, as we have seen, none of our societies can provide personal life with its full expression. Group comes into conflict with group ; and as consequence there is maladjustment between each group and the members composing it. Freedom is yet thwarted and incomplete ; not because social life is "organized" but because its organization is still fragmentary. There are genuine clashes of interest, some of which seem to admit of no compromise. There are grievances and animosities which separate groups from one another and thus mutilate and impoverish individual life within the groups. On the level of economics and politics these conflicts seem to defy solution. But until they are solved, personal life is spoiled by what should be its instrument and expression. Freedom remains unreconciled with Community.

All these conflicts and separatisms—whether racial, political or economic—seem to be in their own nature insoluble. The group loyalty which informs each group is the spirit or purpose recognized by that group ; so that the very bond of society seems to involve exclusion and opposition. There is no way of transcending this finitude unless the purpose informing all groups is the will and purpose of the Whole. That is what the Christian religion offers. The Holy Spirit redeems Community from the bankruptcy of human statesmanship. It leads men to trust one another through all differences of race and temperament. Christ, says St. Paul " slew the enmity ". It cleanses hearts from fears and suspicions. It demolishes the walls of partition and throws down the barricades of privilege. It begins to draw men across all that divides them, and the apparent conflicts of cross-purposes, into a fellowship which is universal because it is centred in the love of God. That is the holy universal Church—articulating all our communities at their different levels of development in a common life which is fully personal because it lives in the Spirit of God Himself. There Community is fulfilled in freedom and freedom perfected in Community. For in the communion of that society, perfectly responsive to the divine will, all men and women find their true freedom—" the glorious liberty of the children of God ".

That society is the work of Christ, the King of the Communion of saints. It is His unique and incomparable creation. He, as the centre of redeemed humanity, is the source of the new moral order, expressed and embodied in that Divine Community which is even now present in the world, and awaits its victorious manifestation. The Church, thus conceived and interpreted, is no merely " optional extra " to the faith of individual disciples. It is the bearer of the Divine Purpose, penetrating this world of necessity with the freedoms of the life eternal, gathering our fragmentary communities into the Community of the Holy Spirit. It is, indeed, the sacrament of Community—the symbol and the redemptive instrument of the social order in the Coming Age. It is, in St. Paul's metaphor, the " earnest " of human life as it is in the Mind of God ; though it is never left without witness wherever the Spirit of Christ rules our hearts.

The actual " Churches " which exist on earth, despite all their sins and dissensions, are yet pledges of the Coming Kingdom. Wherever a " little flock " is redeemed from worldliness, sustained in fellowship with the living Christ and kept faithful to its Christian loyalties, there is the promise of perfected Community.

Where He is in the heart
City of God, thou art.

CHAPTER X

SPENDING AND GETTING

1. Christianity and Wealth

NOTHING at first sight seems further removed from the spiritual and supernatural than the sphere of financial and industrial enterprise. Such phrases as "value for money", "hard cash", "business is business" and similar twentieth-century catchwords suggest a hard-headed practical realism and an eye to the main chance in worldly success which are commonly thought of as almost antithetical to all that spiritual religion cherishes. Money at least seems concrete and tangible, while the unseen realities of religion are remote, abstract and probably unverifiable. Thus too often the Christian ethic appears to be incurably sentimental. It appears to be asking the world of business to desert those irrefutable facts over which we have at least some control and on which our continued existence depends, for the sake of hypothetical satisfactions and principles which, however idealistic, cannot be sustained in the bank and counting-house. It has indeed come to be taken for granted that religion can have no effective message for the hard world of economic reality. Thus the whole kingdom of modern industry has tended to repudiate any allegiance to the moral sanctions of Christianity, while Christianity on its side has been too ready to acquiesce in weak and pious aspirations which are merely irritating and ineffective. Thus Christian teachers are apt to observe that if everyone would accept Christianity our economic difficulties would solve themselves. Such assertions may be quite true ; but unless the Churches show themselves capable of constructive and realistic thinking to vindicate these enormous generalizations they are bound to appear futile and almost meaningless. It is scarcely surprising that "hard-faced" men demand that religion shall stick to its last and not interfere in those practical concerns about which it has nothing useful to say.

The eclipse of religion by economics has not resulted so much from lack of earnestness as from lack of practical insight and realism. It has not sufficiently valued or appreciated the changing demand of a changing world order. Mr. Tawney's well-known remark about Christianity in the sixteenth century is full of warning for our own time. "In England, as on the Continent, the new economic realities came into sharp collision with the social theory inherited from the Middle Ages. The result was a re-assertion of the traditional doctrines with an almost tragic intensity of emotion, their gradual retreat before the advance of new conceptions both of economic organization and of the province of religion, and their final decline from a militant creed into a kind of pious antiquarianism. They lingered, venerable ghosts, on the lips of Churchmen down to the Civil War. Then the storm blew and they flickered out."[1]

We succeed only in making ourselves ridiculous if we go to the world of banks and factories with their vast plants, their tape machines and dictaphones with murmurs of "pious antiquarianism". It is too much like the Professor in *Punch*. If Religion is to be vindicated in the midst of these magnificent enterprises two conditions seem to be postulated. It must first be strongly and thankfully maintained that the economic activities of the world are not alternatives to the life of religion (so that people must make their choice between them) or hindrances to the cause of Christianity, but essential ways of doing God's will and co-operating in His

[1] *Religion and the Rise of Capitalism*, p. 135.

creative Purpose. It must then be shown that spending and getting, which must in the nature of things occupy a large proportion of mortal Man's existence, presupposes the spiritual order and can only fulfil its functions effectively when it is projected on supernatural backgrounds. To seek first the Kingdom of God and righteousness does not mean working with obsolete machinery ; but it does mean bringing the organization of Industry into touch with those realities of human life which at present are so disastrously forgotten.

But strange things have lately been happening in the sphere of finance and economics ; and these suggest a fruitful analogy with recent developments in natural science. It was taken for granted not so long ago that the one certain and tangible reality was the concrete order of the material. This at least was indisputably real, as all waking experience could verify. For the thinkers of the last generation the difficulty was to find room, in a Universe determined mechanically by the physical configurations of matter, for any effective function for mind and spirit. But to-day matter is by no means so tangible. It is now beginning to melt away into a series of mathematical formulas. Nobody can tell us what " matter " is. We know only that its constant behaviour is in fact due to the work of our minds ; and we are beginning to ask the old question in exactly the opposite of its earlier form. The problem for us is less to discover the place of spirit in the material order than to find the place of " matter " in the spiritual.[1] Something of the same kind has occurred to the supposed realities of hard cash. We thought that at least we knew the meaning of money. It is something that we can carry in our pockets, hoard in a teapot, or entrust to a bank. Here at least there is something more real than the hypothetical forces of spirit.

[1] I am not of course suggesting that the resolution of hard atoms into electrical forces means that matter has become " spiritual ". That is surely a quite fatuous argument.

But in the complexity of the modern world if we ask the question: What is money? we shall be at a loss to find a convincing answer. The one fact which seems to emerge quite certainly from the confusions of large-scale undertakings is that money has no actual existence. It is not so much cash, but so much credit. But credit is nothing material or tangible: it is something to do with purpose and character. Thus the existence and functions of "money" are more and more clearly inter-related with certain moral and spiritual realities. The claim therefore which is so frequently made that Business ought to have complete liberty in the administration of its own province without interference from ethics or religion, is not merely morally "wrong": it is in the very nature of things impossible. Indeed it will scarcely now be disputed that behind our existing economic difficulties both on a national and an international scale there lie fundamental maladjustments in political, moral and spiritual relationships.

Thus religion becomes supremely relevant to the preoccupations of the present hour. And the order of economics, on its side, is of vital import to Christianity. It would be a poor, anæmic religion which remained aloof from our pressing financial anxieties. The cause of God's Kingdom in the world is at present intimately related to those immense economic issues which so largely control the direction of policy. The existing economic situation thwarts God's will for His human family. It impoverishes the manhood of nations, it imperils spiritual brotherhood, and is a menace to the peace of the world. The immediate will of God for mankind must, without any doubt or qualification, be that it should be dealt with creatively as a means to the liberation of spiritual life. Adequate economic resources are obviously the precondition not merely of physical existence but of all the higher reaches of spirit. If it is God's will to give us our daily bread, then the creation and distribution of wealth is one of the surest ways of co-operating with the purpose of God as revealed in Christ. We need to see the bank and the factory as instrumental to the divine Kingdom no less than the school, the hospital and the Church. The economic order, like the political, has thus its own relative independence and justification in its own right. The Christian ethic gives its blessing and sanction to every legitimate industrial enterprise: but it claims that all must be controlled by reference to the needs of spiritual personality and the final End of Man's life.

This is the only possible justification for the institution of private property. There seem to be certain spiritual values which are best sustained and preserved through a guaranteed freedom of private possession. A man's life, it is true, does not consist in the abundance of things which he possesses: yet normally if he possesses nothing he cannot rise to the full stature of manhood. He will be deprived of an indispensable aid to self-fulfilment and spiritual development: and thus some right of property tenure is normally and as a general rule a condition of citizenship in the Kingdom of God. As spirit must be incorporate in a body or remain ghost-like and ineffectual, so spiritual personality must embody itself in material possession. But this very recognition clearly involves a stern limitation on the rights of individual ownership. Too much wealth, no less than too much poverty, may be fatal to spiritual health. Undeniably the thought of our Lord was more sensitive to the former danger; though it must always be borne in mind that the poverty which came within His experience was not that of modern proletariats. The "anxiety" against which He warned men as destructive of spiritual poise, and which seemed to Him to be fatally bound up with "the cares and riches of this world", is in our day caused no less injuriously by the desperate sense of insecurity and the harassing worries of the casual wage-earner.

But to recognize that possessions are justified by the needs of spiritual personality is to recognize also the moral corollary that wealth can be sanctioned by Christian ethics only so far as its distribution and use serve the ends of life in Community. This, as is well known, has been the standpoint of the Christian ethic as expressed in the Canon Law. It has insisted that but for the Fall private possessions would not have been justifiable. In an ideally Christian society all wealth would be owned and administered communally. But as a concession to Man's fallen nature it has given its sanction to private possessions, yet only under the strict reservation that no man has a moral right to possess more than was needed for his true personal well-being and the due discharge of his social functions. What was more was of the Evil One. Luxury, avarice and exploitation were reckoned among the deadly sins. The law of the Church offered the sharpest contrast to the theory of Dominion in the Civil Law. The Church has persistently denied that a man has a right to do what he wills with his own. It allowed wealth no moral justification apart from the needs and welfare of the community. The particular regulations and prohibitions by which the Church sought to enforce its principles on the economic life of the Middle Ages can have no relevance to our situation. But its cardinal conviction remains, that wealth has its place within the life of the Christian only in virtue of its contribution to the service of personal life in Community.

It is this ultimate standard of Christian ethics which the modern world most needs to recover. For it is the merest commonplace to observe that the underlying assumptions of modern life stand in diametrical opposition to it. We all assume that the making of profits and the unlimited increase of possessions is the chief if not the sole end of man and the only completely intelligible motive. It is true, of course, that the making of profit is indispensable to a modern business: if it failed to do this it would quickly come to an end, and involve its shareholders in its own ruin. But current events are making it glaringly obvious that the economic life of the world cannot be maintained in health or efficiency in the strength of merely economic motives. Behind the mystifications of the Economists, who use phrases such as over-production, under-consumption and so forth, to obscure facts which we all know in experience, there are certain indisputable truths which belong to the province of religion and ethics. Industry is producing many commodities which consumers either do not want or are not wealthy enough to buy there is, we are told, a failure in adjustment between consumption and production. Meantime, while millions are on the point of starvation, foodstuffs are being destroyed wholesale in the hope of thereby keeping up prices which an impoverished world cannot pay. But this is brigandage rather than industry. And if we compare the alleged falling prices with those charged by the chain stores and retailers we come upon further suggestions of piracy. Now these are not technical matters of economics: they are elementary issues of right and wrong. Can it be denied that the fundamental factor in our economic depression is moral? The present organization of industry both on the national and the world-wide scale bears no relation to ultimate human need. The moral issues are the decisive issues. The supreme interest of Christianity is that the creation of wealth should be controlled by a more searching sense of corporate human responsibility, and be made to minister to the fuller enrichment of human persons in fellowship with God.

For the Christian ethic cannot despise wealth. It is quite insincere and unreal to pretend that in the circumstances of modern life the needs of Man's spirit are independent of sufficient material supply. God's will for men cannot be realized in a world of economic disorganization. Spiritual values are frustrated by grinding poverty and incessant worry. The moral and spiritual development of India, for example, or tropical Africa, must be inextricably bound up with a raising of the general standard of life, the exploitation of natural resources and the more effective organization of Industry. And we in Europe know by bitter experience what moral and spiritual wastage results from lack of sufficient material wealth to give personal life its full chance.

Thus I cannot believe that "holy poverty" is the true ideal for twentieth-century Christians. Our task is rather to sanctify wealth. Our Lord's injunctions to "sell all" cannot, obviously, be regarded as law universal for modern disciples. Nor are we in much danger of so regarding them. The extra-canonical Saying: "Be good bankers," appeals more immediately to our taste. Yet it may be urged that the sayings in the Gospels ought to ring in our ears and make us feel uncomfortable. The besetting temptation of present-day Christians is not that they should esteem wealth too slightly. And while Christians ought, as we have suggested, to regard the due increase of the world's wealth as an integral part of doing God's will, they must yet endeavour to keep alive in their hearts that otherworldly sense of detachment which alone redeems economic enterprise from secularization and worldliness. And it may be that in times like the present, when covetousness has become an idolatry ruinous to soul and body alike, we can only recover the true Christian values by some signal and voluntary renunciation. It may be that wealth can be made holy only by demonstrating its unimportance by comparison with the riches of mind and spirit. Prosperity may be purchased too dear. "In the currency of the soul as in that of states, spurious coin drives out good. . . . The chief enemy of the life of spirit, whether in art, culture or religion or in the simple human associations which are the common vehicle of its revelation to ordinary men, is itself a religion. It is, as everyone knows, the idolatry of wealth."[1] Now there can be no true Community where wealth is either so far deficient that many lack the means to a complete life, nor where it is so inequitably distributed as to divide a man against his neighbour, class against class or nation against nation. The gravest peril that now besets England is that political lines of division should be drawn by distinctions in economic status, so that rich and poor form the two parties. The achievement of spiritual Community, both within nations and between them, is thus bound up with a redistribution of the available wealth of mankind and a rational agreement about its increase. "Though the ideal of an equal distribution of wealth may continue to elude us, it is necessary, nevertheless, to make haste towards it, not because such wealth is the most important of man's treasures, but to prove that it is not."[2]

Such an ideal is, of course, served in part by taxation and similar forms of State action. But it remains true that the greatest need of the world is some such radical redirection of motive as religion alone is capable of inspiring. Unless we change our hearts and our habits we and the world may go down together. We call Russia "materialistic", and it is so in the sense that it recognizes no values other than economic. The Russians admit that they live for material ends: we pretend to ourselves that we do not. Yet one outstanding difference between the Russian system and that of the other countries of Europe is that the Soviet Government has the courage, and can call upon the brains and imagination, to *plan* its life to achieve its avowed ends, while we and others drift inertly along. But though the Soviets show themselves cruelly hostile to all religious and non-material values, is there another instance in modern history of such nation-wide repudiation of the motive of *individual* gain? "In our Soviet Union, citizen, we have deposited the

[1] Tawney, *Equality*, p. 290.
[2] Tawney, *op. cit.*, p. 291.

word Riches in the archives."[1] The entire people may be preoccupied with the increase of material goods, but the pursuit of personal wealth and aggrandisement is counted as the one unforgivable sin, and is punished not only by fine or confiscation but by social ostracism and the contempt of friends.

Those sickening persecutions and cruelties which at present stain the rule of the Soviets make it appear to us in a devilish light. But let any Christian in Western Europe who has cleansed his heart from the motive of personal gain take the first stone to cast at it. Indeed it is no fantastic speculation that despite those brutalities and oppressions, those elemental passions and furies, which haunt the life of a still backward people, yet out of Russia will " come forth a law " which may change the whole attitude of the world. At present they are a people driven desperate by a race against time and the hatreds of neighbouring states. But I would venture to hazard the prophecy that in due course, when the plan has been put into practice and the nation is freed from its fierce preoccupations and able to live calmly and peaceably, Russia may yet prove itself the matrix of such a rebirth of the Christian spirit as may give a new leadership to the civilized world.

As things are now, the temper that animates Russia is a deadly foe to true human welfare and the cause of spiritual freedom. It starves the spirit of its own citizens and it unites them in fierce antagonism to those who live under other forms of government. It makes for disunion, not for Community. But we have here at least a signal suggestion of what may be achieved by the Christian faith if it can inspire the life of spending and getting, and clothe itself in an economic order of common devotion to common good, as the one Spirit that dwells in the one body.

Of that consummation of the divine will, each group of

[1] Quoted from M. Hindus in the *Week-end Review*, August 15, 1931.

Christians is meant to be sacramental—its standing witness and its effective instrument. In the central rite of the worship of Christianity, where Christians meet to share in the New Life, that obligation is solemnly accepted. They take the bread of man's common need, they offer it before their God and Father and partake of it in fellowship in Christ's name—that the economic life of mankind may be no more that for which men kill one another, but the pledge and expression of unity in the Spirit and the vehicle of life eternal. "Thy will be done—in the earning of our bread—on earth as it is in heaven."

Such aspirations are merely sentimental unless they are harnessed to concrete suggestions for beginning to make our loyalties effectual. I append one elementary proposal.

2. The Standard of Life

History has now reached a point at which no nation can hope to be saved by any merely national policy. All our problems are international, and only resolute international action can provide any effective solution. Till we disarm we shall all be beggars. The lesson of facts is thus in complete agreement with the axioms of Christian thinking. To recognize this leads almost inevitably to a certain critical detachment from the rival proposals of economists and political leaders in our own country. Moreover the situation changes so rapidly that whatever might be truly said now would be obsolete by the time it appears in print. Such considerations are apt to make discussion seem slightly unreal; and so complex are the technical issues that it is scarcely possible for the private citizen to form any judgment worth having on the existing economic position. Experts disagree so perplexingly that the plain man is left inert and bewildered, as though faced by a blind catastrophe which no human power can control ; and this is destroying our sense of responsibility. Nothing, however, could be more fatal than that we should allow the complexity of the crisis to become an excuse for supine inaction. This country may yet recover its moral initiative and lead the world back to sanity and freedom. But it cannot take its place in the divine Purpose without convinced and creative leadership, which at the moment we need more desperately than at any recent period in our history. Christianity has a unique chance to guide our people towards its future, to offer that touch of fundamental conviction which alone can heal us of our paralysis, and to purge and strengthen the soul of the nation by a courageous reassertion of its own essential values.

For the Christian values are frankly incompatible with those which our civilization takes for granted. During the hectic years since the Armistice there has been a disastrous shifting of standards. It has come to be assumed in all classes that spending-power is the chief aim of Man ; the lust of possession has seized on our whole people, and the worse things are the more reckless do we become. The standard of life is constantly rising, and nearly the whole employed population spends out of all proportion to its income on eating, drinking and amusements. Thus while millions are unemployed the amount expended per head of the population on the luxury trades is colossal. An entirely unjustifiable percentage of the aggregate income of our people is spent on smoking, drinking, betting, and the "movies." This is the scale on which England is living while its foundations are being undermined. The unpleasant truth must be faced : our present standard of life cannot be justified or endorsed by the Christian scale of values unless sustained by harder work and informed by a more searching sense of obligation. The fundamental demand of the Christian ethic is for a drastic simplification of life.

In general principle it is probable that a rising standard of life is desirable, and may serve many vital Christian interests. Nor need Christianity be suspicious of the insistent demand for more leisure, unless this proves to be incommensurable with the social necessities of the hour. Work for work's sake is not a Christian ideal. But there is a law of diminishing moral returns. The desire for heightened standards of living may advance true moral well-being; but (as appears to be true at this moment) its effect may be found to be the exact opposite.

An artificially protected standard of life, such as has been established in England chiefly by the enterprise of Trade Unions, is at present involved in a vicious circle. It is maintained partly at the expense of the poorest classes in the community, the semi-skilled and the agricultural workers. The excessive toll of fixed money wages tends to render industry unremunerative; while the increasing drain on taxation caused by the consequent unemployment means that the latter grows steadily worse. Meanwhile the land goes out of cultivation; and the population can be fed only by mass produced urban industries which, in turn, survive only by their success in suggesting that the more we spend the better for trade. Yet this suggestion defeats its own object. For the more recklessly we spend on demands thus artificially stimulated, the less we can invest in productive enterprises. Crushing taxation has the effect of making us prodigal rather than thrifty and postpones still further the hope of a lasting solution. Yet it seems as though, within this situation, production can be continued only by inducing people to spend unrestrainedly.

But Christians may lead a moral sortie from the vicious circle in which we are all imprisoned. There is, it is clear, no way of escape save by deliberate and personal sacrifice; and this offers Christians an open opportunity. It may be found that sheer bitter necessity will compel some reduction in money wages as the sole way of maintaining real wages at any tolerable level, and controlling the epidemic of unemployment. It may be that the pocket-money expenditure of wage-earners must be cut down, as the condition of saving their standard of life as expressed by education and the social services. But it is not endurable that the professional classes should call upon the wage-earners for sacrifice so long as they assume (as we all do) that whatever changes may become necessary, their own standard must remain constant. Not only do they themselves spend on a scale which cannot be morally justified, for against the background of our present distress the smart shops and fashionable restaurants are a scandal to a Christian country; they also establish fashions and tastes in expenditure for the rest of the population to emulate.

Here, it may be urged, is a straightforward and direct challenge to Christian society. There is no more obvious way of testing our allegiance to the standards which we profess, and none of contributing more effectively to the nation's moral and economic well-being. Christians should set themselves deliberately to a simplification of their standard of life, helping to create a social opinion which regards reckless expenditure as vulgar, and thus giving a lead to our fellow-citizens out of the prison-house of false values. The demand for one amusement after another springs chiefly from lack of imagination, and from identifying happiness with ostentatious luxury and excitement. Those who know but little of the life of the spirit and the secrets of joy and simplicity must seek their satisfactions more grossly. Christians should not be in that predicament. Moreover, the tyranny of social conventions tends towards an enforced conformity under pain of misjudgment or ostracism. Christians should be sufficiently independent not to be at the mercy of female snobbery. At least they should measure by real valuations. A strong Christian social standard on all such matters as dress, entertaining, theatres, week-ends and so forth, would make an exceedingly rich contribution to some of our most recalcitrant difficulties. We cannot continue to live on our present scale without incurring the danger of bankruptcy, or being forced into such reckless inflation as would fall most cruelly on the most defenceless. But Christians of the professional classes are in a position to give a strong lead, and to draw the sting from wage cuts and restrictions (if these should unhappily become unavoidable) by a voluntary simplification of our standards.

It is true that "saving" by individuals, if that involves withdrawing employment, is a false policy in the existing circumstances. We ought, probably, to spend all we can. But some retrenchment will be imposed on everyone, except the few very rich people, by increased taxation and diminishing dividends. In such situations our natural tendency is to save what we can in various ways, but assuming always that we keep the same amount free for spending on our pleasures and luxuries. Our first move as ratepayers and taxpayers is to cut down the educational estimates: as private citizens our first step is to cancel subscriptions or dispense with the gardener. Such "saving" has little merit; it means that we impoverish other people without cutting into our own enjoyment. This can have no Christian value and no sort of economic justification. The right course is to spend what we can in such a way as enriches the lives of others; and this must mean for almost everybody a cutting down of accustomed indulgences.

Luxurious living corrodes the soul and has no economic justification. "It curses him that gives and him that takes." The Christian should so direct his spending-power as to strengthen genuinely productive industries and those financial and economic enterprises which minister to the glory of God. This cannot be claimed for Parisian cosmetics, the ermines of fabulous Film stars, or ostentatious, extravagant entertaining.

"Be not made a beggar by banqueting upon borrowing, when thou hast nothing in thy purse."[1]

[1] Ecclesiasticus xviii. 33.

CHAPTER XI

THE LIFE OF THE WORLD TO COME

1. The Eternal Hope

"TOUCH Me not for I am not yet ascended," says the Risen Christ in the Fourth Gospel. Most modern Christians, if they are candid, would probably admit that this saying freezes their blood as they read the story. It seems to chill the atmosphere of that garden as the spring sun is beginning to warm the flowers, and the Conqueror comes striding through the lilies, and the loved tones speak the name of greeting, and in that rapt moment of recognition she turns herself and says to Him "Master"! The scene is so unimaginably lovely, so perfectly and divinely satisfying, that His response to her seems to leave us frozen. It seems to withdraw Him again from our contacts, to make Him remote and unapproachable, out of the range of our faith and love. It seems to hold the disciple at arm's length. Yet it is indeed just that sense of *distance* on which depends all Christian faith and the Christian interpretation of Man's destiny.

For Christ is only completely real to us as a vivid and lifegiving Presence, just because He is not confined within the sequences of history. So the Fourth Gospel insistently maintains. "It is expedient that I go away . . . that where I am there ye may be also." If we "cling to" Him, if we hold Him down to our transitory, contingent world, we shall never possess Him as our own. What is described in mythological language as the Lord's Ascension into heaven is the precondition of His abiding presence as the Companion of our passing days. To recognize this cuts very deep, and not only into our theology but into onr conception of Christian ethics and indeed our whole attitude to life. The failure of "commonsense" ethics, no less than that of popular Christianity, is due to the loss of just this sense of distance. Without it, our apprehension of human life is blurred, because it is set in false perspective. And, if the otherworldly emphasis is not central in our religious thought, then in truth what we are thinking about is not religion at all but something else.

"Speaking broadly," writes Professor Gilbert Murray, "apart from certain religious movements, the enlightened modern reformer, if confronted with some ordinary complex of misery and wickedness, instinctively proposes to cure it by higher wages, better food, more comfort and leisure; to make people comfortable and to trust to their becoming good. The typical ancient reformer would appeal to us to care for none of these things (since riches notoriously do not make men virtuous) but with all our powers to pursue wisdom or righteousness and the life of the spirit; to be good men, as we can be if we will, and to know that all else will follow."[1] Either attitude, taken in isolation, is (as we have insisted) inadequate to the richness and complexity of the problem. But no one can doubt that it is the latter insistence which is needed most by our generation as the corrective of its dominant ethic. "This (he adds) is one of the regions in which the ancients might have learnt much from us, and in which we still have much to learn from them, if once we can shake off our temporal obsessions and listen."

The accepted ethic of the twentieth century is avowedly eudæmonistic. At its best, it is not self-regarding. It is controlled by a fine ideal of devotion to the common good. But the latter is conceived almost exclusively in terms of

[1] *Five Stages of Greek Religion*, p. 149.

social amelioration, of political and economic reforms, and of Man's earthly and temporal welfare. Time is the limit of its horizons. At its highest, it fosters a noble spirit of sacrifice, at its lowest, it is apt to degenerate into a mere deification of comfort. But in all its grades of refinement it is dominated by the assumption that the improvement of Man's earthly estate is the end and goal of moral action. It is therefore apt to demand of religion that it shall vindicate its claim to respect by ability to " deliver the goods ", to shew direct and immediate returns in its contribution to social welfare. Only on such terms can its value be recognized. Christianity is respected or repudiated almost entirely from this point of reference. The advanced thinkers base their rejection of it on the ground that its teaching and its way of life no longer conduce to social improvement in the changed conditions of modern history. The mass of kind, duty-loving Englishmen still hold it in genuine honour, as more likely than any other religion to rectify our human relationships and inspire a more perfect order of society. The Christian way of life, it is held, if men had grace and courage to follow it, would lead to that idealized world-order of peace, justice, health and freedom which we describe as the " Kingdom of God on earth ".

Now all that has been said in this volume rests on the resolute conviction that the Christian religion holds within it a transfiguring power in the world of history. It is a false and anæmic Christianity which takes refuge in mere pietism and claims a private religious experience as a victory for the religious ideal.[1] Such a " flight " is glaringly inconsistent with the prayer : " Thy will be done on earth ". But this book has been equally controlled by the certainty that the popular Christian belief in a " good time " to be realized in this world (however " refined " our conception of the good time) as the goal of Christian endeavour and the fulfilment

[1] Cf. *supra*, Chap. II, pp. 25–27.

of the Kingdom of God, is yet something less than Christianity. The Christian ethic is a religious ethic, with an otherworldly hunger and thirst at the heart of it. It presupposes the Christian conception of God and Man and therefore of human destiny; that Man is an immortal spirit and that his true end is only achieved in communion with God in a life eternal. It is valid only on that assumption. There is too much secularized Christian teaching, too many little books which suggest that if the world would accept Christ's way of life we should all be rich and prosperous and comfortable. Even if this were true, which is highly doubtful, it is the degradation of Christianity.

The organization of the material order is a vital Christian concern. It is not possible to save souls without regard to their environment, or that social and economic context which, while it certainly does not determine character, equally certainly moulds and conditions it. But I see no way of evading it—a certain austere strain of asceticism is indelible in authentic Christianity. For if indeed it is true, as Christians believe, that the spirit of Man is designed for eternity and can be fulfilled only in the eternal, then we cannot surrender ourselves wholeheartedly to any satisfactions of this world, however rich and however ennobling. We must use the world but not use it to the full. Yet if we do not accept with reverent gratitude the gifts of this life and its opportunities, then we refuse the divine invitation and shut ourselves out from the King's banquet. For the Spirit is disclosed to our spirits through those manifold values and interests which are the substance of spiritual life. Moreover, to shirk the demands and tasks of helping our fellows and serving our generation is to empty the moral life of all meaning; and to do these things for the sake of our own salvation is to negate both religion and morality. "If the light that is within us is darkness, how great is that darkness!"

We argue that this apparent contradiction is resolved by the Christian insistence that the Good for Man and his soul's salvation is in God Himself and in nothing else. The Christian ethic does not say: "Be virtuous for the sake of being virtuous"; still less: "Be virtuous that you may be saved." Such self-conscious morality is alien from it. It does not teach a contempt for this world that we may enter into a better; nor does it suggest that we ought to serve this world in order to earn an eternal recompense. It says: "Love God with all your heart and mind." This is the first and great commandment; the second is its spontaneous expression. But there are two commandments, not one; and to substitute either for the other is to empty both of significance.

These two poles of the Christian ethic are determined by no arbitrary dogma. This double movement of world-affirmation and world-denial is intrinsic in the very nature of moral life, and reflects that inseparable duality which is inherent in all human experience. We are at once temporal and eternal, at once under law and under grace; we are under necessity and yet free, both natural and supernatural. All our tragedy and all our grandeur comes from this central fact about us. Few among us can find true bearings on these twin poles of man's consciousness. What we know in our own experience is to be seen pre-eminently in Christ. He moves about, a Man among men, vividly concerned with human interests, bound by our human limitations. Yet He lives in detachment from the world, looking out upon it from the centre of unbroken intercourse with the Father. He is in the world but does not belong to it, in history and yet transcends it. He is completely at home in this world because His Spirit dwells in another. That impression is clear in the Gospels; yet the portrait has baffled all its interpreters. Christian thought has always been one-sided, either in this direction or that. In the past it has been so overwhelmed with the consciousness of the divine Redeemer "coming down from heaven" into this world, as to obscure Jesus of Nazareth in a haze of unreal timelessness. Yet equally false is the modern reaction which tends to make Him purely historical.

But our failure to interpret Him truly corresponds to our one-sided emphases in the explication of our own consciousness. On one side life has been impoverished by the false measures which would weigh and appraise it as though wholly eternal and spiritual. In our age, by reaction from this, we attempt to assay Man's worth and destiny by exclusively sociological standards. And here, it may be urged, is the radical cause of the moral confusion of our day. If we persist in thinking of Man wholly in terms of biology and history, wholly within space-time horizons, our philosophies end in contradiction and our nostrums of salvation do not save us. We must go back again to the cross roads and ask yet once more: What is Man?

Thus what most needs rediscovery and revived emphasis in this generation is that wellnigh lost sense of distance, that homesickness for eternity, which may never be extinguished in Christianity without adulterating its essence and devitalizing its power. The Christian ethic cannot redeem and vivify the rich tasks and values of civilization but by the saving knowledge that Man's *home* is in that which is unseen and abiding. We cannot even make a success of this world unless our hearts are fixed in another. We cannot worship God in His creation save by "detachment from the creatures".

No ethic of which the guiding motive is conformity to God's holy will can find its goals in this world of time. No utilitarian scheme of ethics (however nobly "idealistic") can ever do justice to what is implied in it. "If our moral achievement always ends only in the attainment of the slightly better, that of itself is proof that we can never attain the good."[1] If the Kingdom of God which we seek is the perfecting of a temporal condition, somewhere to be realized in time, then it will always be exposed to the relativities of the temporal process. It follows that the goal of moral endeavour is an infinite but never completed progress, and the good life is inherently self-frustrating. But it is the very nerve of religion, at least of a fully moralized religion, that the good which the moral will seeks is an abiding rest for the people of God. This aim cannot be described adequately in terms of personal freedom or fulfilment. That imports a self-regarding suggestion which is far removed from the Christian genius. The Kingdom which is the goal of the Christian ethic is a good, final, absolute and eternal in the "fruition of the glorious Godhead". It is a "Kingdom which cannot be shaken". Only this transcendent finality in the ultimate convictions of faith gives the Christian his spontaneity in welcoming the gladness of this life, his firmness in accepting its duties, his sureness of attack on its moral tasks. God for ever "makes all things new, yet Himself abides for ever the same", and the Christian seeks to renew this present world, ever changing and ever passing away, by "the powers of the world to come".

The point was seized admirably by Troeltsch, in a passage which refuses translation but may be roughly Englished as follows:

"The Christian ethic sets before all social life and effort a Goal which lies beyond all the relativities of earthly life, and presents it in relation to values which can never be more than approximations to it.

"The thought of the coming Kingdom of God, which is nothing else than the thought of the final realization of the Absolute (in whatever forms it may be conceived) does not devalue the world and the life of the world, as short-sighted

[1] A. E. Taylor, *op. cit.*, p. 99.

critics contend ; on the contrary it braces its energies, and through all the stages of its journey makes the soul strong in its certainty of a final, absolute meaning and goal of human enterprise in the future. It transcends the world but it is not world-denying. This underlying thought and meaning of all Christian asceticism is the only means of maintaining energy and heroic renunciation in one psychological unity, which immeasurably deepens and sublimates the life of instinct, and irremediably destroys the merely natural motives of heroism or simply attempts to call them into life again out of the biological impulses. From it issues both intense activity and certainty concerning the goal of action : it is thus the true source of inner health. All social Utopias then become superfluous ; the constant warning of experience, that it is impossible to grasp and realize the ideal in its completeness, does not then bewilder the seeker or throw him back into that scepticism which results so easily from a sincere realism, and is everywhere overwhelming the finer spirits of our time. The ' beyond ' is the dynamic of the present."[1]

The moral End is eternal and final. But it is clear that more is implied if the Christian ethic is not to be illusory. The individual seeking to do God's will must himself be an immortal spirit ; else his own moral fruition is forever and in the nature of things sacrificed to an end in which he can never be a partaker. That is to say, in effect, that human persons are, even at their highest and best, no more than means to the fulfilment of a Purpose which scraps them as Man scraps his tools. But that is blankly irreconcilable with the revelation of God in the mind of Christ. If persons are of infinite worth in God's sight, then they are not merely means or instruments to an end which is ultimately independent of them. That persons are ends in their own right is almost the definition of personality. "How

[1] Das Jenseits ist die Kraft des Diesseits : *Sozial-lehren,* p. 979.

much better is a man than a sheep." That God is one to whom persons are dear is utterly central in our Lord's mind. Nor is it really possible to conceive a will to personal perfection, as a will directed to any purpose other than the perfecting, and fulfilment of those who share and co-operate with it. The Kingdom is a communion of persons in life eternal "in" the Father, enjoying God and one another in God.

There is here no available way of compromise. Here the Christian faith demands decisive committal to one alternative. The Christian belief in immortality is not in my judgment demonstrable. Nor can it be deduced or even supported by any empirical investigations into the nature of human consciousness. Indeed modern psychological theory makes it frankly much harder to believe in it. But the natural immortality of the soul as expounded, for example, by Plato is not and has never been Christian doctrine. The so-called "resurrection of the body", which means the survival of personality, was intended by the Church to supplant it.[1] Nor in the end are Christians concerned with proofs and arguments for "survival". The Christian hope is essentially *religious :* it is bound up with the Christian thought of God and of the meaning of the divine Kingdom.

It is not part of the scheme of this book to examine this doctrine or to seek to support it.[2] But it cannot end without an emphatic assertion that this is the fundamental postulate presupposed in the ethic of Christianity. If it is repudiated or invalidated the Christian ethic cannot be justified ; its characteristic stresses are then misleading, and its deep, otherworldly chords are discordant with the melody of experience. Indeed the case should be stated more

[1] See Lake, *Earlier Epistles of St. Paul*, pp. 215–219.

[2] It is being treated by my friend, the Rev. J. S. Bezzant, in another volume in this series.

strongly. For if men serve their day and generation and pass out, like the swallow, into the night, then the whole perspective and orientation of the Christian moral outlook is false. For it is thus wholly at variance with the pattern of Man's moral and social life. "Plato's *Republic*," says Professor Taylor, "is, for good or bad, intensely 'otherworldly'. Man has a soul which can attain everlasting beatitude, and this beatitude it is the great business of life to attain. The social institutions or the education which fit him to attain it are the right institutions or education: all others are wrong."[1]

Christianity, as we have observed, does not envisage the doctrine of immortality in the same forms as the Platonic philosophy. It would not say that Man has a soul but that he *is* a soul in the making. There is, moreover, in the *Republic* a certain irreconcilable discord between the eternal salvation of the philosopher and the welfare of all in the social order. Only in the Christian idea of God can this discord be completely resolved. But the central point made by Professor Taylor is of permanent and supreme importance. The eternal hope of Christianity imbues its ethical values and judgments with their ingrained, characteristic colour. Christianity, which is a way of life rooted in a spiritual *Koinonia*, will always invest the life of Community with a certain measure of eternal significance. Yet, because of its unequalled sense of the supreme value of individuals as the subjects of an eternal destiny, it can never acquiesce in their being sacrificed to the claims of an omnicompetent State.

This is the ultimate issue at stake between the Vatican, for example, and the peremptory demands of the Fascist State. Obscured as it is by humiliating manœuvres to retain the shadow of temporal power, which in fact force the Pope to surrender vital positions at point after point, the Vatican

[1] Taylor, *Plato: the Man and his Work*, p. 266.

nevertheless is making a stand for the Christian conception of Christian loyalty based on the Christian conception of human destiny, against that of an absolutist secularism. Here is an actual illustration of the dependence of Politics on Theology.

It must, however, be freely admitted that the Christian attitude on this question involves a trenchant separation from the "liberal" thought of our contemporaries. To hope for personal immortality is thought to be not merely obscurantist but intrinsically immoral and selfish. The individual, it is now taken for granted, must expect for himself no survival. He must devote himself to the social good; though he will perish the race endures, and the only immortality he can hope for is that he will live on in the "undying race", permanently ennobled by his devotion. Now this sounds stupendously emancipated: but if it is examined more narrowly it is found to have no meaning at all. For we know, or think we know, with fair probability what the future of this planet is likely to be, how the slow diffusion of temperature in a distant but not incalculable future will cause life to shrivel from the face of it and leave it empty in the silence of death. Where will the "undying race" be then? The tides of time will sweep it away, it and its sand-castles together. No more for the race than for the individual can the world of nature and time ever be more than a temporary lodging-house. There is here no ultimate security for any belief in personal life, which is then but an evanescent reflexion on the moving waters of mutability. And thus the good we seek ever eludes us, and we perish frustrate and unfulfilled. The popular notion of racial immortality offers, therefore, no kind of equivalent for the personal immortality which it repudiates. If anything be in truth immortal, it is men and women as individuals, not a generic noun called the Race.

2. Worship and Christian Ethics

But the central concern of the Christian ethic is not speculation in personal futures. Its hope, and goal, is in God Himself. The vision of God in Christ is its inspiration, the touch of the living Spirit its dynamic, and to possess God its ultimate reward. Hence, as Dr. Kirk rightly insists, " the principal duty of the Christian moralist is to stimulate the spirit of worship in those to whom he addresses himself, rather than to set before them codes of behaviour."[1] This is the key to the whole position which I have tried to establish in this essay. "Without institutionalism or cultus (as Troeltsch said in an impressive sentence) Christianity can be neither evangelistic nor convincing."[2] But it involves heart-searching questions both about the form and the content of our worship. All awakened Christians are sensitive to the need for intellectual restatement and the reshaping of our moral prescriptions : few of us have begun to face seriously the demands which are made by the changed conditions on the methods of Christian public worship. Yet, it seems to me, it is here chiefly that the Church, as an organized institution, can express a creative conception of Christianity and regain its hold on the lives of the people. It is not possible in the space that is left to me to elaborate on any adequate scale what needs to be said on this burning question. That would require a further volume. Yet it cannot be altogether ignored. For everything that I have attempted to say is leading to certain practical conclusions, which are directly applicable to worship. And it is, on the other hand, in worship that the double movement of the Christian life is best evoked and sustained, and its twin stresses held in a living poise.

[1] *The Vision of God*, Preface, p. x.

[2] " Ohne Gemeinde-organization und ohne Kultus ist das Christentum night fortpflanzungs-und zeugungs-fähig," *op. cit.*, p. 980.

It has been argued that Christianity is essentially and at heart otherworldly, a hunger and thirst for the living God, and a measurement of Man's experience by the grand dimensions of the eternal order. This, if it be accepted, involves that deep note of detachment and asceticism which must always ring through the Christian life. The order of this world can never satisfy it. Yet, on the other hand, our whole effort has been to insist that the Christian religion implies a welcoming, outward-moving response to the rich values, tasks and opportunities of this world of movement and colour and human interest. Where it lacks such spontaneity, where it cannot accept with reverence and gratitude the gifts of life in their manifold forms of goodness, there it falls short of its authentic character. Yet it can only redeem these good gifts from worldliness, triviality, or corruption, if it is so centred upon the Giver as never to yield itself utterly to the gifts. Else the lump will overwhelm the leaven. Now these two inconvertible "moments" in the fully developed Christian ethic are admittedly hard to maintain in a real unity, either of thought or of life and conduct. It is the test of heroic Christian living. But in Christian worship they may be richly harmonized. For Creator and Redeemer are one God.

The liturgical worship of the Anglican Church does maintain that ascetic emphasis which is inseparable from all real religion. But it is, in my judgment, the wrong kind of asceticism. It does not suggest the surrender of spirit to the ultimate and eternal Perfection which invests all that is real with its reality; that is far from our English temper. It suggests rather a restriction of interest, an avoidance of life's vivid concreteness, a relative non-concern with the world about us and a devaluing of its worth and richness. Yet worship is the recognition of worth. We pride ourselves rightly on our "restraint": but much of our worship is so restrained as to be almost a barren formality.

It lacks colour and spontaneity ; and if our services fail to awaken a sense of God's nearness and reality, it is because they are too little related with the concrete values of everyday experience to fill the worshippers' thought of Him with content. Our worship, like the life of the Church, tends towards something merely institutional. It does not spring vitally out of the sap of life as at once its blossom and its consecration. We are worshippers without an offering : we bring nothing to lay upon the altar. Thus, on the one hand, men's thought of God is impoverished almost to the point of vacuity ; on the other, the worship of the Christian society fails to awaken in the hearts of its members any rich, expectant responses to the gifts and opportunities of the Creator.

A religion is rightly judged by its worship. People are right in judging the Christian religion by what they observe in our Christian Churches. And if they conclude that it is largely irrelevant to the values which inspire and sustain their lives, we give them only too much justification. The recent revision of the Anglican Prayer Book had as one of its aims the "enrichment" of worship. But, though it gave us much to be thankful for, it was in truth a sorry instalment. We cannot meet the demands of the Christianity which is emerging in the new age, by inserting a few more "prayers for special occasions" or by mere rearrangement of existing offices. What is needed is a courageously new approach to the meaning of worship in the Christian community. Urgently we need to recapture the "experimental" stresses in public prayer, as well as those that are merely given and historical.

The whole conception of Christianity which is embodied in the Institution, and expressed in its liturgical worship, is almost exclusively historical. It presents the disclosure of God and the presence of the divine Spirit almost wholly in the context of history, and thus in predominantly Jewish forms. It assumes that Christians in modern England will express their recognition of God's goodness in Jewish Psalms and Hebraic canticles. That is to say, it preserves almost exclusively the "Synoptic" element in the Christian tradition. The "Johannine" or Hellenic element is disastrously unrepresented. But the Christain faith is, after all, not that there has been an Incarnation but that God is at work in the world through Christ.[1] And correspondingly, modern Christian worship ought to preserve and incorporate such stresses as witness to, and strengthen recognition of, the immanent work of the Spirit in the world. The primitive, Synoptic tradition had to be translated and refashioned in the language of an enriched Christian experience; and a fresh retranslation is called for in our vocabulary and in our worship. The God of Abraham can be no longer the only or even perhaps the central background of Christian faith in the twentieth century. The Christian experience, as we conceive it, is not solely or exclusively mediated by traditions and events in past history. It is a flame which leaps to life in the heart when the Spirit of the living Christ touches us.

If this be true—and if it is untrue this book is built on a misapprehension—then it would seem to lead unmistakably to a changed emphasis in our methods of worship; not by way of supplanting the ancient forms, but by way of amplifying and interpreting them. We should seek, for example, by all available means to express our sense of the Spirit's presence in the life and movement of God's world; to acclaim the pressure and touch of the Spirit in all those manifold values and excellencies in which He invites the spirits of men to respond to and rejoice in His perfection. "The Spirit beareth witness with our spirits that we are the sons of God." Thus we should clothe the

[1] Cf. W. R. Matthews, *The Gospel and the Modern Mind*, p. 72.

idea of the will of God with a precious fulness and definition, and help to rescue the Christian faith from its penury and its danger of formalism. We should also help to re-enthrone worship at the living centre of Christian experience, gathering all the values of life within the shrine of religious consecration, cleansing and enriching its good things as they are uplifted in religion—their fairest flower and their sanctification.

Yet the balancing stress must be safeguarded. Such experimentalism in worship must be jealously protected against becoming "chatty" and "bright" and trivial. If the ultimate sense of the Numinous ever evaporates, then we have abandoned religion and substituted a mere ephemeral "Uplift". The "ascetic" note must have its essential place; but we should seek for more positive ways of expressing it. It is less a non-concern with the temporal order, than a thirst for the Eternal God and, as result, the deliverance of our spirits from entire immersion in time; an opening of grander horizons, and a drawing of our earthbound affections from finding their complete satisfaction in the dear fascinations of this world, to seek their fulfilment in God's life eternal. Thus the gathered and stored associations of the historic, liturgical forms of worship, culminating in the Eucharist, will remain as indispensable media for symbolizing the unseen immensities and evoking the sense of the Divine Presence. To evoke and awaken response to this Presence must be the prime concern of all worship. We have yet to explore further means of doing this. There are new sacraments yet to be discovered in the Spirit's still inexhaustible resources. In particular, we have still to appropriate in the public services of our Church the lesson which the Friends are able to teach us concerning the sacramental uses of silence. The Cathedral builders knew that the sense of the Presence could be evoked by great unfilled spaces. We have yet to learn the equivalent value, in the midst of our clamorous civilization, of unfilled intervals of time.

Such a seeming arrest of the time-process is what most helps to deliver us from its tyranny.

INDEX

I. INDEX OF SUBJECTS

II. INDEX OF NAMES

Wisdom defined - pg 3. –
Christianity - ineffective - pg 8.
Conversion defined - pg 10.